HISTORY OF ARUNACHAL PRADESH

About the Author

Prof. M.L. Bose has been teaching in the Dibrugarh University for about thirty years and has contributed more than thirty papers in Regional and National Seminars and Journals of Repute. An Aurobindite Prof. Bose has guided many research scholars to produce Ph.D. thesis. His earliers published works *Historical and Constitutional Documents of North East India,* 1979, *British Policy in the North-East Frontier Agency,* 1979, *Development of Administration in Assam,* 1985, *Social History of Assam,* 1989 and *Social and Cultural History of Ancient India,* 1989 were well received in the academic world.

HISTORY OF ARUNACHAL PRADESH

M.L. BOSE

Department of History,
Dibrugarh University,
Dibrugarh - 786 004 (Assam)

CONCEPT PUBLISHING COMPANY, NEW DELHI 110059

ISBN 81-7022-665-1 (HB)

First Published 1997

Published and Printed by

Ashok Kumar Mittal
Concept Publishing Company
A/15-16, Commercial Block, Mohan Garden,
NEW DELHI - 110059 (India)

Phones: 5554042, 5504042
Fax: (011) 5598898

In the Memory of

My Father

Late Sri Sisir Kumar Bose

PREFACE

This book attempts to draw, in seven Chapters, a connected history of the North-East Frontier which is now known as Arunachal Pradesh. In the first five Chapters, the period from annexation of Assam in 1826 to the end of British rule in 1947 in order to provide an understanding of the development of the North-East Frontier during the British period from a historical angle. Then in last two Chapters post-independence developments leading to the creation of the Arunchal Pradesh has been shown.

For the British period, the relevant proceedings of the revenue, judicial, police and political departments of the Government of Bengal between the years 1826-1874, and the Secret Consultations of that Government, in the West Bengal State Archives, Calcutta, as well as the Home, Public, Judicial, Police, and Foreign Political proceedings of the Government of India, in the National Archives of India, New Delhi, for the same period were examined. (The history of this period has been laboriously written by Sir Alexander Mackenzie, who served under the Government of Bengal and the Government of India and had full access to all the official papers of these Governments. The book is well written, though with a purpose.). Besides, the following have also been thoroughly studied: all the proceedings of the Chief Commissioner of Assam between 1874-1905 in the Foreign Department of the Government of India; all the relevant proceedings of the Government of Eastern Bengal and Assam in the Political Department between 1906-12; and all the proceedings of the Government of Assam for 1913-20, 1921 and 1937 have also been consulted. Subsequent developments have been studied from the proceedings of the Tribal Affairs Department of the Assam Governor's Secretariat. The study was considerably facilitated by the author's discovery of the records preserved in the Lakhimpur Deputy Commissioner's Record Room at Dibrugarh; all the original papers relating to the Frontier, particularly of the period between 1874 and 1914, and all the reports on the administration of the North-East Frontier till the end of the British period are available there. Finally, all the relevant proceedings of the Government of India in the Foreign Political and Secret Department had to be consulted for connecting the missing links in the development of the Frontiers. The study at the National Archives of India was, however, greatly handicapped by restrictions on the use of records relating to certain periods and certain aspects of the subject. But the difficulty has been partially removed by the publication of some White Papers by the Ministry of External Affairs. To the study of the unpublished documents was added a thorough survey of reports and articles on the Frontiers published from time to time in different journals as also books which have been published in recent times, particularly those mentioned in the preceding paragraphs.

The last two Chapters have been written mainly on the basis of data called from the statistical Hand Books prepared by the Arunachal Government and an official publication called *Arunachal Pradesh—An Overview* written by Dr. P. Datta, Director of Research, Arunachal Pradesh, (1989), besides my new work entitled *Historical and Constitutional Developments of North-Eastern India* (1979), V. Elwin's *Philosophy for NEFA* (1957) and P.N.Luthra's *Constitutional and Administrative Growth of NEFA* (1969).

Thus, the present study may claim originally in respect of collection of new facts from hitherto unexplored source materials as also in respect of new interpretation of some already known facts. It is an original work also in the sense that it has treated the history of the Frontier from a fresh point of view. It is a comprehensive study of: (i) relation of the Government with the Frontier Tribes up to the end of the British period; (ii) emergence of the Inner Line, Outer Line and McMahon Line; (iii) the evolution of the Constitution and administration of the North-East Frontier, in the perspective of the land and the people. Secondly, an attempt has been made to study British policy against the background of political realities. Adverse criticism of that policy is usually based on the charge that it was because of the British neglect that the present problems have cropped up. This is true in a general sense, but then it is only one aspect of the issue. We cannot, as students of history, overlook the fact that British interest was concentrated on the plains—and not on the hills—for practical reasons. No threat of foreign aggression across the eastern frontiers seemed possible after the British had come to Assam; what caught their attention were the raids of the tribes from above the hills. The British were anxious to ensure safety of the plains below the Frontier Hills and for this purpose they strengthened the security measures on the foothills. Then after 1910, when the Chinese appeared across the frontier and foreign aggression became possible, the frontier was delimited and development and security measures began to be provided. It was already too late; the frontier people, deprived of governmental attention for about eight decades, remained far behind their brothers in the plains in respect of social and economic development. Administrative and security measures were thought of and provided for by the British Government during the last three decades of its rule. But this was only a beginning, and they left a complicated legacy for free India. Indian measures resulted in the emergence of Arunachal Pradesh.

The book is based mainly on my thesis submitted for the Ph.D. degree of Jadavpur University which was awarded in 1976.

For the help I received in preparation of the book, I am indebted to many, particularly A.C. Banerjee, Ex-Centenary Porfessor of International Relations, Calcutta University and retired Professor of Guru Nanak University. I am also grateful to P.C. Sharma, Keeper of Records, Assam Secretariat; the authorities of National Archives and West Bengal State Archives and Dibrugarh District for permitting me to collect research material from their respective archives and libraries. I am also grateful to B. Datta Ray and his family in Shillong who extended warm hospitality to me during my stay there in connection with the preparation of the book.

Department of History
Dibrugarh University,
Assam

M. L. BOSE

CONTENTS

Preface vii
Map 1: North-East Frontier Tracts, 1919 xiii
Map 2: North-East Frontier Tracts 1947 xiv
Map 3: Tribes and Rivers with River System 3

1. Arunachal Pradesh: Land, People and Culture 1
2. British Relations with the Tribes of the North-East Frontier 53
3. The Inner Line, the Outer Line and the McMahon Line 111
4. Administration of the North-East Frontier 154
5. British Policy in the North-East Frontier 193
6. Constitutional and Administrative Growth of Arunachal Pradesh 230
7. New Profile of Arunachal 250

Appendices

A — The Inner Line Regulation, 1873 264
B — India-Tibet Frontier, 1914: Exchange of Notes between the British and Tibetan Plenipotentiaries 268
C — Scheduled Districts Act, 1874 270
D — Assam Frontier Tract Regulation, 1880 275
E — Rules for the Administration of Justice in the Dibrugarh Frontier Tract 276

Bibliography 286
Index 292

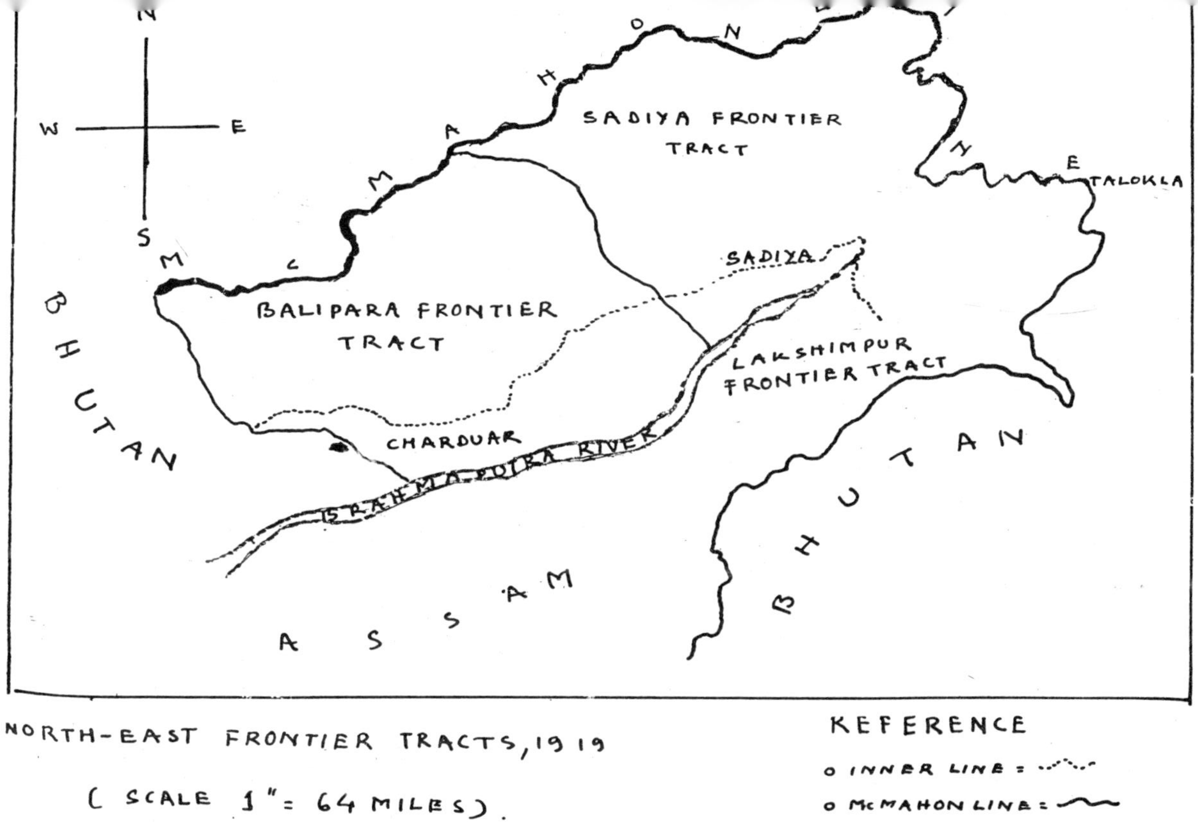

MAP 1: North-East Frontier Tracts, 1919

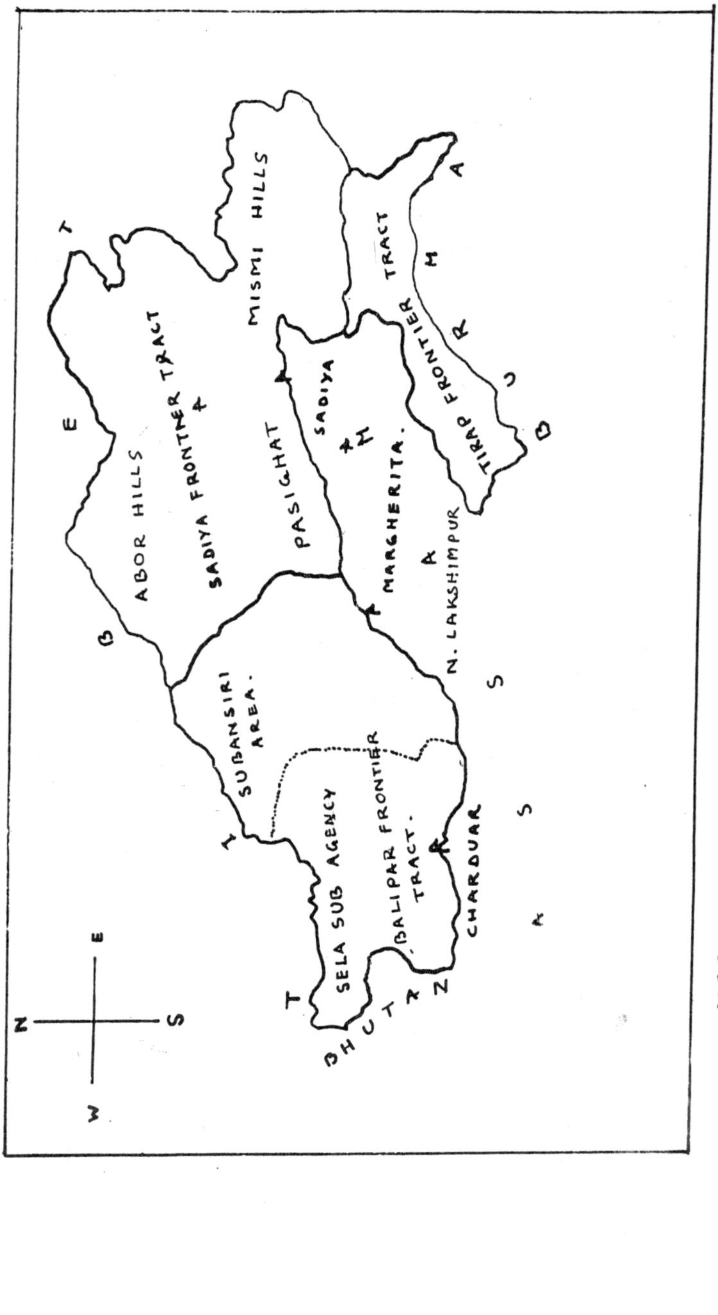

NORTHEAST FRONTIER TRACTS, 1947 (SCALE 1" = 64 MILES).

MAP 2: North-East Frontier Tracts, 1947

1

ARUNACHAL PRADESH
Land, People and Culture

THE LAND

Arunchal Pradesh, erstwhile North-East Frontier Agency (NEFA), comprises mountainous territory on the southern slopes of the Eastern Himalayas with the spurs coming down from north to south from the crest of the main range to the valley of the Brahmaputra in the State of Assam, except in the district of Tirap where the territory consists of the north-eastern slopes and spurs of the Patkai range, the crest of which divides India and Burma. Thus, the province is separated on the north by the province of Khams or Khamsyul of Tibet along the 700 mile long crest of the eastern Himalayas, known since 1914 as the McMahon Line,[1] to the Talok (Diphuk) Pass to the north-west of Burma, from the tri-junction of Bhutan, Tibet and India to the tri-junction of India, Tibet and Burma; on the west by Bhutan; on the east through the crest of the Patkai range which separates India and Burma; and on the south by Assam and Nagaland. The province is the home of twenty-five major tribes with a number of sub-tribes totalling a population of 6,31,859 according to the 1981 census. The total area is said to cover 83,743 sq. kms. divided into eleven districts from west to east: West Kameng, East Kameng, Tawang, Lower Subansiri, Upper Subansiri, West Siang, East Siang, Dibang, Lohit, Changland and Tirap.[2]

Geopolitically speaking, the province was regarded as unimportant[3] till 1910 when the contingent of Chao Er-feng, after occupying Tibet, appeared at Rima and demanded the submission of the Mishmis to their orders, bounded as it was on three sides by states which were neither powerful nor intentially dangerous for the British Empire. The Himalayas always provided India with natural defences and the Eastern Himalayas were regarded as barrier against the invaders from the north-east. To the east, Burma, after the first Anglo-Burmese war (1824-26) was regarded as an aggrieved and powerful state and to stop an immediate attack on the British territory by Burma, a hedge of semi-independent petty states was created between Burma and the British possessions in Assam. In the north-east—the Kampti and Singpho tracts—were the Ahom principality of Upper Assam and Manipur. As the earliest approach from Burma to British India lay through the Kubo Valley, a contingent called the Manipur Levy equipped, paid and commanded by a British officer was maintained there. To strengthen and gratify Manipur, some tracts of Cachar were made over to the Raja of Manipur.[4] But after the second Anglo Burmese War (1852), when Lower Burma was annexed to the British Empire, the dangers of Burmese aggresion receded to naught; finally, the Chinese overlordship over Burma was brought to an end by an agreement between China and Great Britain in 1876.[5]

To the west of the province, along a frontier of 159 km lies Bhutan which was a petty vessal of Tibet. The location of Bhutan, between the Tibetan plateau and the plains of Bengal and Assam, gives it a highly strategic importance. But Tibetan control over Bhutan had become extinct and Bhutan had become independent for all purposes; the Bhutanese ruler became practically sovereign. The British had come to the rescue of the ruler of Cooch Behar in 1772 when the latter had been carried off by the Bhutias. The East India Company's army marched into Bhutan and defeating the Bhutia army not only brought back the Cooch Behar prince but also got a treaty signed by the Bhutia authorities

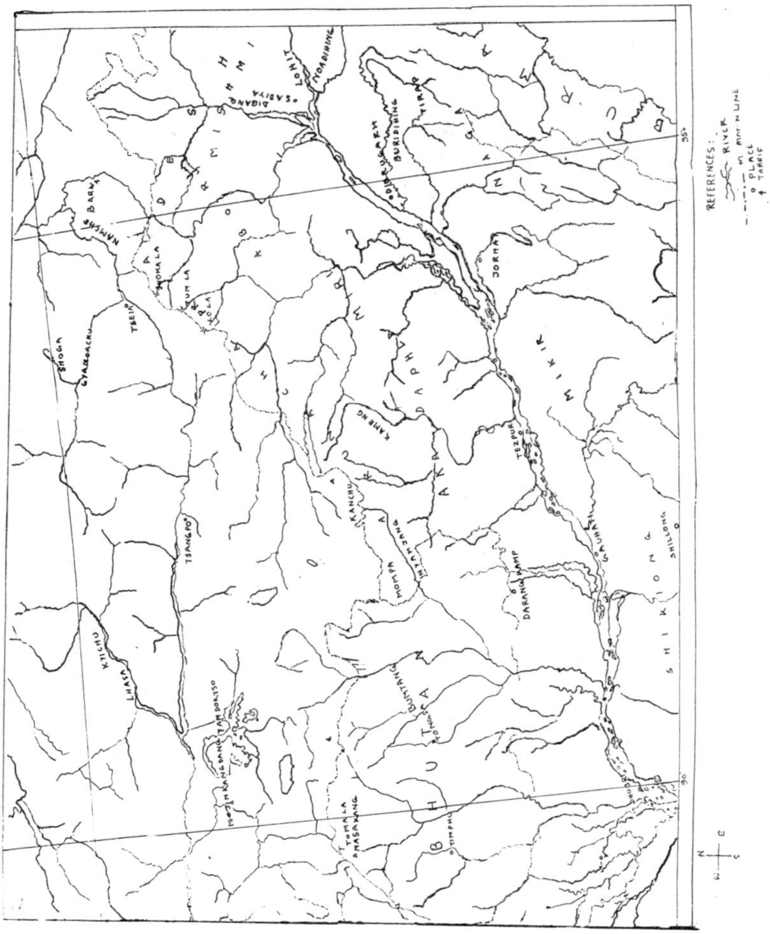

MAP 3: Tribes and Rivers with River System

to the effect that they would never entertain hostility against the British nor would they give asylum to any enemy of the British.[6] Gradually Bhutan Duras were annexed to the British Empire. In 1857, the Bhutia sympathy for the Sepoys in the Mutiny, antagonised the English. After the suppression of the Mutiny, the English deputed Ashley Eden, then Secretary to the Government of Bengal, on a Mission to Bhutan to obtain a fresh teaty on favourable terms. The Bhutias instead got Eden to sign a treaty which pledged the restitution of the Duras to Bhutan. On the return of Eden, the English declared war on Bhutan. The Bhutias were defeated; a fresh treaty was concluded. This ceded Kalimpong to the British and the Bhutias agreed to refer disputes between them and Sikkim and Cooch Behar to the English arbitration. The English agreed to raise the subsidy to Bhutan to Rs. 50,000 per annum. Since then peace was not disturbed till 1910 when the army of Chao Er-feng invaded Tibet. The British, suspicious of the Chinese motive, got a new treaty signed by Bhutan. The Bhutias agreed to be advised by the English in the conduct of foreign affairs and the Bhutia subsidy was raised to Rs. 1,00,000 per annum.[7] The threat on the Arunachal area from the Bhutan side thus disappeared altogether.

To the north of the Eastern Himalayan range lies the eastern division of Tibet known as Khams or Khamsyul extending from the frontiers of China in the east to the Tibetan province of U in the west.[8] The region was regarded as ethnographic Tibet rather than political Tibet as the Tibetan Government exercised jurisdiction in the province only in certain places and at irregular intervals. For the most part, the local lay or monastic chiefs ruled the districts of varying size at their discretion.[9] Again China, Tibet's suzerain, herself showed symptoms of decay and disintegration and till 1910 her control or direction of affairs in Lhasa was nominal rather than real. Neither Tibet nor China showed signs of virility or aggressive propensity. No danger thus loomed across the northern frontiers. Therefore, the British, instead of guarding the frontiers and arranging for their proper defence, remained unconcerned about the province[10] and left the affairs there to the helpless people themselves.

Geographically, the Eastern Himalayan range of Arunachal from the eastern border of Bhutan through the gorge of Tsangpo (Dihang) up to the syntaxial bend in the Mishmi hills lies entirely within Tibet and Assam.[11] The Mishmi hills and that part of the Patkai range which falls within the Tirap district of Arunachal are within Burma and Assam. Compared with the Sub-Himalayas, the information about the more interior parts of the Himalayan mountains is restricted and vague. The main trafficable trade route from south to north runs along the Kameng Valley through Bomdi La, Se La and Tawang; along this route, the Dalai Lama fled into India in 1959 and then three years later the Chinese troops made their major thrust into Assam. Further east, no important trade routes cross the range and that factor accounts partially for lack of full information about this region of the Himalayas.

According to Augusto Gansser, the Eastern Himalayas can be divided into four structural units: (i) The Sub-Himalayas consist of Siwalik sediments of the Tertiary period, lying mostly in the southern part of the region; (ii) the Lower Himalayas lying between the main boundary fault and the main central thrust comprise varied sedimentary and metamorphic rocks ranging in age from Palaeozoic to Mesozoic; (iii) north of the central thrust lies the basal crystalline thrust sheet of the Higher Himalayas; (iv) a great thickness of fossiligeorous Telhys sediments cover the crystalline thrust sheet of the Higher Himalayas.[12] The geological structure and process of erosion have influenced the surface appearance of landforms, which are intricately related to man's use of the land. But in this part of the country, the natural environment has remained inhospitable and adverse features have seriously impeded human development over large areas.

Very little information is available about the soils. The rocks are generally of the Himalayan type—shabs, schists and conglomerates; the derived soils are sandy and progressively clayey in the lower reaches of the valley. Soil acidity caused by heavy rainfall is high. The recently cleared forest lands exhibit a thick layer of leaf mould, rich in organic matter, but as a result of early rains the top soil is easily washed off. Soils in the foothills are alluvial in nature, being either loam or sandy loam mixed with pebbles, brought down by rain from higher altitudes. Soils in the valleys are clayey alluvium and rich in crganic content.[13]

At least three major climatic zones can be recognised on the basis of temperature although temperature, pressure, precipitation and winds vary with altitude. The foothill area is hot and humid and has a sub-tropical climate; the lesser Himalayas enjoy cooler or microthermal climate; and finally in the higher region, a Himadri type (Alpine) climate is found. The flora and fauna of the province vary with the climate and soil. The forest types range from tropical evergreen in the foothills, through temperate evergreen in the middle ranges, to the coniferous in the higher elevations and the high Himalayas in the extreme north.[14]

Be that as it may, the hills of this province up to the Mishmi hills may be sub-divided into sections based on the major tribes that inhabit the respective mountains. From the west at the eastern border of Bhutan to the east, they are the Mompa, Sherdukpen and Aka hills, the Nishi hills in the Subansiri district, the Miri hills and Adi hills in the Siand district, the Mishmi (Idu, Taraon and Miju) hills in the Lohit district; the Daphabhum and Patkai ranges are known by their names even to the tribes that inhabit them. The Daphabhum range is populated by the Singphos and the Singphos, Wancho, Nocte and Tangsas populate the Eastern Patkai range of the Tirap district.[15]

THE AKA, SHERDUKPEN (THONGJI) AND MOMPA HILLS

Former Kameng district which is now divided into three districts named West Kameng, Tawang and East Kameng covers 14,000 sq km and is the habitat not only of the Mompa, Sherdukpen (Thongji) and Aka tribes but some other tribes live there as well. The Mompas live in the Tawang district as well as in the Dirang and Kalaktang circles of the Bomdi La sub-division, that is to say, in the hills of west north-east region. The Sherdukpens (Thongji) live largely in the Rupa circle and some parts of the Kalaktang circle, that is to say, in the hills east of the Mompa, but covering the hills of the south-western part of the West Kameng district. The Aka hills are bounded on the north by the Miju hills, on the west by the Sherdukpens, on the east by the Bengni hills and on the south they stand above the Darrang district of Assam. In between the Nishi hills to the east and the Mompa, Sherdukpen and Akas to the west, and bounded by the northern border of the Darrang district of Assam on the south and the territory of the Bangros and Sulungs on the north, lie the extensive Bengni hills. From the Bengni hills on the south to the McMahon Line on the north and between the Mompas of Tawang and the Tagins of Subansiri stand the Sulung and Bangro hills. Besides some Mijis live in the hills near central Mompa tracts and a few Buguns are found in between the Sherdukpens and Akas of East Kameng district.[16] Thus, the territory of the district is bounded by Bhutan on the west, the Tibetan province of Khams on the north along the McMahon Line, the Nishi hills on the east and the Darrang district of Assam on the south.

On the west, from the Mompa region of Tawang, flows the Nyamjang chu (Dargong) drawing the waters of the Mela ridge. It flows from north to south and a number of tributaries having their origin in the Mela ridge debouch their waters into it flowing eastward. The waters of the Namka chu, which assumes the name of Tawang chu and receives the waters of the Thangla ridge, are discharged into the Nyamjang chu.[17] After flowing through the Mompa hills, the Nyamjang enters into Bhutan and flowing through that country discharges its waters into the Brahmaputra through the Manas river. East of Tawang through Se La flows the

Dirang which draining the western Mompa hills feeds the Kameng river. From the south-west, the Rupa river through the Sherdukpen hills sends its waters to the Kameng which with the waters of the Dirang flows into plains under the name Bhorali and discharges its waters into the Brahmaputra.[18] So the rivers of the eastern Kameng hills flow in the south-westerly direction and the rivers in the eastern region flow in the south-easterly direction.

The altitude of these hills is comparatively lower except in the north than the other hills of this region of the Himalayas. The hills in the lower region on the plains are steep and inaccessible. The pass leading to Tawang along the Kameng valley and then through Bomdi La and Se La lead through higher altitude; at Se La the elevation is 4,680 m. But the Tawang region is relatively lower and the altitude of the Tawang itself is, 3,000m above the sea level.[19] The climate of these hills is humid up to 1,200m, temperate up to 2,100m, and cold with heavy snowfall beyond that. Rich with evergreen deciduous forests, the hills in the upper region are dressed in pine, oak and fur. Carpeted with wild strawberries and a display of rhododendrons and a score of other multicoloured flowers, these hills are the most picturesque of all the Arunachal hills.[20]

NISHIS AND APA TANIS

Former Subansiri district covers 20,042 sq km and is now divided into two districts of Lower Subansiri and Upper Subansiri is the habitat of the Nishis.[21] Only a few Apa Tanis are found engulfed in and about Ziro, the headquarters of the district, and a few Hill Miris are found on the north-eastern extremity of the Nishi hills, adjacent to the Adi hills of the Siang district. The Miri hills are bounded on the south-east by the Dirjemo river which separates them from the Abors inhabiting the low hills north of Dibrugarh; on the north-east by a low range of hills forming the southern boundary of the Dihang valley; on the south by the Sub-division of North

Lakhimpur; on the south-west by hills to the east of the Ranga river which separate them from the Nishis. The Subansiri river divides the hills east and west. To the north up to the McMahon Line and between the Bangros and Sulungs of north Kameng in the west and Membas and Gallong Adis in the east are found over extensive territory the Tagins who are regarded as Tagin Daflas.[22]

Robinson places the Nishi hills between 90°50" to about 94° north longitude and forming the northern boundary of the valley of Assam from the Kuriapara Duar to where the Subansiri debouches into the plains. G.W. Dun, in his preliminary notes on the Nishis, holds that the Nishis are a tribe of the "outer hills" of the southern slopes of a spur of the Himalayas which divides the Bhorali from the Subansiri Drainage. "This spur is well defined as far as a peak called Lollupo, but at the point it is split into numerous minor valleys and spurs among which the Daphalas have established their villages. On the west, a very distinct ridge coming down from Lollupo separates the Daphalas from the Akas, who inhabit the basin of the Bhorali. On the east, another district ridge starting from Lollupo pesk divides the Daphalas from the Miri of the Khru river (an afluent of the Subansiri) and of the Subansiri."[23] Thus, the Nishi hills are bounded on the north by the McMahon Line, on the west by the Bhorali river, on the east by the Sundri river and on the south by the Naoduar of Darrang and Cheduar of Lakhimpur districts of Assam.

The hills of the region are rugged and the lower region is covered by dense forest. The hills rise towards the north to 6,000m (20,000 feet) on the Tibetan border and remain snow-covered all the year round.[24] The valley in the hills lies east and west. The distinguishing feature of the territory of this district is a remarkable level valley, 4 km × 125 km (or 2.5 × 7.5 miles) at Ziro which is 1,500m high.[25] Between Bhutan and the Subansiri river the Kandgu massif (7,089m) forms the only major culmination. It forms a marked southward-directed spur and it seems possible that this culmination coincides with a southward-extended 'bulge' of the main thrust zone. From the Subansiri river to the east-north-east, the main range is surprisingly straight and no river flowing to the south crosses it. The Tsangpo, flowing from south of Lhasa in an easterly direction has approached the range to as near as 15 km and now follows its north-eastern track.[26]

Two principal streams drain the interior of the traingle enclosed by two spurs of the Nishi hills, *viz.* the Humderi or Ranga on the east and the Dikrang. The Dikrang has a small tributary from the east called Barpani, and further west are the still smaller stream of the Buroi with its tributaries the Poma and the Papum, and still further west the Borgang, a stream of the other slopes. The general direction of the rivers in this triangle is easterly.[27] But, by far the largest river of the district after which it has been named is Subansiri. It has a long course through the Himalayas and flows through a series of gorges and rapids. This river cuts the main Himalayan range in Arunachal Pradesh east of Bhutan and sends its headwaters into Tibetan territory pushing the actual watershed almost to the Tsangpo river. It is known as Tsari chu in Tibet and in the upper course of Arunachal as Mara where in the Tagin territory the Galen, a tributary, discharges its waters.[28] The principal tributary of Subansiri in Arunachal are the Kamla and Sidan draining the west and east respectively. The range from which the Sidan flows is a comparatively low one on the south-west of Dihang. The Kamla flows from the high mountains of the north-west.[29]

ADI HILLS

Between the Nishi hills on the west and the Dihang river which borders on Mishmi hills on the east and in between Lakhimpur district of Assam and the McMahon Line on the north lie the extensive Adi hills of East and West Siang districts which covers 18,518 sq. kms.[30] These hills constitute the slopes of the main Himalayan ranges which at the very eastern extremity rises to the highest elevation of the whole eastern Himalayas in the still practically unknown Namche Barwa (7,755m).[31] The northern region is full of high, steep and inaccessible mountains and wild valleys. The southern part is comparatively flat. But the mountain in the south running north-east to south-west stand as a solid wall and shut the Brahmaputra valley from the north.[32] The passes along the northern boundary on the main range are surprisingly low; the tree studded Tum-La is only 3,600m high and the more eastern Shoka La apparently still lower. We have here one of the lowest passes crossing the whole Himalayan range, similar to or even lower than the Zoji La in Kashmir (3,529m) and only 600m higher than the Tsangpo river which meanders in a rather steep gravel-filled valley, flanked by impressive terraces.[33]

The Tsangpo known in Assam as Dihang (now known as Siang-Brahmaputra) turns its north-easterly course into a southern and south-western direction at Namche Barwa. As the counterpart to the famous Indus gorge at the western end of the Himalayas north of Nanga Parbat, the Tsangpo cuts exactly through the highest culmination of the eastern end of the Himalayas. Down to Pe or Timpa, just west-south-west of Namche Barwa, the Tsangpo flows placidly in a gravel-filled, though rather steep-walled valley. From here downstream, the river which was previously over 1 km wide suddenly narrows to a mere 90m and tumbles through a deep gorge with enormous boulders in most impressive cataracts.[34] The Tsangpo-Brahmaputra is one of the longest rivers of the world traversing a distance of 2,900 km through Tibet, India and Bangladesh.[35]

The Siang-Brahmaputra (Tsangpo-Dihang) flows through the centre of the Adi territory. Those living on the left or east bank of the Siang river up to the Dihang are called Bar Adis or Great Adis. Those living on the right or west bank of the Siang are known as Pasi-Meyong and formerly only Meyong Abors.[36] With the variation in altitude, the topographical and climatic conditions vary from south to north. The whole ranges are covered by dense forests and between October and January gorge wind occurs.[37]

MISHMI HILLS

South-east of the Siang (Tsangpo-Dihang) valley, the Mishmi hills form the still very obscure eastern syntaxial bend of the Himalayas.[38] Divided into two districts of Lohit and Dibang covering 24,431 sq kms it consists of a continuous chain of hills which in the higher region of the northern boundary remain perpetually covered with snow. The firs, and the highest in the horizon is the turret-form which is commonly known as the Sadiya peak; its base extends to Dihang on the left, and to the right it covers a considerable extent, allowing a more distant class of mountains to peep above its sloping sides. The next is the huge three-peaked mountain; the Mishmis call it as Thigritheya. It is succeeded by a wall after which Thathutheya, a round-backed ridge, rises high above the ranges near Parasuram Kund. Then there is a fall filled in by low mountains. Immediately to the east, at about a distance of 65 km the ranges are high and snow is seen above them throughout the cold season. The last peak in that direction is known as Beacon or Daphabhum as it is called by the Singphos. The lofty mountain retrogrades to a considerable distance beyond Daphabhum and forms a deep basin, the southern and eastern sides of which are alone visible; through the centre of this basin, the Dihang winds, having its source in the most distant point.[39]

Thus, the Mishmi hills are flanked on the west by the Dibang river, on the north by the McMahon Line and on the north-east by Burma, while in the south-west it is bounded by the valley of the Brahmaputra and the Patkai range. The hills and mountain ranges up the Lohit river from the Parasuram Kund as far as the Tibetan frontier on the east and round to west as far the Digaru up to the Tibetan frontier on the north are inhabited by the Digaru Mishmis.[40] The territory to the south-east is occupied by the Mijus, and to the west of the Digaru up to the Dibang on the west and

Tibetan border on the north live the Idu or Chulikata Mishmis, to the south-east of whom, up to the foothills, live the Bibijias.[41] Some Khamptis live on the plains just below the Mishmi hills and a few Singphos inhabit the Daphabhum range part of which lie in the Lohit district. These areas have been brought under the Lohit district (23,191 sq km or 9,059 sq miles).[42]

The altitude of the hills of the Lohit district ranges between 600m and 5,100m. The craggy hills and blue green valleys are very narrow and steep. High river terraces, some 200-300m above stream level, border the valley.[43] The hills in the Dibang valley are generally more pointed and the hill slopes are steep and precipitous.[44] The plain areas in the foothills are covered by tropical jungle and are intersected by numerous ravines and water courses. Because of the inaccessible nature of the terrain, population in the Mishmi hills is sparse, particularly in the eastern region which embraces a number of high mountain ranges. The majority of the population is concentrated in the western part, chiefly in the southern portion of the Lohit valley.[45]

The principal rivers drain the Mishmi hills; both originate across the border within Tibet and flow down from south-eastern slopes of the Namche Barwa. The Lohit, known in Tibet as Zayul chu, flows into the Mishmi hills from the Tibetan post Rima, and through Menilkrai it approaches the Parasuram Kund across the high mountain and debouches into the wild valley below at a short distance from it.[46] A number of tributaries both across the Indian border and from the Digaru and Miju Mishmi hills feed it to make it a mighty river. From the western side, the Dibang, similarly, drawing waters of tributaries of Tibet and upper hills of Bibijia and Chulikata or Idu territories, flows into the plains and unites with the Lohit below Sadiya.[47]

The climate of the Mishmi hills is generally moderate throughout the year. The foothill areas are warm during the summer, but the temperature in the high region goes down even in summer. As a result, innumerable varieties of trees grow in the district and some of them make good timber.[48]

DAPHABHUM AND THE EASTERN PATKAI RANGES

South of the Mishmi hills lay the districts of Tirap and Changland where the Daphabhum and Phunganbhum meet, the Patkai range begins covering 7,024 sq. kms. It separates Assam and Burma and stands in a south-westerly direction projecting spurs on the Assam side in the northerly direction. The portion of the range in Arunachal is almost uniformly high, 1,500m above the sea level. Only the Pangsau Pass connecting the upper valley of the Brahmaputra with Burma stands at 1,238m above the sea level. The elevation of the range varies from 2,040m at Maium Peak in Upper Burma to 924m in the Sympana Saddle.[49]

Towards the north-east fringe along the Daphabhum and Phunganbhum and the Patkai live some Singphos who have been in close connection with the Kakheyans of Burma.[50] Adjacent to them in the northern spurs and slopes of the range live the Tangsas who were known as Sarkari Nagas; next to them along the main range and the middle spurs are found the Wanchos who were known as Rangpangs and further south-west along the Tuensang district of Nagaland live the Noctes known as Namasangias.[51] The Noctes, Tangsas and Wanchos were regarded as Nagas and they still have close connections with their Burmese coutnerparts across the Patkai. A few Lisu or Yobins, Chakmas, Huzongs, Deonias, Kacharis and Miaos also live on the hills of the Miao sub-division on the north-eastern extremity of the Tirap district. These hills borders on Burma on the east, Nagaland on the south-east and Assam and the Mishmi hills on the north-east.[52]

Towards the north-east originates the Namphuk river which drains the north-eastern spurs and valleys and discharges its waters into the Buri Dihing river. The Tirap river, after which the district has been named, drains the huge valley along the eastern flank of the Patkai and after a long course falls in on the left bank of the Buri Dihing.[53] But the Buri Dihing is by far the largest of the rivers of the district that drains the entire basin of the northern slopes of the Patkai and receiving the waters of all the streams that flow from the north-eastern slopes of that range discharges its water into the Brahmaputra south of Dibrugarh.

The altitude of the hills of the district varies from 400m in the Daphabhum range to 150m in the foothils of the Patkai range.[54] The general relief over the entire north-western part of the Tirap district is low and the district is highly dissected by a number of wide river valleys like those of the Tirap and the Nou-Dihing. It is in these river valleys, particularly along the Brahmaputra plains, that the major part of the population is concentrated. The eastern part of the district is comparatively sparsely populated.[55] The climate conditions also vary to a great extent. The climate of the foothills and plains valley is hot and humid whereas that of the higher hills is moderate and pleasant. As a result, the district is rich in sub-tropical evergreen forests and varieties of fauna.[56]

INFLUENCE OF GEOGRAPHY

The physical features of the territory of Arunachal have restricted the mingling of the people of different tribes and retarded the growth of national consciousness among the people; geography of the area favours retention of local identity, and lack of transport and communication facilities had kept the tribes separate from each other. Much of the land in the northern region of the Greater Himalayas has remained virtually empty; the middle zone is moderately populated; but the foothills and valleys are relatively closely populated and are characterised by the scattering of population clusters. The uneven distribution of population among several small valleys without adequate communication with each other hinders cohesiveness among the people. To the people the tribal loyalties come first and national allegiance—if there is any such sentiment at all—comes second. The environment is largely responsible for the multiplicity of language and customs of the tribes which do not have easy communication with the neighbouring areas.[57]

Geography has influenced the cultural development of the province to a great extent. The northern region had little contact with the lower region, particularly the valley of the Brahmaputra, and has been greatly influenced by the Indo-Tibetan culture. For the past many centuries, the Tibetan traders crossed the borders and traded in the region; many of them settled down in the valleys of the Greater Himalayas. This accounts for the large Buddhist settlements in the Siang districts and the Buddhist impact is visible in the way of life in the higher regions. The southern belt of the foothills has had similar contact with the plains of Assam. The results are manifest in the religion, language, clothing, food habits and mode of agriculture. But the middle zone has remained comparatively backward and both Tibetan and Assamese influence are visible in their way of life there. The tribes living in this region had very little contact with the outside world and even today they are living in extremely primitive conditions.[58]

But nature nas endowed the land with beauty and hydro-electric potential which, if developed properly, can more than offset the physical difficulties. The province is full of scenic beauty and can attract tourists from all parts of the world. If transport facilities are improved and the restriction on the movement of visitors is removed, a flourishing tourist trade will develop. The hydro-electric potential, if developed to its logical capacity, will transform the face of the land. If human efforts come to the aid of nautre, Arunachal can develop into a second Switzerland.[59]

PEOPLE

ORIGIN AND MIGRATION OF TRIBES

History furnishes a very imperfect insight into the origin and descent of the tribes of the North-East Frontier. Robinson in his *A Descriptive Account of Assam* observes : "It seems almost vain to attempt to lift up the dark veil which conceals the origin of the tribes, to trace back their history, or to gain any information of the various revolutions by which they have been influenced; these subjects belong to times and circumstances which are beyond the limit of certain knowledge. It would be most cautious and perhaps the most philosophical course, to abstain from any conjecture relative to their origin or from any attempt to penetrate into the nautre of causes of which even the most distant results are but partially known to us. Therefore, we must depend on the reflected light which is obtained by the comparison of language, by the analysis of civil and religious institutions and mythological fables, or by tracing clearly marked affinities in the manners and customs of different tribes."[60]

Indeed, it is very difficult to arrive at any definite conclusion regarding the original home, the routes of immigration and the dates of settlement of the myriad tribes of the North-East Frontier. Even the names by which they were popularly known were attributed to them by the neighbours in the valley of the Brahmaputra and were quite unknown to the tribal people themselves who had no contact with the plains.[61] The tribes of the present Kameng districts were collectively known by a generic name Bhutia, except the Hrussos who were known as Akas for their custom of tattooing their bodies.[62] The Nishis were known as Daflas but the reasons why they were so called are still to be ascertained. The inhabitants of the present Siang districts were called Abors, perhaps for their unruly nature, but they call themselves "Adi" which means "hillmen".[63] The tribes of the Lohit district were called Mishmis, but they have objected to be known as such and are now known by their group names, e.g. Idu, Miju and Taraon. Of the North-East Frontier tribes, only the Khamptis and the Singphos do not express any objection to being called by their agelong popular names. The tribes of the Tirap district were called

Nagas; they are now recognised by their group names like Wancho, Nocte and Tangsa.[64]

But the identification of the tribes by their proper names has not in any way established the link with their past history. It has been pointed out that the assumption of the present nomenclature is perhaps more due to the rise of a sense of dignity and pride among the tribes who no longer like to be branded by their plains fellows in any manner they want.[65] It is not due to a tendency to identify themselves with a glorious race or kingdom elsewhere in the past or present as is the case with the Ahoms who now establish their connections with the empire of Pong which existed to the north of Burma and the Shan tribes who live in Thailand or Siam.[66]

The tribes of the North-East Frontier trace their origin in the north-east. George A. Grierson holds: "North-western China between the upper waters of Yang-tse-Kiang and Ho-ang-Ho was the traditional cradle of the Indo-Chinese races, and from that starting point successive waves of immigrants entered Assam. The first were the Maan-Ahoms who have left Khasis and are now to be seen in Annam and Cambodia. Second came the Tibeto-Burmans, the ancestors of the Bodo tribes with whom the Abors, Miris and the Daflas are clearly connected."[67]

C.H. Hesselmayer says: "The Himalayan mountains as they form the northern boundary of Assam are inhabited by two distinct races of men. Originally probably one and the same race, they seem to have undergone a change sufficiently marked to authorise their being considered at the present moment as two distinct races. The mountaineers who occupy the eastern half of these frontier hills seem to be original occupants, or first arrivals, and to have retained their original habits and customs. Those who live to the west appear to belong to a later period of immigration, subsequent to their descent from Central Asia."[68]

It is very difficult to ascertain the date of immigration of tribes. But the statement of Hesselmayer also seems to be untenable. Beginning from the west, we know that the father of the Mompa tribe, Rupati of Kameng, had migrated to its present home in the hills from the plains of the Brahmaputra valley in the tenth century and is said to have married the daughter of a prince of Kamrup.[69] The progenitor of the Sherdukpen tribe is the grandson of an eighth century king Srongtson Gempo; he again is an immigrant from Tibet and is said to have come from the ancestral home in the eighth century.[70] According to a tradition recorded by Capt. Kennedy, the Akas trace their origin from the east. They trace their descent from Arima who migrated from the plains below the hills in remorse for having killed father in ignorance.[71] The date of their immigration is not known, but it must have been after the decline of the dynasty of Bana, whose relics are found in Bhalukpong and Tezpur sometime after the twelfth century."[72]

The origin of the Nishi is not known. They trace their descent from a legendary ancestor whose three sons are believed to have been the forefathers of the three clans known as Dapum, Dodum and Døl respectively.[73] The first mention of Nishis is found in the *Ahom Buranjis*. Their atrocities caused the Ahom kings to hold a portion of their territory and erect a line of fortifications along their hills.[74] But no account is available regarding their migration and origin elsewhere. It seems possible that they came from across the McMahon Line from the Khamsyul division of Tibet. To the north of the Nishis live the Tagins who are definitely immigrants of Khams. Some Tagins are to be seen across that Line in Tibet. The Nishis in the north are called Tagin Daflas and the Tabins, though a separate group, are off-shoots of one and the same stock.[75] The two other tribes, Apa Tanis and Sulungs, have been overwhelmed by the Nishis. They seem to have been living in the region before the coming down of the Nishis from across the McMahon Line. The Apa Tanis have remained independent, but the Sulungs have been reduced to the status of serfs in relation to the numerous and powerful Nishis. The Apa Tanis trace their migration from a valley of two rivers Supupad-Pudpumi. They have cultural affinities with the Adis and Nagas.[76]

The tradition of origin among the Adis, as recorded by R.C.R. Gumming in 1931 for the Census Report, is as follows: "In none of these tribes there are any traditions of origin which go back very far. All claim origin from one race or tribe settled at Killing in the Bomo-Janbo country. From Killing, part of the tribe journeyed south across the Siyom river and occupied the hilly country between that river and the Subansiri and the Brahmaputra. These are now known as Galong. Others crossed the Dihang (San Fo) or settled on its bank or neighbourhood."[77] In the Census Report of 1961 they have been stated to be immigrants from the Khams province of Tibet.[78] The Abors probably had close relations with the Ahoms of the Brahmaputra valley, for during the Moamaria rebellion of 1792-93 twenty to thirty thousand Abors are said to have assisted the Ahom monarch.[79]

About the Mishmi immigration, J.P. Mills wrote that they were immigrants from Burma who entered Assam 500 years ago.[80] The Mishmis were followed by the Khamptis and the Singphos. The Khamptis began to migrate to Assam from Khampti-long from north of Burma, somewhere in the 18th century.[81] The Singphos followed them from north Burma much later. During the decay of the Ahom kingdom the Singphos crossed the Patkai *circa* 1793, entered into Assam, and capturing Assamese slaves settled down on this side of the Patkai range.[82] The Wanchos and Tangsas of the Tirap district perhaps were preceded by the Ahoms who entered the valley of the Brahmaputra along the Buri Dehing valley crossing the Patkai range in the vicinity of present Vijaynagore, *c*. 1226.[83]

Thus, it seems that the present tribes of the North-East Frontier in Arunachal had entered into their present homes at different times and from different directions. The Sherdukpens, Nishis and Adis had come from across the McMahon Line from Tibet and settled over territories displacing the tribes who were already living there. The

follow Buddhism; the Buguns and Akas of Kameng, the Dhammain of Susbansiri and the Singphos of Lohit and Tirap have been influenced considerably by Buddhism. Common artistic pursuits, including making of wooden masks, are distinctive feature of this group. The second group consists of the Nishis, the Adis, the Mishmis and sundry tribes inhabiting the hills stretching from Se La in Kameng through the greater parts of upper Subansiri, Siang and Lohit districts. These tribes have varying traditions but are culturally united by their attachment to weaving, absence of wood-carving and a degree of excellence in fine works of cane and bamboo. The last group is confined to the present Tirap district of the Nort-East Frontier and are composed of the Noctes, Tangsas and Wanchos of Tirap.[96] All these tribes have still wide contacts with their brethern across the Patkai in Burma and have been influenced to a great extent by them. They inter-marry with the Burmese tribes and do their hair and dress in imitation of them. They also are experts in wood-carving and personal decorations.

TRIBAL SOCIETY

Notwithstanding these cultural divisions, the tribes of the North-East Frontier have some common social features. The social organisation among them without any exception is patrilineal and the oldest male member is regarded as the guardian of the family; marriage is usually negotiated and the groom has to pay a bride-price to the guardian of his wife; members of the tribe marry within it but members of a clan outside it; polygamy is permitted but monogamy is the usual practice; polyandry is restricted to only some Adi tribes and is practically dying out; women in general enjoy a good deal of respect in society; slavery existed among all tribes throughout the British period. There is no casteism or racialism in any tribal community though social grades exist.[97]

Each tribe of the North-East Frontier lived an exclusive

life of its own which the difficulties in communication and terrain had fostered to some extent. Each tribe, however, is divided into endogamous clans. The Nishis are divided into exogamous groups; clan divisions hardly exist among them.[98] The Adis are subdivided into exogamous clans which are further subdivided into smaller clans or families among which endogamy is strictly forbidden.[99] The Mishmis are endogamous and are divided into sects rather than clans.[100] The Khamptis, Singphos, Wanchos, Noctes and Tangsas are also divided into exogamous clans.[101] Each clan breaks up into numerous families each of which consists of husband, wife and their children. A grown up son, when married, sets up a separate house unless he is the eldest and becomes a member of the village community which allocated a plot of land for his subsistence.[102] Families of the same clan may live in separate villages over which there is one chief or Gam or Gaobura, as he is known now a days. The villages in the Apa Tani plateau and Wancho and Tangsa are the largest and houses are built close to each other. The Apa Tani villages accommodate even 100 families.[103] The smallest villages are seen in the Mishmi Hills where a village is practically the home of a single family.[104] Social habits and customs are peculiar to a particular tribe, but there are some basic similarities though there may be difference of details from group to group. Every tribe has club houses or dormitories where youths are trained in civic duties, tribal disputes are resolved in meetings of the village elders, youths sleep in the night. Tribal guests are accommodated in these Morangs.[105] The accommodation of the youths in the Morangs served some other useful purposes as well. If the village is in danger and the youths are required to be mobilised to face the emergency, then the youths from the Morang could be given instructions quickly. In the Tirap and Siang districts, these Morangs serve as meeting places for youths to select their marriage partners. Among the Tirap and Siang tribes, their were separate Morangs for girls.[106]

The position of women in North-East tribal society is

respectable is not very high. The system of polygamy, particularly among Nishis and Mishmi tribes, no doubt has lowered their position, and sometimes wives are foresaken without being divorced. In spite of laxity in sex relationship, prostitution is practically unknown in the North-East frontier.[107] Ordinarily, women lead a busy life, helping the menfolk in all walks of life. They wake up early in the morning and prepare meals for the family. Taking their morning meal, they proceed to the fields carrying their noonday meal and drinks. They work in the fields and return home in the evening. Again, they cook the meal for the night. Women took part in folk-dance where it existed and the entertainment of the guests was their privilege.[108]

Life of the People

The tribal people have a knack of celebrating festivals with a mounting crescendo of activity. Generally these festivals are connected with deaths, marriages and sowing and harvesting of crops. The Mompas of Kameng celebrate the Losar festival which is a kind of new year's festival on the occasion of Buddha Purnima.[109] The Adis celebrate Arau and Mopin festivals for a good harvest.[110] The Khamptis and Singphos celebrate Buddhist festivals. But the tribes of Tirap usually celebrate the settlement of disputes with feast and drinks.[111] Individual dances are practically unknown among North-East Frontier tribes; but community dances are also unknown among the Nishis, Apa Tanis and Mishmis. The Mompas and Sherdukpens of Kameng are most skilfull dancers. People in colourful make-up and gorgeous costumes perform dances representing the world theatre in various religious functions to teach moral lessons to the people.[112] The Adis and Hill Miris of Siang and the Wanchos and Noctes of Tirap perform community dances or folk dances during community feasts. During these occasions, people drink liquor in large quantities so as to become intoxicated.[113]

The staple food of the people in the North-East Frontier consists of rice, millet and wheat which are supplemented by vegetables and forest produce. Fish and meat are consumed by all tribes, whether followers of Buddhism or of a tribal religion. Even Buddhist monks eat fish and meat but they do not catch and kill any fish or animal.[114]

Tribal houses are made of bamboo, timber, leaves and grass. Stones and mud are used extensively in Kameng where houses are comparatively small. In other parts, the houses are long and are raised on posts of cleft timber. The Adi houses are raised about 5 feet from the ground and posts are not used.[115] Four or five pieces of wood at an angle resting on the surface take the place of a post. Houses are constructed indiscriminately either on the top or side of hills, but the levels of the floors are maintained. The floors are of split bamboo not woven and walls are made of rough planks. For the roofs, palm thatch and wild plantain leaves are used. Roofs of the houses come down so low that externally the wall is not seen. But division of a house into compartments depends on social customs of the tribes and there is no distinction between individuals. The Wanchos and Noctes have two rooms in each house, one for the men and the other for women;[116] the Mishmis have as many rooms as the number of wives of the master of the house;[117] the Apa Tanis and Hill Miris have only one long room.[118] The houses of the tribes are 18 to 20 feet wide and 100 feet long; the interior is divided into chambers for private use and reception, and at the front there is an open balcony, a prolongation of the floors beyond the eaves providing for an airy place for the family to sit or work or lounge in (this is not so in the case of the Khamptis, whose chiefs possess two houses contiguous to each other).[119] Every house at the rear is provided with a veranda with a hole in the floor where the domestic stock is accommodated and these serve as scavengers. There are no sweepers and scavengers among the Frontier tribes.

Slavery

As mentioned above, slavery as an institution existed in the North-East Frontier all through the British period; slaves were objects of merchandise liable to be bought and sold. The unyielding and unproductive terrain of the Himalayas was perhaps conducive to slavery; it was strengthened by tribal beliefs and the superstition that a person would get after his death as many slaves as he commanded in this world. People fell into slavery for many reasons. War captives might be sold as slaves in accordance with the custom existing in India from primitive times. The children of slaves became slaves automatically. Sometimes people committing offences against the community were condemned to slavery. The tribal people, however, treated their slaves quite well and their hardships were not as severe as depicted in *Uncle Tom's Cabin*. The positon of the slaves in the tribal community is well described in a letter of the Chief Secretary of the Chief Commissioner of Assam : "Word (slave) connotes nothing more than a very mild form of servitude. The so-called slaves in the unadministered areas usually live in the house of the family for which they work, though occasionally they have separate houses of their own. Their clothing, food, house accommodation and general domestic equipment do not differ in any way from that of the ordinary hillman. They not infrequently possess private property which they obtain by trading during the months of the year when they are not required to work in the fields or in the case of women, by weaving clothes and rugs. A slave, in the event of the death of all the males inherits his master's property including his house. A master during his life time often sets up a slave in a separate house, finds him a wife, and gives him livestock and fields for his support, allowing him to live an independent life. It is true that slaves receive no actual cash wages, but money is exceedingly scarce in the hills and is used very little by the hillmen in their ordinary transactions. The slaves live in the same style as other hillmen and take as well as they do and it might, therefore, not unreasonably be urged that the wages which they receive in kind are as good as any servant can expect in such a quarter of the world. Moreover, there seem to be good grounds for holding that in the immense majority of cases, these so-called slaves remain with their masters of their own accord. No physical restrictions are placed upon their liberty and there is nothing to prevent them, if they wish to do so, from coming down and settling in the plains. In spite of this, the number of slaves who actually leave their master is very small."[120]

Political Organisation

The tribes of the North-East Frontier know no kingdom or king; but each tribe or clan or village has its own head styled as Gam or Gaonbura, that is the village head, who is sometimes known as Sat Raja, as is the case with the Mompas and Sherdukpens, or Raja as the case with the Aka chiefs.[121] But the management of the internal affairs of the village or clan and its relations with the neighbours is vested in the village council which consists of the elders of the village. In such a village council, all members have equal powers and each such council is independent of all external influences.[122]

The most conspicuous of these village councils is the Adi Kebang. Its members, known as Kebang Abus, are chosen for their experience, ability and capacity to present and decide cases according to the traditional customs and conventions of the tribe. The Kebang controls the entire village activities and punishes those who deviate from the right path. The allocation of plots out of the *jhum* land of the tribe to each family, including plots for residential houses, and settlement of the village disputes—are all discussed and decided in the meetings of the Kebang. In settling disputes the view points of both the parties are taken into account after a careful hearing. Inter-village disputes are composed in the meetings of the inter-village council known as Bangos. All villages are divided into several groups for this purpose. The Bangos are composed of all the Gams of the member villages and such other members as have distinguished themselves in Kebang meetings and a secretary. Money collected in Bangos as fines are spent for the welfare of the village under the Bango. The inter-Bango disputes are settled in the meeting of the institution known as Bogum Bokang which is temporarily created for a particular case with members of all the Bangos and some distinguished persons who do not have any interest in the dispute and are impartial.[123]

Though the composition and functioning of the village councils differ from tribe to tribe, it is the main administrative, judicial and political institution throughout the North-East Frontier. Among some tribes, like the Wanchos, and the Noctes of Tirap, the Khamptis and the Singphos of Lohit, the Akas (Hrussos) of Kameng, the chief of the tribe or clan is hereditary and possesses more power and influence over their tribesmen. The Dafla chiefs are less influential as they are divided into innumerable petty divisions.[124] But the Tagin chiefs seem to be little more influential than their fellow Daflas.[125] Among these tribes, inter-village disputes and political decisions are within the jurisdictions of the chiefs.

But the Mompa and the Sherdukpen set-up is a little different. There were chiefs known as the Sat Rajas who were subordinate to the Governor of Tawang. In between the Governor of Tawang and the Sat Rajas of the different regions, there were some Gellings who were appointed by the Governor of Tawang for three years.[126] Under the Sat Rajas operated the village councils (Tsorgens) in different areas. The villagers elected the village council for a term to manage the affairs of the village according to the tradition of the tribe. But inter-village disputes and political decisions lay in charge of the Sat Rajas and their superior, that is, the Tawang Deo.[127]

ECONOMY

AGRICULTURE

The economic life of a country is largely conditioned by its physical and topographical features. Man tries to adapt himself in his natural surroundings with his technological equipment and social resources. The tribes of the North-East Frontier testify to the truth of this natural law. The mountains of this region are of younger age and break up into soil easily. The rainfall is heavy except in the north-east of the Kameng district with an average of more than 100 inches per annum. This has made the economy of the hills jhum-agricultural, which is supplemented by hunting and fishing. Generally, by the end of the winter an area is selected for cultivation and the jungle is cleared and fire is set to burn the dry bushes and trees that are felled. Before the onset of the reiny season, the soil is prepared with primitive implements, *e.g.* dao, axe, iron-hoe, pointed bamboo, and seeds of various crops are sown in the same plot. Seeds are often placed in separate holes with pointed bamboo but broadcasting of seeds is not uncommon. Different crops are reaped at different seasons from the same field. A clearing is used for two or three years and when its fertility is lost, it is abandoned and a new site is selected.[128]

Wet-rice cultivation and terrace cultivation are also prevalent among some tribes. The Mompas, the Khambas, the Membas practice terrace cultivation, wet-rice cultivation is popular among the Apa Tanis of Subansiri and the Wanchos, Noctes and Tangsas of Tirap and the Khamptis and Singphos of the Lohit district. The Mompas, Khambas and Membas plough their fields with yak or mithun and the tribes practising wet-rice cultivation employ cattle for ploughing their fields like the people of the plains.[129]

All tribes grow paddy, maize, millet, and vegetable of different varieties. The most popular and widely grown vegetable is *aram* which is grown in abundance all over the hills and is a common item of food of many people. The Adis and Mishmis grow tobacco; cotton and some barley are raised in some places.[130] The Wanchos and Noctes grow tapioca and cotton.[131] The domestic animals are pig, cow and mithun; the Mompas, the Khambas and Membas keep horses and are very fond of them. But the mithun is, by far the most important and valuable domestic animal and usually the yardstick of wealth of the rich.[132] Fowl are found almost in every household along with pigs.

Land is said to be more important to an Indian farmer than his wife and there is no exception in case of the North-East Frontier tribes. Land is the bedrock of the tribal economy in the hills and it is the mainstay of their subsistence. On land, the tribes grow their food and rear their herds, and from the forests around their villages they gather their housing materials like timber, bamboo and grass and collect firewood and fuel and go for hunting. Since the tribal people live on hill sides and cultivated the hill sides which are subject to erosion and land slides, the importance of land is more keenly felt.

There are three kinds of ownerships of land : personal land, clan-land and village-land. The land which is held in individual ownership and is inherited through the father is personal land; the land which is utilised by different villages of a particular clan for burial or grazing purposes is clan-land; the land on the fringes of villages where there are forests providing the villagers with firewood, roots and herbs as also hunting or fishing is the village-land property. The Apa Tanis and the Mompas who practice permanent or terrace cultivation have strong attachment to personal lands. The individual's status in society is determined by his possession of land. But the burial ground and the pasture are in all cases the property of the clan or the tribe. The forests on the periphery of each village is the property of the village.[133] The tribes who practise jhumming hold the agricultural land in common and the village council allocates to each individual family a plot of land for its use in each clearing.[134] The family enjoys it as private property till it moves away for a fresh site.

TRADE

Almost all the tribes grow all that are necessary for them and yet barter or trade is quite familiar. The Mishmis and the Khamptis are inveterate traders;[135] the Akas and the Mompas carry on extensive trade and act as middlemen for their neighbours;[136] the Adis trade with their brethren living behind them. What the tribes do not produce and require to procure from outside is salt. A small quantity of clothes, utensils and agricultural implements and some ornamental beads were the other items that they purchased at the fairs or from traders or businessmen are gold, yak-tails, wool and woollen blankets, ponny, sheep, dogs musk, ginger, Mishmiteeta, wax, honey, chillies, spices, madder, walnuts, rock-salt and oranges. Rubber and elephant tusk were at one time objects of a prosperous and lucrative trade.[137] But the introduction of synthetic rubber and indiscriminate tapping of rubber trees brought the rubber traffic to an end, and the government's policy of wild life preservation has stopped elephant catching.

INDUSTRY

Industry in the modern sense practically did not exist among the tribal people of the North-East Frontier. But cottage industry to produce the household requirements existed almost among all tribes. Marketable surplus of cottage industry products consisted of wooden-musks and utensils, carpet and tribal dresses, painting and religious scrolls called "thang-kas." In addition, there were a little handmade paper from the Mompa tribe,[138] cotton balnket of artistic design called "Jom" from the Adis,[139] coats and houses from the Mishmis,[140] and at one time artistic jewellery inlaid with stones from the Khampti tribes.[141] The Nishis produce fine hats from cane and bamboo but they did not have a market.[142]

FAIRS

Inside the hills there are practically no daily or weekly bazars or marts where the tribal people may sell their products and purchase their requirements excepting some

permission to send an envoy to Lhasa by the same route from Assam.[151] Unfortunately, the British Government did not take any step to implement the idea though the issue was discussed time and again. The specification of the Inner Line on the Darrang frontier again put a barrier on Indian traders to trade freely with Tibet and the hills leading to Lhasa.

RELIGION AND CULTURE

MIXTURE OF RELIGIONS

To satisfy his mental and spiritual hunger, man has through the ages built up a spiritual world from which he derives guidance for every-day life. The people of the North-East Frontier are no exception; they also have developed a supernatural world to brighten the stark realities of life. They believe in a world of good and evil spirits hovering in the air about them and on the earth below, and long to appease enmity or enlist the aid of these secret powers by sacrifice.

Unfortunately, the European officers on whose reports we have to depend mainly for our information on the North-East Frontier during the British regime have not left any favourable account of the religious practices of the tribal people. "In no field are our old records more imperfect than in that of religion", observes Elwin.[152] The general attitude of the European writers towards the tribal religion is that the tribes did not have any religion at all, or that it was a mixture of all the various idolatries and superstitions.[153]

But a careful study of te religious practices of the tribal people show that in building the spiritual world the people of the frontiers have been influenced by the religious practices of their neighbours and have adapted some of their practices or beliefs to their requirements. The Mompas, the Khambas and Membas profess the Mahayana form of Buddhism.[154] Khamptis follow Hinayana Buddhism which they brought with them from Khampti Long, while others worship the Hindu goddess Devi or Durga.[155] The Singphos who have accommodated the religious practices of their neighbours follow Buddhism and Brahmanism and have decorated their temples with images of different gods and goddesses.[156] Some Noctes of Tirap profess the Mahapurushia form of Vaishnavism propagted by Srimanta Sankardeva in Assam, while the Wanchos and Tangsas of Tirap follow their tribal religion.[157]

The people who have been influenced by the religion of their neighbours have also built temples or sanctuaries like their neighbours. In the Buddhist region of Kameng, every village has a Gompa or temple and every house has its own chapel and altar with a statue of the Buddha. The Buddhist monastery of Tawang, which accommodates a magnificient statue of the Buddha, is the largest of its kind in India.[158] During the Buddha Purnima, the Mompas celebrate the Losar festival in a spectacular manner with the accompaniment of musical instruments, like clarionet — made of silver, brass and wood, reed-pipes, horns, shells cymbals, drums and gongs. There are many shrines and temples in Khamba and Memba villages of Subansiri.[159]

But still a considerable number of people of the North-East Frontier follow what may be called tribal religion or the so-called animism which is a sort of primitive religion to be found anywhere in the tribal societies. The characteristics of primitive religion, as Will Durant has observed, "are an animistic fear and worship of spirits lurking anywhere, a poetic reverence for the impressive forms and reproductive powers of earth, and an awed adoration of a heaven whose energising sunlight and fertilising rains are parts of the sky."[160] This definition of animism is corroborated by Prof. E.O.James who writes : "The doctrine of animism represents a complex attempt to interpret the material and spiritual aspects of the phenomenal world by revolving the universe into a fundamental dualism of Body and Soul."[161]

The Adis of Siang, the Akas and Khowas of Kameng, the Nishis of Subansiri, the Mishmis of Lohit and the Wanchos and Tangsas of Tirap believe in a number of heavenly spirits and offer sacrifices to propitiate them. The Akas regard the sun and the moon as the male and female god and goddess respectively who have the powers of peace and prosperity, and they offer sacrifices to enlist their support.[162] The Nishis regard moon as male and sun as female deity and trace their descent from their union.[163] The Adis of Siang and the Mishmis of Lohit regard Donyi-Polo or the Sun-Moon god as the supreme reality and offer sacrifices for his favours.[164] The Wanchos believe in Rang, the benevolent god of the skies, who cares for men and beasts, and Baurang, the Malevolent god of earth and destroyer of living creatures, and offer sacrifices to appease them.[165]

The remarkable feature of the tribal religion as practised in the North-East Frontier is the absence of shrine or temple, as also of image worship. Nor is any organised clergy or priesthood dependent on religious performances as distinct from the rest of the community to be found among the tribes except some religious functionaries like the Epak Miris and the Nyibo[166] of Adi society and the Tumsawa of Singphos[167] and the Opa or Nampa Aja, Rampa and the Rammi of the Wancho society.[168] Women usually do not take part in religious functions; worship among them means prayer and offering sacrifices. Sacrifice is followed by community feast and wine is consumed on the occasion of offering sacrifices.[169]

Emile Lasbax, in an article on *Rhythm of Sacrifice and Prayer*, has observed, "Primitive sacrifice is always an offering under one aspect or another; it is a sacrifice of the firstlings. The sentiment which inspires it is that the materials should never be used without some reserve; for it becomes an absolute master who has himself produced them to sacrifice them without some reserve. It should not be forgotten that their true creator is God, and therefore, it is equitable to offer Him the first fruit, which it has permitted to us to gather, in gratitude for this first gift. The sacrifice of man thus appears to be the exact counterpart of the creative work of God."[170]

But the tribes of the North-East Frontier are practical people. Their attitude to religion might originally have been influenced by the sense of awe and reverence, but it is now based on the system of barter and purchase. So the sacrifices performed by them are mostly performed for worldly gains. The agricultural ceremonies and sacrifices are performed with a view to ensuring good growth of healthy crops and preventing disease and failure of crops.[171] Other rites are performed either to keep away the evil spirits or to bring in prosperity.[172] Thus, their sacrifices have nothing to do with the firstlings as suggested by Lasbax.

The world of the spirits is not confined to the forces above the earth alone; it extends to the world of the dead as well. Most of the tribes believe in a separate world of the dead. The Akas believe that the spirits of the dead go under the earth and proceed westward until they come to the place where the sun and the moon set; then they ascend to heaven. But the souls of those who die unnatural death and of the children too...... ascend direct to heaven without undergoing the pilgrimage under the earth.[173] The Nishis have similar notions about the dead, but they hold that there are villages under the earth for those who die a natural death and villages in heaven for those who die unnatural death and for the children's spirits.[174] The Misings and the Mishmis also ascribe an abode underneath for the spirits of the dead.[175]

Since the tribes believe in the existence of the spirits of the dead, they put in the graves of the dead some food, clothes, weapons and other items of daily use to aid the journey of the spirits. The Adis place in one hand of the dead a small knife as an aid for getting food on the way to the spiritual home. A gourd of rice beer is tied under the grave and various garments of the deceased; any heads of mithum, etc. killed by him and used to feast the community are suspended on the posts nearby or under the shelter.[176] The Akas and Nishis hang a basket of rice, meat, beer, etc., near the grave of the departed.[177] The Mishmis put the corpse on a wooden couch, fully clothed and armed and with food, money, utensils etc. under the grave.[178]

In fact, the religious philosophy of the Arunachal tribes, be it Buddhist or Hindu or Animist, is based on a strong sense of history, a pride in the descent of the race from a great ancestor, and a belief in the value of sacrifice for the common good.[179] This is again founded on five cardinal tenets. First, the tribes believe in a supreme God who is just, benevolent and good. Their religion emphasises the spiritual realities behind the daily life. The tribes have faith in kind tutelary spirits and emphasise the spiritual cause of tragedy. Religion in North-East Frontier, as elsewhere, is closely associated with social ethics that unites the tribe in its discipline and promotes virtues like generosity, hospitality, truth, kindness and devotion to work. Finally, their religion gives them the power to reconcile themselves to the frequent emergencies of life.[180]

The study of the Arunchal tribes, thus, reveals strange contrasts. Some of these tribes, like the Mompas and Sherdukpens of Kameng and the Khamptis of Lohit, together with the Khambas and Membas of Subansiri, possess a remarkable culture and an advanced form of religion in contrast to the rest who follow more or less their ancestral religion which is again typical of primitive society everywhere in the ancient world. In some areas, the tribes practise what may be called permanent cultivation on irrigated terraces and valleys, whereas in others, tribes follow jhuming or shifting cultivation. In some tribes, workmanship in cane and bamboo shows remarkable dexterity while in others it is practically unknown, but then they are far more dexterous in wood carving and painting. It is quite difficult to state categorically whether these people are Hindu or anything else, for the terms Hindu is so catholic and elaborate as to embrace not only the followers of Gautama Buddha and Mahavira, the great teacher of Jainism, but also the worshippers of snake and spirits, supposed to be the presiding deities of natural forces or calamities and diseases.

But the recent excavations at the foothills of NEFA have brought to fore yet another problem. The ruins of Bhismarkanagar about thirty miles from Sadiya,[181] the Tamreswari temple nearby and the ruins of a palace at Malinithan, a place near Likhabali in the Siang district, prove conclusively that these are of Hindu origin and construction.[182] Besides, there are some relics of Hindu culture at Bhalukpong in the present Kameng district to the north-west of Tezpur; a Buddhist gompa or cave exists at Dirang in the Subansiri district, a stupa has been found at Vijaynagar in the Tirap district, and there is the Bhairav Kund on the western tip of Kameng district.[183] Parasuram Kund, a famous place of Hindu pilgrimage in the Lohit district, still attracts numerous Hindu pilgrims from all over India. How do we relate these sites to the present tribes?

A recollection of the traditions associated with these places may suggest some solution. In the sacred Vaishnava work, *Srimad Bhagavata,* there is a story that the king of Vidarbha, Bhismaka, had a beautiful daughter Rukmini by name. The king had arranged her marriage with a prince named Sisupala, the ruler of a kingdom in the neighbourhood; but Sri Krisna, the lord of Dwaraka, carried her away by a stratagem and married her.[184] The present Bhismaknagar on the river Kundil near Sadiya was known in ancient times as Vidarbha. The ruins are said to represent the palace of the king Bhismaka alluded to in the Bhagavata.[185] Excavations in 1967 brought to light a phallic stone representing lord Siva. The Chutias of Assam claim to be descendants of the same king. The copper temple near Bhismaknagar is also attributed to the Chutia kings of Vidarbha. The temple is the shrine of Kechai Gohaini which still now is revered by the Chutias and Cacharies of Assam. Two copper plates in Sanskrit have been restored from this place.[186]

The next important site excavated is Malinithan. It is not at a great distance from Bhismaknagar. Local traditions say that Krishna while going back to his home, Dwaraka, rested here with Rukmini, the daughter of Bhismaka, whom he had married, as the guest of Lord Siva and his consort Parvati. During their sojourn, Parvati had offered garlands of beautiful flowers from her garden. Lord Krishna, who was overwhelmed with the charm and beauty of these flowers, addressed Parvati as Malini or mistress of the garden. Since then the place was known as Malinithan or the abode of mistress of the garden. The *Kalikapurana* says that when the body of Sati, wife of Siva, was cut to pieces by Vishnu with his holy discus, her head fell somewhere on the Akasi Ganga. Some hold that the same river flowed once by the present site of Malinithan. The North-East Frontier Agency authorised L.N. Chakravarty, Deputy Director of Research (History), who had traced out the Sivalinga or the phallic stone at Bhismaknagar in 1968, to undertake the excavation of Malinithan. He has already exhumed over one hundred images of various gods and goddesses of Hindu pantheon, Yaksas in dancing postures, figurines, sculptured panels, animal motifs such as those of bull, lion, elephant, etc., and some iron dowels or clamps used to hold building materials instead of mortar; some geometric and floral designs have also been discovered by him. An eight-foot high plinth of a temple, most beautifully and florally decorated, has also been unearthed. Images of Indra, seated on elephant, Kartikeya on a peacock and Ganesh have also been found, besides Sarawati and Nandi, the vehicle of Lord Siva. The excavations have proved conclusively that the ruins are of Hindu civilisation that flourished perhaps before the tenth century.[187]

Moving westward up the hills one comes across the cave temple of Dirang associated with the Buddhist religion in Subansiri. But further west at the foot of hills below in the Kameng district at Bhalukpong there are the ruins of yet another palace with temple sites in and around it. This place is associated with the name of another Puranic king Bana. In the *Vishnu Purana,* we have a reference to king Bali whose son Bana was contemporary of legendary Naraka of Kamakhaya. The king Bana, who had a palace at Bhalukpong, had a very beautiful daughter Usha by name. Krishna's son Aniruddha was charmed by her beauty and she consented to marry him; the two lovers secretly escaped from the palace. Bana, enraged at this, chased the fugitives, but they were rescued by Krishna who had meanwhile arrived on the spot and defeated Bana's contingent.[188] Besides, the Bhairav Kund of this district is associated with the king Bana who was a devotee of Lord Siva.

Parasuram Kund, where the holy river Lohit, known as the Brahmaputra, descends on the plains, is regarded by the Hindus as a place of pilgrimage, and on Magh Bihu in the middle of January pious people and pilgrims from all over India came to take a dip in its holy waters. There is a story that Parasuram had killed his mother with an axe at the command of his father and had thus committed a great sin. His father told him to take a dip in the Brahmakund at the place now known as Parasuramkund which would absolve him of his ghastly sin. He did accordingly and was purified by this act.[189]

Now the association of Hindu legends with these places, references to these places in the Puranas and Tantras, and excavations carried out so far prove beyond doubt that people of these places were influenced by Hindu religion and civilisation right from very ancient times. But when and how Hindu civilisation penetrated into Assam can only be conjectured, for no connected history of Assam in its religious and cultural aspects till the advent of Ahoms in 1226 A.D. is available. Then we have only accounts of Ahom warfare with the Assam valley chiefs with occasional references to some customs and costumes with artifices. The condition of Assam at the time of the Ahom incursion is not known in its all aspects. The remains of civilisation that have been unearthed are said to be remnants of the culture of the Chutia, Kalitas and Bhuyans, who have almost merged their identity with the rest of the people of the valley. The problems of identity of the people with this civilisation can be solved in the light of "Sanskritisation" theory of Srinivas.[190] Then the claim of the Mishmis that they descended from Bhismaka, the legendary king of Kundil, and the tradition of the Akas who regard themselves as descendants of king Bana can be resolved.

An analysis of the culture and the people involved may help an understanding of the problem. The Chutias who are identified with the Kacharis of the south bank of the Brahmaputra are a people of the Mongolian stock without any doubt. Again, it is a proved fact that they had come to stay in the valley right from the beginning of the Christian era. The present state of their (Chutias) culture and living may lead to the conclusion that the culture which flourished at Bhismaknagar, Malinithan and Sonitpur (Tezpur) could not have been developed by them alone; there must have been some outside Aryan influence over them. But at the same time it is also clear that they continued to be the predominant people before the flood of C.A.D. 1750, and were gradually dispersed thence by the Ahoms and other people.

The Kalitas and Bhuyans were almost the same people and perhaps were pioneers of the Aryan elements in the Assamese population. If we accept the view of Gait that the Aryans penetrated into the Kirat country and established petty kingdoms we may assume that these Aryans established themselves among the Kirat people and in course of time became princes, as their counterparts did in the Malay peninsula and archipelago.[191] S.K. Chatterjee also holds the same view.[192] Thus, a new type of culture began to generate in the upper valleys of the Brahmaputra and it subsequently flourished at places like Bhismaknagar and Malinithan.

A critical appreciation of the stories relating to the origin of the ruling dynasties of the localities brings one to the conclusion that these kingdoms and culture were the results of the labours of the indigenous Kirat people who had immigrated from Mongolia in China to the valleys of the Brahmputra and the Aryan people who fused themselves with these people. Stories of union of the native princes with Hindu gods in the guise of some kings or princes and queens with Brahmanas or some Aryan chiefs are frequently brought forth in tracing the origin of different powerful chiefs. Thus Gourinarayan, the celebrated Chutia king, is said to be an offspring of the union of Kuber in the guise of Bispal with his queen Rupabati.[193] Another powerful prince of Arimatta was born of Ramchandra's wife Chandraprova when she eloped with the Brahmaputra.[194]

J.P. Wade narrates an account of origin of the Jaintia Raja in the following words: "Zointeh Rai had no children but solicited Takoor Ranee by pious exercise to bless him with a son. Devee in a dream visited him and informed him that destiny had determined that he should not have offspring, but that she would supersede his destiny as a recompense for his devotions at her altar and grant his request. She accordingly promised to be herself the child, and to be born of the princess, his wife.... In due course of time, a most beautiful child saw the light in his family. The king sought in vain a husband worthy of her and ultimately married the daughter to his confidential adviser Sundobur's son Sundahburra, a Brahmin."[195]

In tracing the origin of Kacharis also the same author observes, "Deongdana had paid her assiduous devotion to Sioo to obtain the favour of a male child. The god appeared to her in a dream and directed her to receive a stranger who should visit her the ensuing day into her embraces, promising her a son who should become prince of that country". The two former races of princes are also said to have descended from the conquerer Bhim (an Aryan chief of the *Mahabharata*).[196] A similar origin is attributed to the Koch king Biswa Singh. His father Hurria Mundal had two wives, Leela and Heera. The latter was carrying some repast for her husband who was at work in the field. On the way, Mahadeo, assuming the form of Hurria, surprised her under a tree and devoured the repast and caressed her on the spot. In due course, a son was born of this union and he became the founder of the kingdom of the Koches.[197]

When we study these stories in the larger perspective of Hindu expansion from the 3rd century A.D. to the 12th century A.D. in the countries adjacent to India, particularly in Burma, Malay, Siam, Cambodia and the Malayan Archipelago, it is quite clear that some adventures from within India made their way into the valley of the Brahmaputra and, like their counterparts, in the South-East Asian countries, succeeded in establishing themselves as either rulers or advisers of the rulers in the region and thus laid the foundation of a new civilisation there. Maybe they were Kalitas and their successors (Bhuyans) who later on were expelled or absorbed by the Shan Ahoms and Khamptis after their incursion into the valley across the Patkai range.

But the problem of placing the present tribes of the North-East Frontier into line still remains. It appears that they came down from Tibetan territories when the Chutia kingdom began to decline and when these tribes originally one and the same came down on the Assam plains. But it may be conjectured that unless there was a major disturbance or upheaval in their original home they might not have migrated to their present homes. It is quite probable that when the Mongol leader Chengis Khan's descendant Godam, who was governor of the Kansu region of China, invaded Tibet in 1239 A.D. looting and killing everything before him, some tribes of the Khams region of Tibet descended on the southern slopes of the Himalayan ranges.[198] The Chutias faced the Ahoms from the south and the Tibetan hordes from the north. When the Ahoms gradually suppressed the Chutias of the north bank, these tribes further came down on the plains and established their sway over the helpless plains people. Further, the flood of the Dehing which submerged the plains of the Upper Assam valley for more than a fortnight in 1750 A.D. facilitated the tribal expansion and weakened the position of the people of the plains.[199] A section of the tribes, now known as Misings, came down to settle on the plains after the recession of the flood waters. Capt. Kennedy, who accompanied the Aka promenade of 1913-14, records an interesting tradition which says that the Akas along with other hill tribes went in search of land; the Akas lost time in resting and drinking beer when others took possession of better lands.[200]

The Linguistic Survey of India has shown that the tribes living in the present frontier tracts speak a language of Tibeto-Burman family of North Assam group with the exception of the Khamptis, who speak a language of Chinese-Siamese family of Tai group. The Khamptis from the Bar Khampti land began to migrate to Assam from the 8th century and gradually pushing the Chutias occupied territories on the Lohit and Dehing; the Singphos came much later in the wake of the Burmese in 1822-23, or just before them, from Burma. Again, the Khamptis profess the Buddhist religion which they brought from their original home, the Bar Khampti country. The tribes of the central tracts follow tribal religion. Therefore, it seems quite clear that the tribes living west of the Khamptis of the Lohit district belong to a separate race and the tribes of the Abor hills or Subansiri district and the Khamptis and Singphos of Lohit had nothing to contribute to the Hindu civilisation that flourished in Bhismaknagar and Malinithan. The tribes of the western district Kameng had not settled on the plains of Assam when these centres of Hindu religion and civilisation developed; they tended to come down when it had begun to decline.

A survey of the land, that is, the physical features and topography, of the North-East Frontier reveals that the natural frontier of North-Eastern India is the crest of the Eastern Himalayas and Patkai mountains which separate the Brahmaputra waterparting from the San Po and the Irrawady-Salwin watersheds. The study of the population shows that the population of the North-East Frontier is Mongoloid and is the pre-dominant ethnic element in the population of North-East India. A review of the culture of the North-East Frontier leads one to conclude that it is an admixture of Indian, Tibetan and Burmese elements, and through the North-East

India has absorbed tibeto-Burman cultural elements to enrich her variegated cultural profile.

It may be concluded, perhaps, without the risk of over simplification, that the Aryan civilisation which penetrated into the valley of the Brahmaputra before the beginning of the Christian era, continued to flourish through centuries of Ahom and British though there can be no denying the fact that the economy and culture of the hills on both sides of the valley influenced that growth. As a result of this mutual give-and-take, the economy and culture of both the hills and plains developed and prospered. As the San Po, orginating from the Lake Manas, becomes the mighty Brahmaputra in the Assam plains, drawing the waters of innumerable tributaries coming down the hills, so also the economy and culture of the plains of Assam have flourished with the contributions of the hills. Again, as a powerful lamp radiates light and expels darkness around, the Hindu civilisation that flourished in the valley of the Brahmaputra enlightened the tribes living on the hills.

REFERENCES

1. The total length of the McMahon Line is 1,312 km (820 miles) of which 192 km. (120 miles) border with Burma and Tibet and 1,120 km (700 miles) border with Tibet. See *Foreign Political (Secret) Proceedings (India)*, October 1914, Nos. 134-396.
2. Administrative Jurisdictions, p. 6.
3. Foreign Secret Proceedings (India), January 1911, No. 239.
4. A.C.Banerjee, *The Eastern Frontier of British India*, p. 365.
5. H. Vinacke, *A History of the Far East in Modern Times*, p. 62.
6. A.Amanatulla, *A History of Cooch-Behar* (in Bengali), pp. 39-43
7. Ram Rahul, *The Himalaya Borderland*, p. 64.
8. G.A. Grierson, *Linguistic Survey of India*, p.136.
9. H.E. Richardson, *Tibet and its History*, p. 1.
10. Foreign Secret Proceedings (India), January 1911, No. 239.
11. A. Gansser, *Geology of the Himalayas*, pp. 227-30.
12. *Ibid.*, pp.227-29.
13. R.L. Sing (ed), *India—A Regional Geography*, pp.82-84.
14. *Ibid.*
15. North-East Frontier Agency, henceforth referred to as NEFA, *The Land and the People*, p. 4.
16. *Ibid.*

17. T.S. Murty, "Historical and de facto position of the Buddhist Pockets", An article published in the *Institute for Defence Studies and Analysis Journal,* vol. 3, No. 4, April 1971.
18. J.P. Dalvi, *The Himalayan Blunder,* pp. 108-09 (map).
19. F.M. Baily, "Explorations on the Tsangpo or Upper Brahmaputra," *The Geographical Journal,* vol. XLIV, p. 357, Nevill's and Dalvi's topographical features do not tally with Bailey's (Dalvi, p. 113).
20. *NEFA, op. cit.,* p. 4.
21. *Administration Jurisdictions,* p. 6.
22. C. Von Furer-Haimendorf, *Ethnographic Notes on the Tribes of the Subansiri Region,* p. 3.
23. V. Elwin, *India's North-East Frontier in the Nineteenth Century,* p.185, henceforth referred to as *North-East Frontier.*
24. *NEFA, op. cit.,* p. 8.
25. Ram Rahul, *op. cit.,* p. 7.
26. A. Gansser, *op. cit.,* p. 229.
27. V. Elwin, *North-East Frontier.*
28. T.S. Murty, *op. cit.*
29. V. Elwin, *North-East Frontier.*
30. *Administrative Jurisdictions,* p. 6.
31. A. Gansser, *op. cit.,* p. 229.
32. NEFA, *op. cit.,* p. 11.
33. A. Gansser, *op. cit.,* p. 230.
34. *Ibid.*
35. S.D. Misra, *Rivers of India,* p. 28.
36. Ram Rahul, *op. cit.,* p. 9.
37. NEFA, *op. cit.,* p. 11.
38. A. Gansser, *op. cit.,* p. 229.
39. V. Elwin, *North-East Frontier,* pp. 9-10.
40. J.P. Mills, *Notes on the Mishmis,* p. 2.
41. *Ibid.*
42. *Administrative Jurisdictions,* p. 6.
43. A. Gansser, *op. cit.,* p. 230.
44. NEFA, *op. cit.,* p. 17.
45. R.L. Sing (ed), *op. cit.,* p. 486.
46. T.S. Murty, *op.cit.*
47. S.D. Misra, *op. cit.,* p. 29.
48. NEFA, *op. cit.,* p. 17.
49. V. Elwin, *North-East Frontier.*
50. A. Mackenzie, *History of the Relations of the Government with the Hill Tribes of the North-East Frontier of Bengal,* p. 61., henceforth referred to as History.
51. Lakhimpur Deputy Commissioner's Collection No. XII, F. 71, 1904-08.
52. V. Elwin, *North-East Frontier,* pp. 25-26.
53. *Ibid.,* p.104.

54. NEFA, *op. cit.*, p. 22.
55. R.L. Sing (ed), *op. cit.*, p. 500.
56. NEFA, *op. cit.*, p. 22.
57. R.L. Sing (ed), *op. cit.*, p. 480.
58. *Ibid.*
59. *Ibid.*, p. 492.
60. W. Robinson, *A Descriptive Account of Assam*, p. 335.
61. Census Report, 1901, vol. IV, Part I, Chap. XI, p. 120.
62. V. Elwin, *North-East Frontier*, p. 438.
63. Assam Census Report, 1881, para 153, Census Report, 1931, vol. V, Part III, p. XIII.
64. Lakhimpur Deputy Commissioner's Collection, No. XII, F. 7, 1904-08.
65. S. Roy, *Aspects of Padam Minyong Culture*, pp. 1-5.
66. P., Buragohain, "Tai Jati" and article published from Assam in a journal named *Tai Sanskriti* in 1956, No. 2, aserts that the Ahoms are from Mongolia and are same with the Mongols of Mongolia.
67. Census of India Report, 1901, Part I, vol. IV, p. 120.
68. V. Elwin, *North-East Frontier*, pp. 435-36.
69. T.S. Murty, *op. cit.*
70. *Ibid.*
71. V. Elwin, *North-East Frontier*, p. 438.
72. E.A. Gait, *A History of Assam*, p. 16.
73. Census of India, 1961, p. 240.
74. W. Robinson, *op. cit.*, p. 353.
75. Census of India, 1961, pp. 246-50.
76. *Ibid.*
77. Census of Indian Report, 1931, Part III, p. xiv.
78. *Ibid.*, 1961, p. 250.
79. W. Robinson, *op. cit.*, p. 353.
80. Census of India, 1961, p. 252.
81. L. Gogi, *The Tai Khamptis*, p. ix.
82. Selection from Bengal papers, No. 23, p. 6.
83. H. Barua, *Asom Buranji*, pp. 11-12.
84. G. Grierson, *op. cit.*, pp. 126, 136.
85. *Ibid.*, p. 568.
86. *Ibid.*, p. 141.
87. *Ibid.*, p. 499.
88. *Ibid.*
89. *Ibid.*, pp. 2-11.
90. Census of India Report, 1921, Part I, Appendix B, p. x.
91. *Ibid.*
92. *Ibid.*, 1931, Part III, p. xiv.
93. *Ibid.*, 1921, Part II, p. xii.
94. E.T. Dalton, *Descriptive Ethnology of Bengal*, p. 11.
95. Census Report, 1961, p. 231.

96. V. Elwin, *The Art of the North-East Frontier of India,* henceforth referred to as the Administrative, pp. 16-17.
97. NEFA, *op. cit.,* p. 1.
98. Census of India Report, 1921, Part I, p. xi.
99. *Ibid.,* 1931, Part III, p. xiii.
100. *Ibid.,* 1921, Part II, p. xii.
101. *Ibid.*
102. S. Johri, *Where India, China and Burma Meet,* p. 121.
103. Census of India Report, 1921, Part I, Appendix B, p. xi.
104. *Ibid.*
105. S. Roy, *op. cit.,* p. 194.
106. S. Johri, *op. cit.,* pp. 170-71.
107. *Ibid.,* p. 155.
108. *Ibid.,* p. 170.
109. V. Elwin, *The Art,* pp. 71-73.
110. J.N. Chowdhury, *A Comparative Study of the Adi Religion,* p. 45.
111. S. Johri, *op. cit.,* p. 169.
112. V. Elwin, *The Art,* pp. 71-72.
113. S. Johri, *op. cit.,* p. 171.
114. A. Das, 'Fish in Arunachal,' *Pines,* vol. I, Part III, p. 24.
115. Census of India Report, 1931, Part III, p. xiv.
116. S. Johri, *op. cit.,* p. 182.
117. V. Elwin, *The Tribal World of Elwin* henceforth referred to as *The Tribal World.,* p. 274.
118. S. Johri, *op. cit.,* p. 182.
119. V. Elwin, *North-East Frontier,* p. 366.
120. Lakhimpur Deputy Commissioner's Collection, xvii, F. 17, 1917.
121. *Ibid.,* Collection No. XII, F. 7, 1884.
122. NEFA, pp. 18-19.
123. S. Roy, *op. cit.,* p. 223.
124. V. Elwin, *Democracy in NEFA* henceforth referred to as Democracy pp. 87-89, 177-78, 171-72.
125. V. Elwin, *The Tribal World,* p. 265.
126. Foreign Proceedings (Assam), March 1885, No. 40.
127. V. Elwin, *Democracy, op. cit.,* pp. 57-59.
128. V. Elwin, *The Art, op. cit.,* p. 20.
129. *Ibid.*
130. Census of India Report, 1921, p. xii.
131. NEFA, *op. cit.,* pp. 23-24.
132. V. Elwin, *The Art, op. cit.,* p. 20.
133. Col. C. Furer-Haimendorf, *op. cit.,* pp. 56-57.
134. S. Roy, *op. cit.,* pp. 121-22.
135. V. Elwin, *North-East Frontier,* p. 350.
136. Census of India, 1961, p. 233.
137. Report on the Trade between Assam and the adjoining foreign countries, 1890.

138. V. Elwin, *The Art, op. cit.*, p. 20.
139. *Ibid.*, p. 10.
140. *Ibid.*, p. 11.
141. E.T. Dalton, *op. cit.*, p. 9.
142. Census of India Report, 1961, p. 240.
143. Report on the Trade between Assam and adjoining foreign countries, 1890.
144. A. Mackenzie, *History*, p. 15.
145. Report on the Trade between Assam and the adjoining foreign countries, 1890.
146. R. Choudhury, 'A Note on the Sadiya Fair', *PINES*, vol. I, Part III, p. 77.
147. S.M.K. Shubani, "A Study in the Trans-Himalayan Trade through North-East of India," *Journal of the Assam Research Society*, vol. XVII, 1963, p. 46.
148. Lakhimpur Deputy Commissioner's Collection, No. XVI, F. 3, 1904-08.
149. Annual Report, Sadiya Frontier Tract, 1937-38.
150. S.M.K. Shubani, *op. cit.*, pp. 39-43.
151. *Ibid.*
152. V. Elwin, *North-East Frontier*, pp. xviii-xix.
153. *Ibid.*
154. V. Elwin, *The Art*, p. 16.
155. Assam Census Report, 1881, para 142.
156. V. Elwin, *North-East Frontier*, pp. 197-98.
157. Census of India Report, 1961, p. 232.
158. *NEFA, op. cit.*, pp. 4-5.
159. *Ibid.*, pp. 14-15.
160. W. Durant, *The Story of Civilisation*, p. 783.
161. O.E. James, *The Beginning of Religion*, p. 15.
162. Census of India Report, 1921, Part I, p. x.
163. *Ibid.*, Part II, p. xi.
164. *Ibid.*
165. NEFA, *op. cit.*, p. 23.
166. S. Roy, *op. cit.*, p. 244.
167. *Ibid.*
168. V. Elwin, *North-East Frontier*, p. 415.
169. S. Johri, *op. cit.*, p. 171.
170. Ramakrishna Mission, *Cultural Heritage of India*, vol. I, p. 176.
171. S. Roy, *op. cit.*, p. 248.
172. *Ibid.*
173. Census of India Report, 1921, Part I, Appendix B, p. x.
174. *Ibid.*, p. xi.
175. *Ibid.*, p. xiii.
176. *Ibid.*, 1931, Part III, p. xiv.
177. *Ibid.*, p. xi.

178. *Ibid.*, p. xii.
179. V. Elwin, *A Philosophy for NEFA,* henceforth referred to as A Philosophy.
180. *Ibid.*
181. R.M. Nath, *Background of Assamese Culture*, pp. 63-64.
182. L.N. Chakravarty, *Malinithan,* A pretty nice illustrated booklet published by Arunachal Pradesh Administration, Shillong, 1974.
183. R.M. Nath, *Glorious Assam,* p. 24.
184. *Bhagabata*, Book 10, chapter, 52-59; *Vishnu Purana*, Chapter 33, Verses 7-50.
185. R.M. Nath, *Background of Assamese Culture*, pp. 63-64.
186. *Ibid.*
187. L.N. Chakravarty, *op. cit.*
188. *Kalika Purana*, Chapter 83, Verses 16-48.
189. *Ibid.*
190. M.N. Srinivas, *Caste in Modern India and other Essays*, pp. 56-57. Srinivas holds that when a social group aspires for higher social status it tries to find a place in the Sanskrit hierarchy.
191. E. Gait, *op. cit.*, p. 15.
192. S.K. Chatterjee, *The Place of Assam in the History and Civilisation of India*, pp. 31-33.
193. Sarbananda Rajkumar, *Chutia, Bhuyan aru Matak Rajya*, p. 44.
194. J.P. Wade, *An Account of Assam,* (ed. B. Sarma), p. 37.
195. *Ibid.*, pp. 38, 59.
196. *Ibid.*, p. 184.
197. *Ibid.*, p. 45.
198. H. E. Richardson, *op. cit.*, p. 33.
199. V. Elwin, *North-East Frontier*, p. 4.
200. *Ibid.*, p. 438.

2

BRITISH RELATIONS WITH THE TRIBES OF THE NORTH-EAST FRONTIER

During the decaying days of the Ahom regime, the diffrent tribes of the North-East Frontier began to come down and establish themselves on the plains below their hills. The Ahom king Pratap Singha, to conciliate the tribes and secure the frontiers of his kingdom, granted them some lands in the Duars through which they came down. These grants were made usually to provide the hill people with articles which were not grown or available in the hills. The grants took the form of land, with people to cultivate the land, and sometimes some marshes were given in grant to enable the hillmen get fishes from them.[1] The *paiks*, as the subjects of the Ahom kings were called, who provided articles to the hillmen or served them, got remission of revenue from the Ahom authorities.[2] After the annexation of Assam to the British dominions, the British found the valley surrounded on the north, east and south by numerous hill tribes who advanced claims to rights, more or less definite, over lands lying on the plains; some claimed tributary payments from the villages below their hills or the services of the *paiks* in those villages.[3] To begin with, such claims had been, to some extent and in some places, formally recognised by the British authorities. The British relations with these tribes show a gradual extinction or commutation of such claims, as we shall see in the succeeding pages of this chapter.

EXTRA-BHUTAN BHUTIAS (MOMPAS AND SHERDUKPENS)

In the north-western part of the North-Eastern Frontier lay the hills inhabited by the so-called extra-Bhutan Bhutias. These tribes are now known as the Mompas and Sherdukpens (thongjis) of the present Kameng Tawang districts of Arunachal Pradesh. They were under the rule of the chiefs who were called the Sat Rajas.[4] But the term was used by the Bhutias to denote the petty local chiefs of the frontier hills. The word 'Sat' (meaning seven) had perhaps no literal meaning or relation to actual number of chiefs. In the Darrang books (Register of Stipendiary chiefs) seven Rajas of Kuriapara were invariably recorded as pension or *posa* holders though the treaty edited by Aitchison shows that it was signed by only three Sat Rajas who perphaps were present at the time of the 1844 negotiations. But in case of the Charduar Bhutias, seven Rajas seem to have been always recognised.[5]

The Sat Rajas, who held Kuriapara, were subordinate to the governer of Tawang whom Aitchison calls 'Tong Debee Raja' and with whom the treaty of 1844 was concluded. The three Sat Rajas mentioned by Aitchison seem to be merely his subordinates.[6] Between the Sat Rajas and the governer of Tawang, there were two Gellengs who held office for three years.[7] The Bhutias of this area during the cold season used to make their headquarters at Amrotal, a place about half a day's journey from the border of the Darrang district, whence they came down to the Udalguri fair. Their houses were supposed to be five easy marches from Amrotal. The two Gellengs stayed at Amrotal and came to Udalguri if the Chief Commissioner or Deputy Commissioner specially sent for them, but usually they sent representatives who were merely traders.[8]

Before the British occupation of Assam, these tribes used to hold the Kuriapara Duars (situated between Bornadi in the west and Deoshan in the east) for four months a year, from the 15th October; during the remaining months these territories were held by the Ahom authorities.[9] Pratap Singha is said to have granted them this right to enable them to procure the commodities which were not available in their hills. The Bhutias paid due tribute for their concession.[10] The Bhutias also came in large numbers from their hills to the fair at Udalguri and exchanged their goods with the merchants of the plains. After the annexation of Assam to the Company's territories, they continued to hold Kuriapara. The Collector of Darrang, Capt. Vetch, proposed in 1838 that the Bhutias should not be allowed to collect *posa* as they did during the Ahom days, and they should, instead, be paid in cash. It was troublesome and beyond the dignity of the British Government to allow the Bhutias to collect dues which they might have wrested from the 'effeminate' Ahom authorities.[11] He estimated the revenue of the area to be somewhere between 10-12 lakhs of rupees, and if the lands were settled with the ryots, they would leave a good surplus after paying the *posa* to the Bhutias. The agreement, he suggested, should provide for recognition of the British army to march through their hills, should that be necessary. The Bhutias should not allow criminals to settle or seek asylum in their hills and should not violate the British territory.[12] His proposal was approved of by the then Commissioner Jenkins and it was also agreed to by the Supreme Goverment of the Company.[13]

But the Bhutias refused the overtures for relinquishment of their rights in consideration of cash payment by the British.[14] Then on the score of a Bhutia raid in 1843-44, a blockade was instituted against the Bhutias of the Kuriapara Duars and negotiations were instituted with their chiefs for relinquishing their rights in the Duars.[15] Three agents of the governor of Tawang came down to negotiate along with the local chiefs with a view to concluding and engagement for settlement. It was finally agreed that the Bhutias would receive Rs. 5,000 in lieu of their *posa* in the Duars and would recognise the limit of the British jurisdiction up to the foot hills. They would not allow criminals to seek asylum in their hills and hand them over if asked for by the British authorities.[16]

The relations between the British and these Sat Rajas remained peaceful till 1852 when a misunderstanding arose. One of the Gellengs who was vested with supervisory powers over other chiefs declared himself independent of his authority and intercepted the money paid by the British Government to the Sat Rajas.[17] For some time, he held his own position but eventually he fled from the hills and took refuge in British territory. The army sent by these so-called Bhutias for the capture of the Gelleng demanded his extradition in peremtory terms from the British and threatened perpetual war in the event of refusal.[18] The British Government mustered 400 troops and a couple of six-pounders to face the imminent invasion of the Durrang frontier. But the effect of British concentration dampened the morale of the Bhutia army and they assumed a compromising tone. Instead of the head of the Gelleng, they now asked for the Governor General's Agent a certificate to the effect that the rebel was no longer alive. This, they thought, would save their honour.[19] The cerificate was denied and eventually they were made to sign the treaty again concluded in 1844, in which they gave an undertaking that the followers of the rebel in the hills would be pardoned.[20]

Since the confrontation of 1852-53, peace between the Tawang Bhutias and the British was never broken. The British Government did not interfere in the affairs within the hills nor did the Bhutias ever raid the plains. The retreating Bhutia army, in violation of the 1853 undertaking that they would not take action against the partisans of the Gelleng, did not honour their word; they brutally murdered supproters of the rebel. The British did not go for satisfaction of the breach of the undertaking as the event had occurred within the hills, outside the British jurisdiction.[21] In 1861, the Gelleng went back to the hills and was reconciled to his master, the governor of Tawang.[22] But once again, in consequence of a quarrel, he fled to the plains; the Bhutias did not pursue him.[23] He continue to live in a house in Kuriapara. But in April 1864 a party of the Bhutias fell upon him by night and murdered him. The British Government did not take any action against the murderer though it had occurred within the British jurisdiction; there was no breach between the bhutias and the Government.[24]

To the east of the Rowta river and the west of the Bhorali (known as Belsiri in 1875) lay the Charduar territory from which the Rupa and Shergaon Bhutias now known as Sherdukpens or Thongjis collected dues along with the Akas (Hrussos) and Nishis.[25] The Bhutias of Rupa and Shergaon were termed Bhutias Roop Roe Gya and Surgyah respectively in Aitchison's *Treaties* (CVI). The hills of these Bhutias were two days' march from the plains of Charduar.[26] These Bhutias were supposed to be independent of the Twang governor till 1875, and were under the authority of the local chiefs styled Sat Rajas like the hills north of Kuriapara as we have already seen. One of these Sat Rajas (who were seven in number) was Darji Raja of Rupa who was considered to be superior to others.[27]

L. Devi, in her book *Ahom Tribal Relations,* mentions that king Partap Singha had probably granted the right to *posa* to the Bhutias to keep uniformity with the other neighbouring tribes of the Akas and Nishis to whom he had granted similar privilege.[28] There is no authoritative record of the grant, however, in any document or in the Ahom Buranjis. Sir Alexander Mackenzie, in his *Memorandum* observes that the 'Assam Rajas' granted them this right to collect necessaries from the Duars in lieu of tribute paid to the 'Ahom Rajas.'[29] The British after annexation of Assam allowed the collection by the Bhutias to continue for some times. The Government of India held the view that the system should not be stopped because that might lead to troubles and since it did not affect its interest immediately the continuance of the practice "however injurious" was allowed.[30] Capt. White, however, was authorised to carry on negotiations for termination of the system.[31] He recommended money payment in lieu of 'blackmail' to be collected by the Bhutias.[32] Capt. Mathai, the Collector and Magistrate of Darrang, also regarded the system as detrimental to peace and prosperity of the Duars and he was authorised to conduct negotiation to substitute cash payment stopping direct collection by the Bhutias. The result was an engagement concluded between the Sat Rajas of Rupa and Shergaon and Capt. Mathai in 1836 wherein the former agreed to relinquish their rights to direct collection in consideration of an annual payment of Rs. 2526-7-0 as compensation. It may be observed that in the negotiations between the tribes and the British, no representative of the Tawang was present and that perhaps led the British to believe that these Bhutias were independent of the Tawang's authority.[33]

The British relations with the tribes of Rupa and Shergaon were strained in 1839 in consequence of the murder of Madhu Saikia a British subject, in a Charduar village. The Bhutias were charged with the murder and payment of *posa* was stopped.[34] The Darji Raja along with his other colleagues protested that for the alleged crime of two or three persons the whole community should not be charged, and promised good behaviour in future.[35] The British authorities were satisfied with this representation and on the recommendation of Capt. J.T. Gordon, the Collector of Darrang, payment of *posa* was resumed. But the amount of *posa* was reduced.[36] Thereafter, the relations with them were never strained during the rule of the British in India.

Next to the Rupa and the Shergaon tribes lived the so-called Thebanga Bhutias, who were later on called Tabang Bhutias or the tribe of Telenigah. They used to come down from their hills which were situated at a distance of 16 days' journey from Charduar. Along with the Rupa tribe, they collected dues from Charduar.[37] It was found later that the tribes of Rupa and Shergaon as also the Thebangas were subject to the Tawang governor but were under local chiefs called Sat Rajas. A resolution of the Chief Commissioner admits that those chiefs were subordinates of the Tawang governor. Their right to direct collection was replaced by the substitution of cash payment of Rs. 145-13-6.[38] The British never came to breach of peace with the Thebengas. In 1915, Nevill wrote to the Chief Commissioner to stop payment of *posa* to them as he considered that it had no effect in keeping them quiet and they hardly realised that they had any condition to fulfil.

In 1872-73 Lt. Col. Graham was authorised to demarcate boundary between Bhutan and the Extra-Bhutan Bhutia hills and the British districts of Kamrup and Darrang. He was instructed to exclude the Bhutia hills and to make the boundary line straight.[40] It appears from the records kept by Graham that the line he fixed up as boundary was accepted by the Sat Rajas of Tawang and Rupa and Shergaon, though the Sat Rajas of Shergaon and Rupa protested regarding the initial demarcation along the foothills.[41] But at the time of the promulgation of the Inner Line Regulation in the Darrang district in 1876, the hill chiefs protested against the restriction put on ryots on their entry into the hills from British territory.[42] On representation from the chiefs, the restriction on entry into their hills from the adjoining Duars were kept in suspension and all traders from beyond intending to go to the hills were granted permission to cross the Darrang Inner Line.[43]

After the division of the North-East Frontier into three charges subsequent to the Abor expedition of 1911 and the promulgation of the Assam Frontier Tract Regulation of 1880, as amended in 1884 and 1898, G.A. Nevill was appointed in 1914 as Political Officer of the Western Section of the North-East Frontier in which were included the hills inhabited by these Extra-Bhutan Bhutias or the Mompa and Sherdukpen tribes. The policy of the government was now to exercise "loose political control" over the chiefs of the hills. Nevill went on tour in 1914 to the hills starting from Jamiri above Kuriapara and through the Aka hills and reached Tawang.[44] Everywhere he was welcomed by the jubilant crowds which had mustered on the way. But though measures of control were contemplated, the outbreak of the First Great Was prevented the government from going ahead with the new policy.

After the war, the freedom movement in India and introduction of reforms in administration kept the hands of the government tied for some time. Again, in the thirties, the government mooted measures for bringing these hills under direct control and Capt. Lightfoot, who had succeeded Nevill as Political Officer, went on tour to Tawang in 1937-38 and proposed measures to bring the hills under control.[45] But the outbreak of the Second World War again prevented the government from taking any effective step to administer these hills.[46] After the war, the British Government withdrew from India and independent India began to set up administrative centres within these hills to the great relief of the local people.

THE AKAS

The Akas, who lived in the hills north of Charduar along with the Rupa, Shergaon and Thebenga Bhutias and the Nishis, collected dues from Charduar.[47] The Akas were independent and had no formal connection with the Nishis or the Bhutias. Both the clans of the Akas—the Hazarikhowas and the Kapachors—lived under the nominal control of the chiefs called Rajas who conducted relations with the outside world and presided over the meetings of the village council. The Akas had received from the Ahom king Pratap Singha the right to collect paddy and other articles which were not available in their hills.[48] The idea behind the grant was to reconcile the fierce hill tribes to Ahom rule and secure for the neighbouring villages immunity from their attack.

After the British occupation of Assam, following the Anglo-Burmese War of 1824-26, the Governor General's Agent, David Scott,[49] allowed the Akas to collect their dues from the Duars. It is found in the records that the Hazarikhowa Akas were entitled to receive from each house of their allotted 'Khels' one portion of a female dress, one bundle of cotton thread and one handkerchief. At this time, the Kapachors were not probably regarded as a separate clan, for the Hazarikhowas were expected to give a share of their collections to the Kapachors.[50]

But the inconvenience of allowing the tribesmen to come down to collect their dues was soon realised by the British authorities. David Scott was the first British officer to initiate the commutation of the system of collection of dues in kind by the tribes by a system of payment in cash. It was he who succeded in making an agreement with the Akas by which they agreed to forego their right to direct collection in consideration of a payment of Rs. 175 per annum by the British Government.[51] But, as a result of the Balipara massacre of 1835 perpetrated by the Kapachor chief Taghi Raja, the payment of *posa* to the Hazarikhowas was stopped because they were also suspected to be involved in the affair.[52] In 1842, when settlement was made with the Kapachors, the *posa* of the Hazarikhowas was restored, but a new engagement was entered into with four of their chiefs. They promised to maintain peace in the Duars for a payment of Rs. 180 to be paid annually to them in lieu of the levy they used to collect from the Duars.[53]

The Kapachors had no relations with the British till 1842 when an engagement was entered into with them. Shortly before the annexation of Assam by the British they had murdered an official of Charduar, and for this David Scott had delcared them outlaw and forbade them to enter Assam.[54] But they continued to collect their dues from the Duars evading the British vigilance as though they were legally entitled to do so. In 1839, their leader Taghi Raja fled to Assam as a result of an inter-tribal dispute. He was captured by the British and sent to Gauhati jail. While at Gauhati he became a disciple of a Hindu spiritual master and through his influence got release from the jail.[55] He went back to the hills and rallying his followers behind murdered all those who were connected with his capture in Assam in 1932. Thereafter to avenge his humiliation at Gauhati he came down in 1835 to Balipura and set fire to the frontier outpost there. Seventeen persons were killed including men, women and children.[56]

All efforts of the government to capture him proved abortive and he continued to raid Charduar repeatedly. In December 1837, he carried off several persons.[57] The government had to set up outposts at the foothills to check his forays and yet he succeeded in evading them and carried on his depredations. In 1838-39 and 1841 he raided the plains of Charduar.[58] At last through the Kotokis an offer of pardon and pension was made to him and he came to the plains to surrender to the British authorities. He was released on a solemn oath that he would not attack the ryots of the plains any more in consideration of a monthly pension for him and three of his chiefs—Seemkolee, Sooma and Nisul. An engagement was entered into in this regard in 1842.[59]

Subsequently other chiefs came down and accepted pensions from the government. In February 1844, Capt. Gordon, the Deputy Commissioner of Darrang, interviewed and granted annual pensions to Chengkolee, Singingkandor, Narsoo and Sarsoo. Again, in 1848, he further granted five more annual pensions to Srigi, Barsoo, Kangsoon, Pasoo, Deekoks and Dhenno.[60]

The British relations with the Aka tribes began to improve after the grant of these pensions or *posa* to the chiefs. The oaths taken by the chiefs to maintain peace and forego collection of dues from the Duars were generally observed though the amount of *posa* was gradually raised to Rs. 668 per annum through peaceful negotiations.[61] The Hazarikhowas had further received a grant of 18 puras of land for their temple in the Darrang district.[62] But in 1857 the Aka chiefs refused to receive their *posa* in protest for getting their *posa* raised. The government ordered to stop the payment of *posa* and closed the markets of the Duars to the Akas. Arrangement for keeping a sharp watch over the border of the hills was made to prevent any disturbance that might result. It had the desired effect of bringing the Aka chiefs to terms and gradually they began to come down for pardon. Some submitted in 1859, and in 1869 Taghi Raja himself submitted to the authorities. The Akas during these years had not committed any raid and, therefore, the Deputy Commissioner of Darrang recommended payment of their *posa* which was paid with all arrears.[63]

The relations with the Akas began to deteriorate from the seventies. They had been protesting for an increase of their *posa* as the prices of commodities had gone up. When the lands in the foothills were being brought within the boundary of the Darrang district by demarcation of the boundary by the Commissioner, Lt. Col. Graham, in 1872-73, the Kapachor chief objected to the boundary.[64] The Hazarikhowas petitioned for a further grant of revenue-free land and the Kapachors asked for a similar grant of 200 puras of land.[65] On the recommendation of the Deputy Commissioner of Darrang, 36 puras were granted to each clan which seemed to have reconciled them. The boundary line was demarcated in 1874-75.[66] Medhi, the Aka chief, even agreed to send two of his relations to schools in British territory where they would read at government expense.[67] But in 1878, his people gave trouble when they came down for their annual visits and three of them were whipped for theft.[68]

Discontent began to manifest itself from the early eighties. In 1882, Medhi's brother who was reading in school at Balipara left his school. It was reported that a large body of Akas and Nishis had come down and set up boundary marks in the forests of Potashali, Diju and Naminimukh which, they held, were within their side of the boundary. They declared that they would not allow anybody to go into their territory. It was known that they objected to the issue of passes to Nepalese coolies who under the passes intended to go to their hills to tap rubber. The matter was temporarily settled by denying passes to the Nepalese.[69]

But the matter did not end there. The Aka remained unsatisfied and continued to press for enhancement of *posa* and redrawing of the boundary. When a party went to their hills to collect some specimens for Calcutta exhibition, the guide of the party, Lakhidhar, with other two were detained by them in 1883. Lakhidhar died in detention.[70] In the cold season of 1883-84, Chandi, the brother of Medhi Raja, raided the Balipara forest range office, the first time after the grant of pensions to the Akas in 1842, and carried off the Ranger and his clerk together with a compass, some money and two guns.[71]

The government sanctioned an expedition to chastise the

Akas and drive them back to their hills. The expedition left for the Aka hills under the Political Officer Capt. H. St. P. Maxwell, Deputy Commissioner of Garo Hills, with a force of 290 Frontier Police under W.B. Savi and Lt. E.H. Molesworth, 571 officers and men of the 43rd Native Infantry drawn from Shillong, 210 of the 12th Khelati Ghilzais from Cachar, 2 mountain guns and a party of Sappers under the command of Brigadier General Sale Hill. A flying column of 150 Rifles, the 43rd Light Infantry and 50 of the Dibrugarh Corps of the Assam Frontier Police started for Medhi's village under the command of Major Bresford.[72]

When the news of the expedition reached the hills, the Akas sent word that they would restore the captives. But when the force advanced into the hills some villages were evacuated and the vanguard was attacked. One sepoy was killed and another was wounded by the shot of poisonous arrow. The expeditionary force easily overpowered and dispersed the Aka force and advanced upon the village of Medhi. The village had already been deserted but the houses were destroyed together with stores and herds. The Aka chief's sent back the captives together with the property they had seized in 1883-84 but did not come in for settlement.[73] Capt. Maxwell stayed inside the hills for some time but due to outbreak of fever among the force left the Aka hills considering the result of the expedition satisfactory. He had succeeded in obtaining a fine of 10 mithun valued between Rs. 700 to 1000 and release of the captives. Villages of the Kapachor Akas had been destroyed with stocks and grains which he considered enough punishment for the offence they had committed.[74]

The Chief Commissioner receiving the reports of the expedition expressed dissatisfaction for not staying longer in the hills to obtain the surrender of the chief Medhi. He instructed the Deputy Commissioner of Darrang to continue the blockade of the hills for getting the surrender of Medhi and also to continue negotiations with the Akas.[75] The Akas continued to represent enhancement of their *posa* to Rs. 20,000, a grant of 200 puras of revenue-free land in the

Duars, and rectification of the boundary of their territory. They represented that the prices of commodities had gone up and the money granted to them was quite insufficient for the articles they purchased from the Duars. The Akas held that they were already in good terms with the government and never meant to kill Lakhidhar who had died in captivity; they had detained him to get their complaints heard.[76] The Deputy Commissioner of Darrang wrote to the Chief Commissioner that really the Akas purchased goods from the Duars with their pension, and as the prices had gone up it was quite inadequate for their purchase.[77] But the authorities did not pay any heed to the solicitations of the Akas and the blockade continued.

At last, the chiefs tendered their submission in 1888 and the compass taken away in 1883 was returned. An agreement of good behaviour was executed with their chief Medhi wherein he accepted the foothills as the boundary between their hills and the British territory. It was stated that the *posa* would be restored after two years if they behaved well as per agreement.[78]

The relations with the Akas began to improve after 1890 when the *posa* was again restored. In 1896, a party of hillmen stayed in the house of Padu Miri near the Inner Line and in the night killed the host and his son and left with four other captives. It was found that the act was perpetrated by the Apa Tanis who lived in the valley of Hong within the Nishi hills. An expedition was sanctioned and sent to rescue the captives and punish the guilty persons under Capt. G.R. Row with 300 men of Lakhimpur Military Police Battalion and Lt. H.F. Norie of 42nd Gurkha Rifles. R.B. MacCabe of the I.C.S. as Political Officer led the team. The captives were rescued and the guilty were punished by releasing six of their slaves. The punishment was light but considered enough in view of the fact that Padu Miri had enmity with the tribe and the tribesmen had acted in the customary tribal way to avenge their wrong. The government accepted the report of MacCabe.[79]

But the question of rights in the forest brought the Akas

into the plains again in 1900. A party of the Akas came to the Balipara market and demanded a sum of Rs. 3000 from a merchant for tapping rubber in their territory. When they were on their way back with the money, the Deputy Commissioner of Darrang arrived there and succeeded in capturing ten of them. He fined them Rs. 3000 for their conduct and released them after payment of the amount.[80] It was decided that to avoid any such occurrence in future, all agreements for rubber-tapping between the merchants and hillsmen would henceforth be executed in the presence of the Deputy Commissioner of Darrang and all payments would be made in his presence.[81]

The British relations with the Akas after this did not bring in any trouble. When the North-East Frontier Tracts were divided into three charges, the Aka Hills were included in the Western Section of the North-East Frontier.[82] In 1913, G.A. Nevill, Political Officer of Western Section led a promenade through the Aka hills with A.L.M. Molesworth as Assistant Political Officer in a party of 1032 officers and men under the command of A.M. Graham. The tour was peaceful except for an attack by the Daflas of Riang. Over 400 square miles of territory of the Miji and Aka hills were explored and surveyed by this promenade.[83] The Aka hills were brought under the control area from 1914 and there was no opposition from the people. Rather the Akas made representations for opening of posts within their hills.[84] Nevill opined that the Akas were an excellent people and capable of improvement; they were much more civilised than the neighbouring Nishis. He recommended to set up a post at Jamiri in the Aka hills.[85] But no steps were taken to implement the recommendations of Nevill. Capt. Lightfoot found the Akas exacting tribute from the Mompa and Sherdukpen villages of Dirangjog and Rupa, and an expedition was sent to punish the Miji Akas for raising tribute from their villages.[86] Practically the Akas were left to themselves till the end of the British rule.

THE NISHIS

As already noted, occupying the hills in Darrang, north of

Noaduar and Chaiduar in Lakhimpur, and between the rivers Bhorali on the west and Sundri to the east lived the Nishis who call themselves *Bangni*, meaning 'man'. They were not united as a tribe and were divided into several clans independent of each other; there were sometimes thirty to forty chiefs in the same clan.[87] The tribes on the borders of Darrang were generally called Paschim or wertern Nishis and those on the border of Lakhimpur, Tagin Nishis.

The Ahom king Pratap Singha had assigned them certain *paiks* to enable them to get supply of rice and other necessaries not available in the hills on condition of supplying him auxiliaries and paying tribute.[88] The *paiks* who satisfied their demands were granted a remission in their dues to the Ahom kings. Thus a *paik* of the Nishi Bhutia Khel, that is, a subject who paid dues to the Nishis, paid Rs. 3 instead of Rs. 9 to the Ahom kings. The difference was remitted to enable him to meet his Nishi engagement. The different Nishi clans did not interfere with each other on the plains, for they knew from which village they were to collect *posa*. But they claimed the *posa* from a *paik* even if he had migrated from one place to another and demanded full dues from the *paiks* without any consideration of their ability to pay.[89]

When the British authority was established over Assam, David Scott allowed the Nishis to collect their dues from the Duars.[90] But as time went on the British wanted to stop these savage tribes' collection from the plains which they wanted to bring within the settled districts. Lt. James mathai, when he was officiating Magistrate and Collector in Darrang, wrote, "the mountain tribes on its (Darrang) northern frontier, *viz.* the Butias, Akas and Nishis, are allowed to collect blackmail from the ryots, and usually come down in February in large parties to collect articles of produce such as rice, sugar and clothes from each house . . . . If we still acknowledge their right to a portion of our revenue, it should be paid in cash for so long as the present system remains in force. I conceive, after what I have witnessed, that the realisation of the government demand is doubtful, and the lives and property of our subjects left in great jeopardy".[91] The Government of India wrote to Robertson, the Commissioner of Assam, that the 'blackmail' collected by the hill tribes should not be stopped but negotiations for commutation of their rights in the Duars might be carried on by Capt. White, the Political Agent of Upper Assam.[92] Capt. White recommended that money payments should be made instead of the 'blackmail'.[93] Thereupon Capt. Mathai, the Collector and Magistrate of Darrang, began negotiations with the chiefs for commutation of their rights in the Duars.[94]

At first, the Nishis seemed to be reluctant.[95] In 1835, some Nishis were suspected of complicity with Aka raiders. The Nishis were then forbidden to enter the plains whereupon they raided Charduar and carried off several persons. An expedition was sent to the hills to rescue the captives and the party brought down the culprits as prisoners. Capt. Mathai then opened negotiations to stop collection of blackmail; eight out of thirteen of the Nishis clans of Charduar came to terms.[96] They refused to accept money instead of articles but agreed to resign the right of collection from individual ryots. In case of any dispute they agreed to refer the matter to the Magistrate; further, they engaged not to aid the enemies of the British and to help in the capture of offenders. The *posa* was fixed now at one coarse askhut sheet, one long cotton handkerchief, two seers of salt, one dao and one goat for every ten houses.[97] After this, five more clans also came to agreement on similar terms. The Government of India felt gratified at this course of action and not only approved of the action of Mathai but praised him as well.[98]

After this, the Nishis of Nao Duar consented to receive their dues also through the village revenue officer. But they insisted on payment of two-thirds of all the revenues paid by the *paiks* of the Nishis Bhutia Khels as they considered them to be their hereditary slaves.[99] In 1838-39, they became very troublesome and the collection of *posa* was entirely stopped. This brought that clans to terms and agreements were entered upon to pay them through the village revenue officer.[100]

But it was only in 1852 that the *posa* was finally

commuted for monetary payment. The Court of Directors had ordered that if the local officers could substitute monetary payment in lieu of 'blackmail' without any disturbance, they had no objection.[101] There were four Mahals in which there were nine Duars from which the Nishis collected dues. The Chaiduar mahal consisted of Nakrang, Boranga and Bar Duars; the Banskata Mahal comprised Kaudarahat, Dalahat Malahat and Ohat Duars; the Lakhimpur Mahal comprised the Manomati Duar; and in Boodoloni Mahal was included Phulpani Duars.[102] A list of the ryots who paid Nishis dues in these Duars showing the chiefs who received them was prepared by Brajanath Bharali Baruah in 1841. Capt. Gordon's letter of 13 February 1844 states that Rs. 2494-0-1 was paid to the Nishis commuting the Nishi chiefs' right to make collection in the Duars. In 1852, Col. Dalton and Lt. Biver modified the list excluding those who did not claim their *posa*, and a list was prepared by the former showing that there were 238 Gams or chiefs who received Rs. 2543. But in 1853-54, the total amount of *posa* reached Rs. 4129-15-0; besides 234 maunds of salt in lieu of 'hat' (weekly market) dues and rights of fishing and gold washing, a diet allowance of Rs. 5 and 26 bottles of rum were also paid.[103]

The relations with the Nishis thereupon began to improve and there was no cause of anxiety till 1870. After this the Nishis raided two Nishi settlements within the Darrang district. In one case the raid was directed to recover an absconding slave and it did not indicate any ill-feeling towards the British authority. But nevertheless they committed an act of violence within the British territory. So all annual allowances were withheld and a reward was declared for the capture of the offenders.[104] In the other case, some Nishis who had submitted a case for settlement to the British authorities became tired of the delay in British justice and they swooped upon their offending brethren and secured justice in their customary way. The case was as follows. One Nishi chief arranged the marriage of his son with the daughter of another chief and gave some presents. But the father of the girl did not honour his word and even did not return the presents to the party to whom he had refused the marriage of his daughter. The offended party filed a complaint with the Deputy Commissioner of Darrang, but being tired of delay and failing to obtain satisfaction, it made a night attack, recovered the presents and took to custody some hostages. In this case also, the allowances were stopped and a reward was announced for the capture of the ringleader.[105] Yet a third raid occurred within the British territory in 1872-73 when some Nishis from the hills carried off some Nishis as they believed that a Nishi of that village was the cause of an epidemic which took several lives. An expedition was sent for the recovery of these British subjects in 1874-75. When the closure of the market proved ineffectual for the recovery of the captives, an expedition was sent and the guilty villagers were punished for their misconduct.[106] Subsequently in 1877 again there occurred a robbery in a Kaya Shop in Lalukadolonee. Lt. Maxwell pursued the Nishis and under threat of closing the market, succeeded in recovering the looted property. The action was approved of by the Chief Commissioner.[107]

Disposition of the Nishis after this was not found to be hostile towards the British. All the raids that occurred subsequently arose out of either inter-tribal disputes or disputes over collection of forest produce by British subjects. In 1887, a party of the Nishis raided the house of the Nishi named Tarang beyond the Inner Line as the latter had quarrelled with hill Nishis. The Government did not take upon itself the burden of punishing the offenders.[108] In 1888, again, another subject Nishi was murdered 10 miles beyond the Inner Line. Again, the authorities declined to punish the criminals as it was not certain whether the British subject was forcibly taken away from his home within the settled district and whether he had quarrels with them.[109] In 1881, the Nishis captured some plain Nishis as they had crossed the Inner Line without passes to tap rubber.[110] Through negotiation the captives were released. In 1896 again the Nishis captured some run-away coolies of a tea garden when they crossed the Inner Line. The British authorities did not send any punitive expedition as the capture did not take place as a result of any raid. When negotiations to release the coolies were conducted the Nishis asked for the restitution of two of their slaves who had escaped into the British territory. The restitution of the slaves was denied and the release of the coolies was purchased by the owner of the garden.[111] In 1899[112] and 1900[113] again the Nishis captured the agents of the Mahaldars; captives were released in the first case, and in the second case the captives were released after the payment of their dues. Two Nishi raids in 1904[114] and 1908[115] are also recorded in the Administration Reports and these show that they had begun to violate the terms of their engagement with the British.

As a part of the general policy of the Government of India, in the North-East Frontier a mission was sent to the hills beyond the Inner Line to increase knowledge of the tribes, establish friendly relations with them, and explore and survey the region between the Subansiri and Bhutan which would enable the Government of India to fix up a boundary between India and Tibet. The party started from Lakhimpur on 11 November 1911 with 75 Rifles under Kerwood, the Sub-divisional Officer of Lakhimpur, as Political officer. Escorts numbered 150, Officers and men, under Assistant Commandant Capt. A.M. Graham. The party, which went up the Subansiri to survey the Khru valley, was attacked but when Capt. Graham opened fire, the Nishi opposition melted and the party came back doing its job successfully.[116]

We have observed that subsequent to the explorations and survey by the Miri mission in 1911, the North-East Frontier was divided into three sections and Capt. G.A. Nevill took charge of the Western Section, in which was included the Nishi hills. Nevill was attacked by the Nishi while he was leading Aka promenade in 1913 at Riang.[117] He observed from his experience that the Nishis as a tribe had not yet recognised the British authority which was evident from their treacherous attacks and petty aggression on the plains of Assam. In 1918, Miripathar Nishis raided the Nishi villages of Gaigaon and Boranipathar in the plains and carried off 59 persons. Nineteen of the captives escaped but 20 had to be released by the Political Officer who imposed fine on the Miripathar. Nishis for the raid.[118] Again, in 1926, the Runganadi Nishis raided Jorum Nishi village and, killing three, excaped with three captives. Again, Nevill with armed escorts visited Runganadi to punish the raiders. He recommended to establish a post in the Nishi hills at Miripathar with a dispensary to bring them under effective control.[119]

Things began to change with the introduction of 'loose political control' from 1914 onwards. Nevill writes in his Administration Report for the year 1927-28, "As years have passed by, the Akas, the Daflas and other tribes have gained confidence and learnt to appreciate the benefits of the new order . . . The growing friendliness has brought about the desire for a still closer relationship. Now a days constant request from all sections of the hills is to establish a garrison in their country . . . . Daflas realise the benefits of peace but owing to their entire lack of combination they are unable to make a united effort to stop this anarchy."[120] But arrangement for direct administration or setting up of Assam Rifles posts in the Nishi hills had not been made during the British regime and the petty inter-tribal raids or raids on the plains continued till almost the end of the British period. In 1931-32, N.L.Bor had to lead three expeditions to punish Chemgung for imprisoning British subjects;[121] in another case to punish the Nishis for visiting Senmara within 5 miles of the Inner Line;[122] the third expedition to punish Midpu for raiding Luluk in the plains of Lakhimpur.[123] The Administration Report for the year 1938-39 shows that the Nishis of Kabeng raided Pinji in which 8 persons were carried off. An expedition succeeded in releasing the captives and a fine of 10 mithuns was imposed on the Nishis which of course had good effect on the Eastern Nishis.[124]

THE ADIS AND THE MISINGS

To the east of the Nishis and west of the Mishmis and

between the rivers Dihang and Dibang live the cognate tribes of the Adis and Mishings. Originally one and the same tribe, the Mishings came down the hills and in course of time became plain-dwellers. They engaged themselves in permanent cultivation on the plains and acted as go-between in trade between the Assamese and Adi traders.[125] But the Adis continued to live in the hills and regarded their co-tribe, the Mishings, as their slaves on the plains and exacted some tribute from them. The exact nature of this tribute is not known, but the Mishings did not decline to pay this impost and their relations with the Adis were constant and intimate.[126]

In the *Assam Buranji,* it is recorded that king Pratap Singha had given some villages to the Adis for the cultivation of paddy and the ryots who cultivated for the Adis were exempted from revenue payment to the Ahom authorities. Besides, some persons were assigned to catch fish from certain *beels* (marshes) for the Adis. But the Adis also paid tribute to the Ahom kings'.[127] With the establish-ment of the British authority in Assam the Mishings became British subjects in all respects; they paid poll-tax for cultivating lands and subjected themselves to the regular jurisdiction of the civil and criminal courts of the British Government.[128] As such, their relations with the goverment need not be studied separately.

In between the Adis of the uphills and the Mishings of the plains lived the so-called Hill Mishings. In the hills west of Dirjimo and to the north of Sisi and Dhamaji lived the so-called Ghesi Mishings; north of Bordoloni and on the course of the Subansiri lived the Sarak Mishings; and on the same river lived the Panibatia and Tarbatia Mishings and all other tribes of the Hill Mishings. They were in no way subordinate to the Adis of the upper hills. These Hills Mishings collected *posa* from the mouzas of Sisi, Dhamaji and Bordoloni of Lakhimpur.[129] The Adis did not collect *posa*, but the Mishings of the plains who saved the Adis were exempted from payment to the Ahoms.[130]

The British authorities seemed to have commuted the

right of the Ghesi Mishings, Sarak Mishings, Panibatia, Tarbatia Mishings and the Bormithuns by granting *posa* to be paid to each as in the case of the Bhutias, Akas and Nishis. It appears from a resolution of the Chief Commissioner of Assam of 1884 that the afore-mentioned clans of the Hill Mishings were in receipt of annual *posa* of Rs. 218-7-5, Rs. 930-4-9 and Rs. 25 respectively, in lieu of their rights of collection in Sisi, Dhamaji and Bordoloni mouzas.[131] No such arrangement or conciliation, however, was made initially with the Adis who were considered distinct from the Hill Mishings and who did not collect any impost from the plains.

The British took note of the Adis in 1830 when Capt. Neufville had recommended to David Scott to erect buildings for setting up guard houses as the Adis had come down to reclaim the Mishings of the plains. David Scott proposed to the government construction of 8 such posts for the protection of plains people, as the proposed measure of Neufville seemed to him highly expedient. He had recommended to recover the expenses from the villagers who were to be benefited by the proposed measure.[132] But in the later part of the same year Neufville wrote again that the Adis were best disposed of all the hill tribes of the North-East Frontier and they had never been down to have committed any act of unprovoked ravage or violence on the villages of the plains.[133] Subsequently, in 1840, when the Khamptis rebelled against the British, the Adis took side with the government.[134] As late as 1847, the Adis remained friendly towards the British; when Capt. Vetch, Political Agent of Upper Assam, paid a visit to their hills, they voluntarily released the captives whom they had carried off from the plains as a gesture of friendship.[135]

Till the middle of the nineteenth century, the Adis claimed and received levies from the gold-washers known as Beehas and fishermen on the Dihang and Dibang rivers and the islands of the Brahmaputra as also from the Mishings who had settled down within the Lakhimpur district of the Brahmaputra valley.[136] But in the later half of the century the gold-washers and fishermen and the Mishings, encouraged by the attitude of the new authorities, that is the British, and feelings a sense of security and protection, began to defy the Adis, some even moved down to remote places beyond the easy access of the Adis.[137] That led to a change of attitude on the part of the Adis; rather, the Adis had to coerce the refractory subjects whom they regarded as their hereditary slaves and thus violated the law of the British which they did not know and considered unnecessary to observe. Thus, began the strife between the Adis and the British.

The friction began on the issue of jurisdiction over the gold-washers. In 1848, Capt. Vetch went to the Adi hills to get release of some gold-washers. The captive, who were detained for non-payment of dues, were released but the camp of Capt. Vetch was attacked in the night and the Adis were sent back after hard fighting. To punish the guilty, Capt. Vetch burnt the villages of the Adis,[138] but this tended to strain the good relation that subsisted between these tribes and the government. The government which began to farm out the right of gold-washing felt an obligation to protect the gold-washers. Escorts were sent to accompany the gold-washers to Dihang and orders were given to station a guard house at the mouth of that river.[139] To conciliate with the Adis, a proposal to start an annual fair was mooted and the proposal to tax the Mishings near Dihang was negatived as it would annoy the Adis further. But the fair did not come to pass and the guard remained on the Dihang for one reason only. In the turmoil of the Second Anglo-Burmese War the Adi frontier was forgotten and guarding of the Adi frontier lost sight of.[140]

Meanwhile the Adis thought of teaching a lesson to the refractory Beehas; in January 1858 the Beeha settlement of Senagajan only six miles from Dibrugarh, to the north of the river Brahmaputra, was massacred by the Kebang clan of the Bor Meyong Adis.[141] The authorities made an attempt to follow up the raiders to the hills, but owing to the inaccessible character of the hills the troops could not overtake the Adis and with discredit they returned to

Dibrugarh. Emboldened by their, success, the Adis now took up an advanced position and threatened the plains below the hills.[142]

The government now was required to prove that it was in a position to accord protection to its subjects and chastise those who threatened their security. Therefore, an expedition to punish the perpetrators of the crime of Sengajan was sanctioned by the government. One European officer of the Navy with fifteen gunners; and Indian officer of Artillery with 12 pounds howitzers, with 50 rounds per gun, and 15 privates; and a contingent of Native Infantry under three Indian officers; an European medical man, 11 non-commissioned officers, 3 Buglers and 88 Sepoys, with the Deputy Commissioner of Dibrugarh left for the Abor hills. But even with such a big preparation, the party returned to Dibrugarh in ignominy without imposing upon the Abors the might of the British Administration, once again losing face.[143] Another expedition was sanctioned on a much larger scale in 1859 to retrieve the lost prestige. It consisted of 4 European officers of the Indian Navy with two Buglers and 60 men; a contingent of Native Artillery under one European officer, three Havildars, two Naiks, one Bugler and 50 men with 12 pounder howitzers and 242.5 masters; and a Regiment of Assam Light Infantry consisting of an European officer, one European non-Commissioned officer, 13 Havildars, 14 Naiks, 5 Buglers and 211 Sepoys. This expedition succeeded in destroying Kebang and its allies.[144] Moreover, the government now took up a proposal to establish a number of posts from Sisi to Pobah Mukh to guard the Adi frontier. Later, in 1859, a strong reconnoitring party passed along the entire Adi frontier. This made an impression upon the Adis and some Gams or Chiefs came in 1860 for peace and friendship.[145] Major Biver, the Principal Assistant of the Lakhimpur district, received the chiefs courteously and asked them to see him next year and referred the matter to the authorities.[146]

But in 1861, the Miyong Adis once again cut up another Beeha settlement, 15 miles away from Dibrugarh but on the south bank of the Brahmaputra. These Beehas had left the north bank of the Brahmaputra after the massacre of Sengajan and settled with a sense of impunity on the south bank.[147] The Adis raid of 1861 proved that unless they were held up within the hills, no place in the district was too distant for them. Biver proposed to construct a number of posts along the foot of the Adi hills.[148] The government thereupon took up a scheme of restraining the Adis by means of roads, forts and effective military command of the whole Adi frontier.[149]

The Adis now began to come in for settlement with the government. As for the proposal of peace, the Government of India wrote to the Commissioner of Assam that peace negotiations might be carried on provided the Adis recognised British jurisdiction up to the foothills and entered into engagements not to molest the British subjects of the plains, to refer all disputes to the Deputy Commissioner of Lakhmipur and to allow to free communi-cation of persons between the Assam plains and the Adi hills.[150] Biver opened negotiations with the Adi chiefs. At first, the attempt at agreement seemed far from success. The Adis claimed sovereignty over the lands up to the Brahmaputra and rights over the Mishings and Beehas. But Major Biver succeeded in impressing upon the Adis the futility of such claims and benefits of peace and friendship. He told them that if they came to terms with the British the country below their hills would be cultivated and communications would improve whereupon population and market would expand. These would benefit the Adis.[151] He, however, promised to pay them in kind some stipend for he understood that money payment would not be welcomed. He thought that payment in kind extending to all individuals would give all of them a direct interest in maintaining peace, for otherwise everybody would suffer from the loss of the *posa*.[152]

The gesture of the government to protect the frontiers did not fail to impress upon the Adis the futility of fighting the British army with its dangerous fire arms. When they heard that the government was willing to compensate their losses by paying small subsidies they came up for a settlement. At length, in November 1862, eight Khels of Miyong Adis concluded agreement with the Deputy Commissioner of Lakhimpur. Major Biver undertook to provide for them their necessaries in kind in specific quantities, on condition of their maintaining peace along the border and handing over the criminal refugees who might take shelter in the Adi hills. Moreover, the British sovereignty up to the foot of the hills was recognised by the Adis who promised not to violate it and molest British subjects. Access to the Adis hills by British subjects for trade and to the British market by the Adis for marketing purposes was also granted.[153] The Kabeng Adis followed the Miyong Adis in 1863 when Capt. Comber, Deputy Commissioner of Lakhimpur, concluded an engagement with them.[154] The Bor Adis from remote parts of the hills then came in for similar agreements in 1866.[155]

After these agreements were concluded, the Adis tended to be conciliatory, but their discontent hardly passed away. In 1863, the Meybo Adis refused to accept the presents as the Deputy Commissioner refused to clasp hands with them;[156] in 1865 the Miyong Adis abstained from coming on the plea of outbreak of small-pox and cholera epidemic;[157] in 1866 again they insisted on the removal of the Poba Mukh guard post.[158] In 1876-77 hostility was shown upon the advance of the Trigonometrical Survey party into the hills.[159]

It was found that the Adis were collecting blackmail from the timber-cutters from forests of the foothills which were considered to be within British jurisdiction. The Chief Commissioner, Keatinge, was of opinion that the government must stop such collection and must assert its right over every square mile of territory in the plains.[160] Lt. R.G. Woodthrope of the Trigonometrical Survey party even asked to advance the frontier to show that the British were not afraid of the Adis.[161] J.B. Goad, who had accompanied Woodthrope, proposed that the *posa* to the Adis should be stopped because the Adis in lieu gave trouble only.[162]

The Deputy Commissioner of Lakhimpur, Graham,

proposed to gradually substitute cash payment of *posa* for that in the shape of articles; he held that, to start with, money instead of tobacco and opium should be given.[163] It is found that in 1877 the payment in kind had ceased and cash payment had been fixed at existing market rate.[164] A guard-post was advanced to Nizamghat up the Dihang river and defences were arranged in 1878 to stop the Adis crossing the river for the other bank.[165] The Chief Commissioner, Sir Charles Elliot, while commenting upon the results of the advance of the post at Nizamghat, proposed to the Government of India to appoint and Assistant to the Deputy Commissioner of Lakhimpur to help him in conducting political relations with the Adis in particular and the other tribes in general.[166]

Jack Francis Needham of the Bengal Police was appointed Political Officer in 1882 and psoted at Sadiya. When Needham visited Adi villages in 1884 they complained of the paucity of the *posa* and British authorities giving shelter to their run-away slaves. They pointed out that the government had been favouring the Mishings and had built a *Namghar* for them. But there was none for the Adis. Moreover, there was no rest house for the Adis at Sadiya.[167]

In 1882, the Chief of Padu in a raid murdered a Sepoy of guard house and killed two Miris.[168] In 1887, some Abors carried off four girls and some articles of domestic use from within the British territory. Subsequently, the captives and articles were recovered when payment of *posa* was stopped, but the guilty persons declined to come down.[169] In 1889, again, four Miris were taken away across the frontier for refusing to pay *posa* and were murdered. The authorities imposed a fine of 30 mithuns on the raiders, instituted a blockade on the Abor frontier and stopped payment of *posa* for a year.[170] Thereupon the Abors came down with mithuns as fine whereupon *posa* was restored and blockade withdrawn.

Early in the last decade of the century, the Adis became most restive in their hills and all combined for concerted action against the British. Several police parties were attacked and in 1893, three Sepoys were ambushed and cut with *dao* and their rifles were taken away.[171] A Mishing village within the British jurisdiction had been attacked and some persons were carried off by the Pasi and Miyong Adis. The usual negotiation for the restoration of the captives proved of no avail, and the government ultimately sanctioned an expedition to chastise the criminals of the hills.[172]

The expedition under the command of Capt. R.M. Maxwell and Political Officer Needham started its journey in January 1894. The force consisted of 100 men of 44th Gurkha Rifles under Lts. J.A. Wilson and G.L.S. Ward; 300 men of Lakhimpur Military Police and 100 men of Naga Hills Military Police under Capt. W.R. Little and 711 guns. The Adis began to retreat and Bomjur was taken without any opposition. The next place Dambuk was stockaded; it was taken after some fight when the Adis further retreated. The villages of Mingsipu and Silluk were destroyed and the party advanced upon Damrah, leaving Bordak as the base of supply with a small guard. The attempt to storm Damrah proved of no avail, and supplies being cut off from behind the force began to retreat without achieving its object. The Adis intercepted the retreat and harassed the force; the base of Bordak was burnt by the Adis and the Guards there were cut to pieces by the Membu and Padu Adis. But no expedition to either burn or destroy the village of Damrah was sanctioned by the Government of India. Though they agreed to the blockade and withdrawal of *posa* deportation of Dambuk and Silluk Gams was refused.[173]

Relations with the Adis did not improve after the expedition of 1894. In 1898, again, some Adis from Silluk came down to Sibyamukh about 3 miles from the Inner Line, with a view to settling there. Needham was ordered to send them back and as they refused to go back, he destroyed their houses and crops and sent them back.[174] In 1899, the Ghesi Mishings raided a village called Chouldhoa and escaped with a girl Yapi. A general blockade of the Adi frontier was now resorted to and in 1900 the Adis were compelled to submit to the British authorities.[175]

But the spectre of Adi hostility continued to haunt the officials; they wanted to bring the Adis under direct and complete control. Noel Williamson, the Assistant Political Officer who had succeeded Needham in 1905, crossed the boundary of the British territory without any escort and succeeded in generating a good feeling among some of them.[176] In March 1908 Williamson made a tour from Pasighat through the foothills south-west to Ledum and then on through Pasi Meyond and the Gallong hills to the Sinyeng River at Dijmur. He proposed a forward policy and establishment of advance posts beyond the frontiers.[177] The Lt. Governor of Eastern Bengal and Assam forwarded the proposal to the Government of India and submitted a scheme of his own. He held that the territories within the Inner Line but up to the foothills should be assessed and a system of presents instead of fixed *posa* in cash should be substituted. The Government of India rejected his proposal entirely; instructions were issued for further exploration of the Adi tracts with a view to ascertaining the reaction of the tribal people to assessment.[178]

In 1911 Noel Williamson and Gregorson went across the British jurisdiction and were murdered by the Kebang Adis. The government could not view the murder as an ordinary crime outside British jurisdiction. An expedition under Major-General Bower to punish the murderers was sanctioned.[179] The expedition was to punish the offending villages, explore the territories and survey the hills on the Dehang. The ring-leaders were arrested; the murderer of Williamson was tried under the Frontier Tract Regulation of 1880 and hanged, and that of Gregorson was court martialled.[180]

What Williamson wanted to do in his life time, i.e., to bring the Adi hills under direct British control, he was able to accomplish it only by his death. Major-General Bower, who led the Adi expedition, recommended the division of the Frontier territories into three charges to be placed under separate officers who would directly control the tribes from within the tribal territories under their respective jurisdictions.[181] Accordingly, the entire tracts were divided into three sections in 1912 and separate officers were posted for each. In 1911, an Assistant Political Officer was posted at Pasighat within the territory of the Adi hills and in 1914 the Adi hills were made part of the Central and Eastern Section of the North-East Frontier.[182]

The Government of India formulated the new policy of 'loose political control' over the frontier tribes as recommended by the Government of Eastern Bengal and Assam. Subsequent to the creation of the new charge of the Central and Eastern Sections of the Frontier administrative posts were gradually opened within the Adi territories and Political Officers began to tour the hills up to the international border. The Administration Report for the year 1917-18 submitted by the W.C.M. Dunda, the Political Officer, states that the Adi villages had been brought under direct administration; but a large area to the north but south of the McMahon Line remained outside the control of the Political Officer of the Adi hills. There was no hostility against the new order, rather inter-tribal disputes were brought before him for settlement. The people were contented and under the new administration it was hardly felt that the conditions were ever different.[183] In 1838, Godfrey, the new Political Officer, wrote that the Tibetans intruded into the Adi territory and it was necessary to prevent them. On his recommendation, posts were opened at Karko and Riga to stop Tibetan incursions south of the McMahon Line.[184] Thus, the control area was extended to cover up the entire Adi hills or the Siang valley, and the Adis were subjected to the jurisdiction of the British Government.

THE MISHMIS

To the eastward of the Adis from the Dibang river up to the Indian borders on the Talok pass the Burma lay the extensive Mishmi hills. The Mishmis, of all the North-Eastern Frontier tribes, did not exact any levy from the people of the plains. Perhaps because of the existence of the Khampti settlement below their hills they could not come down, as the Khamptis were powerful and were in a position to protect their people against any encroachment. During the Ahom times, no formal relation seems to have existed between the Ahoms and the Mishmis. The *Ahom Buranji* mentions that the Mishmis killed four persons of the Ahom kingdom in 1674. The Mishmis produced the murderers to the Sadiya Khowa Gohain and paid some tribute.[185] Again the *Ahom Buranji* mentions that two Mishmis paid tribute to the Ahoms; no *posa*, however, was granted to them by the Ahoms.[186]

At the beginning of British rule, the Mishmis were found divided into three divisions; each of these was ruled by the hereditary chief of the clan. There was no love lost between these clans and the Mishmis were not united. They were engaged in extensive trade with the outside world, the Digaru or Tains had trade intercourse with Tibet and the Chulikatas traded with the plains of Assam.[187] But they did not realise any blackmail from the plains of Assam.

The Mishmis from the very beginning were averse to receive the foreigners, observed Lt. Barlton after he had visited the Mishmi hills to explore the course of the Brahmaputra in 1825.[188] In 1827, Wilcox could persuade them to permit him to go across Tain territory to the Idu tracts. But he escaped from an attack by a retreat overnight.[189] In 1826, Dr. Griffith was hospitably received by the Tains, but they refused to allow him to go to the Miju country, stating that they had a quarrel with them. Tains were anxious to trade, says Dr. Griffith, with Assam.[190]

The unfriendly disposition of the Mishmis is evident from the murder of an Indian *fakir*, Permanand Acharya, who tried to travel to Tibet across the Mishmi hills, and the murder of the French missionary M.Krick. The British authorities, though they did not have any regular intercourse with the Mishmis, could not view the murders silently. In the case of Permanand, a reward was declared for the capture of the murderers, but it was reported that the Tibetan authorities had punished the culprit.[191] M. Krick first visited the Mishmi country in 1851 in the company of the Khampti

Chief of Sadiya, Choking Gohain. In 1854, he went again to the Mishmi hills with a colleague, M. Bourri, and crossed the Mishmi country for Tibet. A Miju chief named Kai-en-Shah by name followed them. He murdered both of them and carried off their property in disregard of the Tibetan authorities. Lord Dalhousie, the Governor General, authorised an expedition to punish Kai-en-Shah. In 1855, a party of 20 Assam Light Infantry personnel with 40 Khampti volunteers and a few hill porters marched from Sadiya under the command of Lt. Eden. After an eight-day journey the party surprised Kai-en-Shah in his village on the river Du and captured him. His elder sons were killed in the fight. The tribal people around were dispersed and awed. Kai-an-Shah was tried at Dibrugarh by the Deputy Commissioner and hanged for murdering the Frenchmen.[192]

But it was with the Chulikatas that the British found difficulty. Between Sadiya and their hills lay about twenty to thirty miles of dense forest through which hillmen came to the markets of the plain. The Chulikatas, who lived in their border hills, took advantage of their situation, surprised the travellers and border villages, and carried off captives from the British territories.

In April 1855, the Apelong Clan of the Chulikatas took away three servants of Lt. Eden from Sadiya. A blockade was instituted against all Mishmi tribes and markets were closed. The other clans who began to suffer as a result brought forth the captives and delivered them to the authorities.[193] Again, towards the close of the same year, the Apelongs attacked a village near Sadiya and, killing two, took off others. Again, the rival clans rescued the captives and this time they punished the criminals.[194] A third time, in 1857, the Apelongs cut up a village in the vicinity of Sadiya. Capt. A.S. Biver, Assistant to the Governor General's Agent, wrote that the prestige of the government would be lost if the raid went unpunished. The authorities planned a punitive expedition but the outbreak of the Sepoy Mutiny kept such petty affairs out of consideration for the time being.[195] At the end of the year again the Chulikatas massacred the women and children of the village of a Khampti Chief, Chauking Gohain, on the plea that some of their clan members had died of cholera after visiting the Gohian. Col. Hannay, who was in charge of the Sadiya stockade, held the view that punitive expeditions into the Mishmi hills were useless; instead, to stop future raids, guard houses should be set up on the Dikrang, and roads along the foothills for patrolling should be constructed.[196]

The raid on the Khampti village roused the spirit of the Khampti people and they armed themselves for their own defence. The government now promised to supply arms and pay one rupee to each Khampti cultivator who would settle to the north of the Brahmaputra. This policy proved to be a success; a strong colony soon developed on the Dikrang. It succeeded in driving back the Mishmi raids in 1861 and 1866.[197]

The sequel of screening the Mishmis was interesting. In 1868, a Chulikata Chief, Kalood by name, came to Dibrugarh to meet the Deputy Commissioner and to seek permission to settle under British protection in the valleys of Dikrang, Koondil and Diphoo in the neighbourhood of Sadiya. The Deputy Commissioner wrote to the government and was instructed that immigration should be encouraged. The Deputy Commissioner allowed Kalood to settle at Habba in the Koondil Valley where they would be under British supervision. He came to settle with his families and later on some 200 followed.[198] In 1880, another Chief, Kaladoi, formally professed allegiance to the British while visiting the Sadiya fair.[199] The Mishmis henceforth began to visit the Sadiya fair in large numbers and began to take to peaceful pursuits.

But the Bebejia clan of the Mishmis became very restive. They were described as "a fierce race of cannibals, a very savage, blood-thirsty and dangerous race." In the cold season of 1878-79, they committed two small raids. In one case, they attacked the house of an Assamese ryot in Patia pathar and killed two persons. The reason behind the raid was known to be an old feud dating back to 1865 when some Mishmis had been killed by British subjects.[200] In the other case, the Mishmis killed two Khamptis and captured four others for tapping rubber 20 miles away from Sadiya in Mishmi tracts. The raiders were pursued by the Frontier Police, but they could not overtake the raiders.[201] In 1884, again, the Bebejias murdered an Assamese ryot in a Dikrang village. A fine of Rs. 2,000 was imposed on them and the Sadiya market was closed to them till they cleared off the dues. The money, however, was paid and the blockade was withdrawn.[202] In 1893, three Sepoys of the Military Police while patrolling near Bomjur outpost were killed again.[203] In 1899, again they made a daring attack on an outlying Khampti village sixteen miles north-east of Sadiya, very near the administrative border. They killed three persons and ran away with four children and three guns.[204]

After the murder of the Sepoy in 1893, Needham wanted to go into the Mishmi hills to punish the offending village; a blockade was imposed on the Mishmi frontier as the Government refused permission for expedition and sanctioned blockade. But after the attack on the Khampti village of Mighaigaon, a punitive expedition was sent to the offending Bebejia village. Needham, with 290 rifles, left for the Mishmi hills under Col. Molesworth. The village was burnt and two Mishmis were captured, but the culprits could not be arrested as they had fled into the interior hills. The captives and one gun were recovered. The British suffered a loss of 34 coolies who died and Rs. 16,000 by way of expenditure. Five Chulikata Mishmis, who acted as interpreters and guides, were given presents of a muzzle gun each and Chulikata Chief Grambon was given an additional reward of Rs. 200 by the Chief Commissioner. One of the raiders, ChenChen, was captured later and given up by the Miris; a reward of Rs. 500 was given to them. ChenChen was tried and hanged at Sadiya.[205] Still in 1905 the Bebejias committed another murderous outrage on the Chulikata Mishmis within the British territory to avenge the collaborators of the expedition 1899, and again blockade had to be restored to.[206]

A new factor was introduced in tribal politics by the advent of the Chinese on the Indo-Tibetan border and the murder of Noel Williamson. Two exploratory missions were sent in 1911-12 and 1912-13 for survey and exploration of the Mishmi hills and to tell the Mishmis that they were under British protection.[207] The last mission succeeded in surveying the entire Mishmi country including the course of the Dibang. The Mishmi hills were included in the Central and Eastern Sections of the Frontier in 1914 when the Frontier Tracts were divided. From 1914, 'loose political control' over the entire Mishmi hills began to be exercised.

The change in policy, that is, the policy of bringing the tribes under direct political control, was not welcomed by all the clans of the Mishmis; the attitude of the Bebejia mishmis continued to be hostile. In 1918, a Sepoy was murdered at Nizamghat to avenge again the death of one of their members in the outrage of 1905 by three men of Elapoin Mishmi. An expedition was sent to punish the culprits in 1920 under O'Callaghan. It not only punished the guilty but also settled many local disputes following the new policy.[208] The disposition of the Mishmis began to change. The British Museum party visiting the Mishmi hills in 1933-34 attested the fact that the Mishmis were friendly. Unfortunately the Chulikatas of the administered area committed on outrage in 1933 in a village within one march, killing four children and injuring others. A promenade was sent in 1934 under a Police Officer from Nizamghat to exact retribution and settle disputes between tax-paying and non-tax-paying villages.[209] This proved successful. Mr. Calvert in 1937-38 toured the unadministered areas on the Du Valley to renew contact with the Taraon Miju clans.[210] In 1940, Godfrey visited Rima, renewed contacts with the Taraon and Miju Mishmis, and succeeded in bringing them under British influence. The extension of the control area thus gradually brought peace and contentment among the Mishmis.[211]

THE KHAMPTIS

Below the Mishmi hills to the south on the Brahmaputra and between them and the Singphos lived the Khamptis. The

British came into contact with them when they came to Assam during the Anglo-Burmese War of 1824-26. The Khamptis were immigrants from the land called Bar-Khampti between the eastern extremity of Assam and the river irrawaddy. At first they had settled around Tengapani in Upper Assam. In 1797-1800, the Barasiriagis revolted in Sadiya; the Khamptis along with other tribes joined them and crossed the Brahmaputra and ousted the Assamese governor of Sadiya.[212] The *Tungkhungia Buranji* records that they occupied Sadiya in 1797, and the title and dignity of the Ahom governor were assumed by the Khampti Chief.[213] The Ahom kings had no formal relation with the Khamptis, nor had any of the Ahom kings granted any *posa* to them. The Khampti Chief ruled like an independent prince.

He had succeeded in keeping his tract free from the Anglo-Assamese turmoil. When Scott, the Agent to the Governor General, came to Upper Assam in 1824, the Khamptis rendered him good service. Therefore, Scott recognised the Khampti Chief 'Chousalan Sadiya Khowa Gohain' as the Chief and permitted him to collect taxed from the Assamese people within his jurisdiction. The Khampti Chief himself did not pay any tax and instead undertook to maintain a contingent of 200 men to be armed by the British, as per terms of an agreement entered into in this regard. But he was required to obey orders of the British Government sent through the Political Officer of Upper Assam to whom they were to bring all serious crimes for trial.[214]

The relation between the Khampti Chief and the British remained friendly and peaceful till 1839 though rumours of Khampti intrigue were reported occasionally.[215] As late as 1838 Capt. White, Political Agent of Sadiya, wrote that they were faithful to their engagements and gave no cause for anxiety,[216] though a report of the year shows that the Khamptis had become disgusted at the long continuance of the British supremacy over Sadiya which they considered to be their own territory.[217] In 1835, a fresh batch of immigrants from the Bor-Khampti land entered Assam and sought permission to settle under the British Government. They asked for remission of taxes for ten years and fire arms. The British were anxious to settle them as barrier between Assam and Burma, because still they were haunted by a dread of fresh Burmese invasion. Therefore, the Khamptis were allowed to settle without payment of taxes for three years, but no fire arms were supplied to them.[218]

In 1838, a dispute arose between the Khampti Chief of Sadiya and the Bor Senapati of Muttack, the Moamaria Chief of Upper Assam, in regard to a tract of land on the south bank of the Brahmaputra. The Political Officer at Sadiya asked both the parties to appear before him. The Khampti Chief took possession of the land in defiance of the order whereupon the Political Agent in vindication of his authority attached the land in dispute. He ordered first the suspension and then the removal of the Khampti Chief from the post of Khawa Gohain. The Khawa Gohain was thereafter removed to a distant station down the river out of the reach of easy intrigue and his post was abolished. His territories were brought under the administration of the British Officer at Sadiya who collected taxes from the Assamese people and administered justice to them. But the Khamptis and Singphos of this territory were left under their own chiefs; no tax was levied upon them.[219]

Apparently the Khamptis seemed content and during the Singphos rising of 1838 they rendered good help to the British. The Ex-Khawa Gohain was allowed to return to Sadiya in his private capacity in recognition of the Khampti service.[220] But their hatred of the British and fear of being brought under regular jurisdiction of the British administration resulted in a premeditated outbreak on 19 January 1839, when about 500 Khamptis in arms attacked the British post at Sadiya, butchered Col. White and his men, and burnt the lines to the ground. The Khamptis on the south bank of the Brahmaputra also rose; but they were put down by the British troops. The successful Khamptis on the north bank, however, retreated with their adherents and took refuge among the Dibang Mishmis. Compelled by distress in their jungle refuge one chief, Chouking Gohain, surrendered and then led a British force to compel others to follow him.[221] In 1839-40, more expeditions were sent to disperse the Khamptis from the hills, and finally in 1843 all the Khamptis surrendered to the British under agreement of good behaviour.[222]

The Khamptis were divided as suggested by Capt. Vetch who suppressed the Khampti rebellion; with a view to weakening them they were dispersed by the British in four divisions.[223] One body was settled at Choonpura, above Sadiya under Captain Gohain, cousin of the late Khawa Gohain. Another division which was formerly near Tengapani was now settled near Saikhowa to the south of the Brahmaputra. A third party under Chowtang Gohain was settled at Dhemaji and the fourth sent to Bhodia, west of Lakhimpur, under the son of late Khawa Gohain. Since then they could not be united and as a result failed to acquire any political importance. They took to agricultural pursuits. Those who settled in Chorapoorah and below Saikhowa did not pay revenues; the rest in Bhodia and Dhemaji paid regular taxes.[224]

The British relations with the Khamptis did not face any strain thereafter. Rather henceforth the Khamptis and their Chiefs always acted as guides of the British officers in their tours in the Mishmis and Singpho hills. Needham, Williamson and Dundas took Khampti Gohains in their tours.[225] The Khampti Chief of Chowkham was granted a pension and a gun in recognition of British favour to him. As late as 1916 he claimed restitution of his independence and title; though the request was turned down, his pension was increased to Rs. 50 from Rs. 30 and his people were exempted from taxation when poll-taxes began to be levied in the Central to Eastern Sections of the North-East Frontier in which some Khamptis were included after 1914.[226]

THE SINGPHOS

Of the North-East Frontier tribes, the British had to come to some sort of relation with the Singphos first. The Singphos were immigrants from a tract of land on the eastern bank of the Irrawaddy whence they gradually crossed the Patkai. In the troublesome reign of Gouri Singha in 1797 the Singphos, together with the Moamarias, began to attack the Assamese villages and gradually occupied the whole territories lying between Upper Assam and Bhamo, driving out the Khamptis beyond the Brahmaputra.[227] When the Burmese invaded Assam in 1817 they set in an era of plunder and misrule. The Singphos began to take advantage of the situation and carried off hundreds of Assamese as slaves.[228] Further, the Singphos were believed to be preparing for an attack over the territories of the Bor Senapati of Muttack and the Khampti Chief of Sadiya. These chiefs now appealed for help to the British. The British succeeded in driving out the Burmese in course of the War, but apprehending another Burmese invasion concluded engagements with the Bor Senapati of Muttack and the Khamptis of Sadiya. Now they were required to come to terms with the Singphos who bordered on the tracts of these two chiefs and Burma.

The British were harbouring an idea of creating a buffer zone to be inhabited by friendly tribes between Upper Assam and Burma. Therefore, the British officer at Sadiya was given strict instruction to give assistance to the Muttack and Sadiya Chiefs only for defensive purposes and not to advance into the tracts inhabited by the Singpho tribe.[229] Meanwhile the Singphos, becoming anxious to protect themselves against possible attack from the Burma side, made overtures of friendship to the British who now realised that to create a tract of tribal terriotry to defend the Burma border was impractical as the tribe itself was afraid of Burmese invasion and wanted their protection. Besides, the question of restoration of the slave and the booty of plunder stood on the way of settlement with them.[230]

Early in 1825, the British informed four Singpho Chiefs that they would be allowed quiet possession of their lands if they surrendered the Assamese slaves, recognised the British supremacy and agreed to inform them of the Burmese activities on the borders.[231] Shortly afterwards, the Burmese appeared on the borders and the Singpho chiefs made over their stockades to them and sided with the Burmese, expressing contempt for the English. But they had also sent message to the British expressing their anxiety to be rid of the Burmese.[232] In June, Capt. Neufville advanced up the Nao Dihing and by a series of attacks expelled the Burmese from the Assam side. During the operations, many Singpho Chiefs who had taken sides with the Burmese were attacked by the English. The Chiefs fled into the hills and their Assamese slaves were set free by Neufville. Bisa Gam, during these operations, moved from his original site on the Nao Dihing to a place called Borhat on the Buri Dihing.[233]

After these raids in June 1826, Scott, the Governor General's Agent, visited the Singpho territories and entered into engagements with sixteen of their chiefs who set free the Assamese slaves and promised to help the British in case of future need and refer all disputes of inter-tribal nature and heinous crimes to the arbitration of the British Officer at Sadiya. Hostages were given for the due fulfilment of these engagements.[234]

But the loss of slave labour had impoverished the Singphos who had become lazy and idlers and dependent on slavery. Therefore, to provide some sort of engagement and income to these Singphos, the British tried to open up a trade route through the Singpho territories wherein the Singphos would act as middlemen in trade.[235] But these attempts did not continue for long as the Company's servants found work elsewhere and the matter was forgotten. Moreover, some Singpho Chiefs were aggrieved by the recognition of Bisa Gam as the paramount Chief and held aloof from the British. One of these Chiefs, Duffa Gam, was a rival of Bisa Gam and he continued to raid Bisa Gam and his dependent villages. In 1830, they, with some Khamptis and Singphos from across the border, attacked the villages of Luttora Gam on the Tengapani river. Capt. Neufville drove them out with the aid of the friendly Singphos and those who had aided him were rewarded. After this incident, the Singphos gradually settled down in agriculture and many took to elephant-catching and hunting.[236] In 1834, an European Officer was posted at Sadiya permanently to conduct relations with these chiefs and gradually the slaves began to be released.[237]

But the raids of the hostile Singphos Chiefs, particularly of Duffa Gam, continued to trouble the Singphos on this side of the border. In 1835, again Duffa Gam made a sudden foray from across the border and took many prisoners including women and children, after killing many. He appeared again from Burma and drew to his side many Chiefs who had owed allegiance to Bisa Gam.[238] A British force was despatched; they dispersed the Singphos, who came from Burma, and all the Cheifs save Luttora Gam, once again came to the side of the English. In 1837, Luttora also resubmitted to the British.[239]

Now the British Government wanted to restrain the raids from the Burma side by pressing the Burmese Government to check their subjects. The Burmese Government agreed to depute the governor of Mogoung to accompany Capt. hannay to visit the borders and see what could be done. But the issue became delicate when the trouble-maker Duffa was received with honour by the Court of Ava, after he had submitted to the Burmese.[240] The Government of India again insisted on sending a second deputation to the borders to close the issue of border trouble and the Burmese reluctantly agreed to it. But settlement became difficult on account of the Burmese claim of sovereignty over tracts of Upper Assam up to Joypore. The British officers rejected the claim as ridiculous and thereupon a military post was established on the Buri Dehing for the protection of the Singpho borders.[241]

Meanwhile, from 1838 the Singphos themselves began to quarrel among themselves and attacked each other. Some even joined the Khampti rebellion in 1839 against the British and the British officers reported that all the Singphos were in a most agitated and discontented condition.[242] At about this time a strong force of British troops was sent through the Singpho tracts and this had a singular effect upon the Singphos who now were awed and had now some respect for the British arms. Many now became friendly and in recognition of their friendship revealed the existence of a brass cannon left by the Mughal force of Mir Jumla as a token of their fidelity.[243] An attempt was made by the government after this to bring the Singpho settlements within the reach of surveillance of British posts.[244] In 1841-42, Capt. Vetch visited the Singpho tracts and found them quiet; thereafter the management of the Singpho was transferred from the Political Department to the Revenue and Judicial Department of the Bengal Government.[245]

But peace on the Singpho border did not last long. In 1843, a fresh raid by Singphos from across the border took place. Simultaneously, the Singphos attacked the British post at Nigroo and the guard post at Bisa. A large body of Singphos and Khamptis threatened the British post at Sadiya; all the Singphos rebelled against the British and sided with the invaders. The Tippum Raja of Hookoom was said to have inspired this movement.[246] British troops were quickly despatched and many chiefs quickly came back to the British side. Ningroota soon resubmitted and Bisa followed him. They protested their innocence and offered to act in future against the Burmese Singphos. The British Government accepted their overtures and agreed to pardon their offences as they had not succeeded in providing them adequate safeguard against the Burmese invasion.[247]

The government now wanted to have thorough probe into the Singpho affairs and appointed Col. Lloyd and Stainforth to enquire into the causes of the Singpho rebellion.[248] As they were unable to do the job, Capt. Jenkins was appointed to do it.[249] He reported that the causes of the rebellion were three, viz., (1) encroachment on the lands and privileges of the Singphos; (2) the seizure and punishment by local officers of some members of the tribes; (3) the orders of the Tippum Raja who was the Chief of the Hookoom province of Burma. The Governor-General in Council, while reviewing the report, set aside the last two causes and accepted the first cause as valid.[250] In the final report, it was held that the main reason behind the Singpho rebellion was the loss of their

Assamese slaves; the loss of land had nothing to do with it as no land had ever been granted to the Singphos or was claimed by the Singphos as theirs. It was concluded that after the loss of their slaves they would be compelled to take to agriculture and they might be left alone for the time being. The government accepted this report.[251]

Gradually the Singphos became peaceful and obedient. The main reason behind their reversion to peace was that after the Second Anglo-Burmese War, when Upper Burma was annexed to British Empire, the Singphos in India did not get either any insinuation or hope of assistance from Burma, and they were ultimately compelled to take to agriculture and hunting. No other Singpho rebellion is mentioned after the Anglo-Burmese War of 1851, when the first Assistant Political Officer of Sadiya, J.F. Michell, pushed up to the Huking valley.[252] He repeated his visit in 1891. On both occasions, he was assisted by the Singphos and no symptoms of hostility were shown to the party.[253] In 1909, Noel Williamson, who succeeded Needham, visited these tracts. He, too, was assisted by the Singphos and they did not oppose the move of the Political Officer.[254] In 1914, when the Frontier Tracts were divided, the Singpho tract were brought within the Eastern Section of the North-East Frontier, and gradually all the Singphos were brought under the 'loose political control' and purview of the Rules for the Administration of Justice in the Frontier Tracts. Poll-tax began to be introduced and collected from the Singpho villages henceforward.[255]

In 1917-18, Dundas, the Political Officer, recorded in his annual report that all the Singpho tribes had been brought under direct administration and all of them paid poll-tax. They were found contented, "hardly realising that the conditions were ever different."[256] In 1943, the Singpho tracts were divided when the Tirap Frontier Tract was created; some were brought within the new charge while others continued to be within the jurisdiction of the Political Officer of Sadiya.[257] The Singphos posed no problem for the British till their withdrawal from India in 1947.

TRIBES OF THE PATAKAI HILLS

Though the British penetrated into Upper Assam in the wake of the First Anglo-Burmese War (1824-26) and proceeded up to Joypur where a garrison post was established after the war, no notice was taken by them of the inhabitants living in the hills beyond. These inhabitants were the Nagas who had been living over and along the spurs and foothills of the Patkai range even before the Ahom advent in Assam in 1226. The Ahoms are said to have crossed the Patkai while marching towards Assam, and they followed a route along the banks of the Noa Dihing and Buri Dihing close by the Patkai. On their way to Assam they first encountered the Naga tribes, these Nagas are now divided into three clans of Tangsa, Nocte and Wancho, and, defeating them, established administrative posts before they marched further towards the Assam plains.[258] Later on, as the Ahom became rulers of Assam, they had to grant concessions to the Western Naga tribes in the form of *posa*.[259] Land grants were made to the Nagas to enable them to procure paddy and other articles which were not available in their hills. Salt wells which abound along the foot of the Naga hills were also shared by the Naga tribes and the Ahoms successively every year.[260] The Nagas visited the Ahom kings with presents, which Mackenzie holds might be supposed to be tribute.[261] It can be safely assumed that during the troublesome days of the Moamaria rebelion and the Burmese invasion, many tribes attacked the Ahom kingdom; the Adis, Nishig, Khamptis and Singphos swooped upon the Ahom kingdom. But the Nagas did not encroach upon the Ahom territories and attack Assamese villages; no such account in either the *Buranjis* or in the British records.

That the Nagas were living in the Patkai hills is evident from the British records of the 1830's. It is recorded in the correspondence of 1835 that the Nagas were raiding villages within the British jurisdiction along with the Singphos and the Burmese. But soon it became clear to the British officers that such raids were reprisals for raids on their villages, mostly perpetrated by the Singphos.[262] In 1837, Capt. Hannay, while marching through the spurs and valley of the Patkai in pursuit of the Singphos, found the Singphos taking the Naga people in captivity in gangs.[263] The Singphos were compelled by the British to surrender the Assamese slaves and the former found alternatives in the Nagas. The British had not yet claimed rights over the Naga territories and did not intervene on behalf of the Nagas. A proposal, however, was mooted to accord protection at this time to the Nagas and to establish a post under a European officer to take effective political charge of the Singpho-Naga tracts.[264] But it was found inexpedient to take charge of such a sparsely populated area, 90 miles long and 40 miles deep, and do it under an officer. As Capt. Hannay reported, it was not possible to accord protection to the Nagas unless they established themselves near the military posts. Then it was decided to leave the Nagas under the care of an officer who would visit the area as and when necessary.[265] Subsequently, the Singphos reduced many Naga villages to subjection to them and levies were imposed on them.

The Nagas did not realise any blackmail or *posa* from the villages of the Assam plains and, therefore, the British were not required to commute their rights over the villages. What caught the attention of the Company's servants was the salt wells of the Naga hills.[266] These hills were within the jurisdiction of the Principal Assistant of Sibsagar. From 1840, the Naga relations with the government were chiefly conducted by this officer; he maintained contact with the Nagas of the western hills which is beyond the jurisdiction of the Principal Assistant of Lakhimpur. Capt. Bordie, the Principal Assistant of Sibsagar, proposed to levy tribute on the villages in recognition of British paramountcy and mediate in the inter-tribal disputes of the Naga hills. He also went to their hills several times between 1840-47 to settle some such disputes. But the government soon decided to follow the policy of leaving the tribes 'alone', and Bordie's proposal as such came to naught.[267]

The eastern hills, or the Patkai hills within the jurisdiction of the North-East Frontier Agency, were initially under the Political Agent of Upper Assam posted at Sadiya and then under the Principal Assistant of the Lakhimpur district when the Political Agent of Upper Assam shifted his headquarters to Gauhati.[268] An Assistant Commissioner from his headquarters at Joypur now conducted relations with the eastern Nagas and occasionally paid visits to Margherita and adjacent areas, as it was decided after the receipt of Capt. Hanny's reports. The Nagas of the eastern hills or of the Patkai caught attention of the government in the last quarter of the nineteenth century when Naga raids consequent upon the encroachment of the tea planters became imminent after the quarrel between a tea planter and the Changnoi Nagas beyond the Lakhimpur frontier.[269] Subsequently, the massacre of Borlangia of 1872 perpetrated by Kamsangias forced the government to establish some link with some chiefs of the Nagas who had leased out lands to these tea planters.[270]

In 1873-74, the government executed agreements with the chiefs of Borduarias and the Namsangias to pay them Rs. 25 and Rs. 450 on account of the lands taken by Minto and Company for the Tawrouck and Hukanjuri tea gardens near Joypur on the Delli river.[271] The object was to bring these chiefs into direct dealings with the government which would enable the government to exert pressure on them in case of raid or any misbehaviour by the Nagas under these chiefs. The Government of Assam, of course, had settlements with the tea garden-owners for realising revenue from them. At the time of specification of the Inner Line boundary of the Lakhimpur district, the line was stretched to bring the tea gardens within the district of Lakhimpur.[272] It is worth remembering that the government held the view that the crest of the Patkai was the boundary between Assam and Burma and the claims of the Burmese over tracts of territory up to Joypur on the foothills of the Patkai was turned down. Yet the government avoided the responsibility to administer the Naga hills of the Patkai range and usually murders and atrocities committed beyond the Inner Line were ignored by them.

The opening of the coal mines in Joypur, Margherita, Ledo and the adjacent areas, extension of railheads to the coal-fields and tea garden areas and exploration of petroleum in Upper Assam brought the government close to the Nagas and roused their suspicion. In 1875, an attempt was made to survey the Eastern Naga hills and that led to a serious clash. The Assistant Commissioner of Joypur, Lt. Holcombe, accompanied by a survey party under Capt. Badgeley, went inside the Patkai range in February 1875. After four days' march beyond Joypur, they were attacked at a village called Ninu by the Nagas (Rangpangs). Lt. Holcombe with 80 men was butchered; Capt. Badgeley with 50 men escaped but was wounded. An expedition was immediately sent to punish the village of Ninu. It destroyed the village, but succeeded in recovering the arms lost and the heads of the men who were murdered in February.[273] In 1876, another expedition was sent to punish the village as it had refused to surrender some more men connected with the massacre of February 1875. The village of Ninu was burnt again.[274]

Meanwhile, in September 1875, the Lakhimpur Inner Line was notified and the Naga area of the Patkai range beyond Joypur was kept beyond the Inner Line. No raid by the Nagas of the hills beyond the Inner Line is reported before 1888 when the chief of Borduarias raided a Delli village near Joypur and took away a British subject. The British subject was killed subsequently together with another hillman whereupon the Deputy Commissioner of Dibrugarh detained the brother of the chief who was in the plains and stopped the payment of *posa* due to the Borduaria chief until he came for trail under the Deputy Commissioner. The chief was fined Rs. 2000 and 15 guns in the customary way; he paid off the fine.[275] The Chief Commissioner commenting upon the report held the view that the punishment was too light in consideration of the crime; but as the measure had already been adopted it was approved of by him.[276]

The government followed a policy of non-interference in Naga affair from the beginning of the nineteenth century.

This minimised the chance of government involvement in Naga affairs. But we find that the tribes beyond Joypur in the Lakhimpur Frontier Tract brought their inter-tribal disputes for settlement to the Deputy Commissioner of Dibrugarh. The boundary dispute between the Namsangias and Borduarias was settled by the Deputy Commissioner in 1905.[277] Henceforth, the main problem faced by the government was that of frequent thefts committed by the Naga tribes. The tribes required iron to make spears and other domestic implements. For the purpose, scrap iron from the mines or workshop of Railways were stolen. In case of theft by the Nagas of the hills beyond the Inner Line they were punished with fines. The offending villages readily submitted to the fines imposed on them. In 1904-05 some Rangpangs had committed a theft in the Ledo colliery and escaped with two captives and a gun with other stolen property. On their way back, some 30 persons of the party were arrested by a Harkara with the help of Sarkari Nagas. These peoples were detained in jail till their villagers came for their release. The Deputy Commissioner punished them with fine of Rs. 200 after the captives and stolen properties were restored.[278] Subsequently, another theft occurred there and this time the Sarkari Nagas were suspected. The Deputy Commissioner proposed to fine all Sarkari Nagas within 10 miles of Ledo with an amount of Rs. 300; the Chief Commissioner, however, declined to approve of the measure, pointing out that the culprits who were British subjects should be duly tried and the whole community could not be punished.[279] Theft of iron scrap cases by the Nagas of unadministered areas are reported as late as 1936[280] and 1937 when Rangpangs took away from Lekhpani Colliery some scrap.[281]

The opening of coal mines, extension of railways and development of Plantation industries had benefited the Naga tribes of the Lakhimpur frontier greatly. Many of the tribesmen came down to the plains during winter season and, serving in the industries, earned wages. Many got employment in the reserve forests and jungle clearings. These facilities kept the Nagas quite. Yet sometimes raids occurred in the Frontier Tracts and in the hills beyond the Inner Line. In 1905, Borduarias were attacked by Kunlungas under the Bormithunia chief, 4 miles within the British territory.[282] Again, in 1907, the Rangpang Nagas committed a raid in the Wakpong village within the Frontier Tract, and in 1908 some Rangpangs attacked and murdered some Longhangs who were going back to their villages beyond the Inner Line after serving in the plains for some time.[283] They later complained to the British for the redress of their grievances. In 1909 Noel Williamson, Assistant Political Officer from Sadiya, went to the Rangpang hills to punish the offenders of the Wakpong raid of 1907 and obtain satisfaction for the Longhang massacre. Willamson's party of 554 persons, consisting of 2 British, 3 Native officers and 142 rank and file of Assam Rifles, with a Hospital Assistant and one Surveyor and his servants and some privates, together with Naga Singpho and Nepali coolies, left for the village of Rashi in November 1909. They reached the village on the 29th and set fire to the village. On December 1, again, the remnant of the village was burnt and the party returned after destroying the village with stock and property.[284] Thereafter no serious raid on British territory was reported from the Rangpang Nagas.

From the beginning of the twentieth century, the government began to bring the Naga villages within the Frontier Tracts and impose taxes upon them. In 1909, Sarkari Naga villages beyond Ledo were annexed to the British territories, and the Assam Frontier Tracts Regulation of 1880 was extended to the Tract. Poll-tax was collected through the chiefs of the villages. In the Lakhimpur Frontier Tract areas, Political Jamadar seems to have disposed of the petty cases, referring serious ones to the Deputy Commissioner.[285] The Naga villages were visited by the Political Jamadar who sometimes went with Harkaras under him to visit the villages and apprehend criminals. The government usually did not provide any welfare measure until late twenties of the present century when one primary school in the Lakhimpur Frontier Tract was taken over by the government.[286] But an agricultural demonstrator was appointed to instruct the Nagas in improved methods of cultivation and some seeds were provided to the villagers.[287]

In 1914, some of the Naga areas were brought within the Eastern Section of the North-East Frontier and others were included in the Lakhimpur Frontier Tract to be administered by the Deputy Commissioner of the Lakhimpur district. In 1937, the transfer of the hill areas of the Lakhimpur Frontier charge to the Central and Eastern Sections was mooted inspite of the protest of the[288] Hill Nagas, but the proposal was, however, dropped. In 1943, again a new charge was created under the name of the Tirap Frontier Tract during the war taking portions of the Eastern Section of the North-East Frontier and the Lakhimpur Frontier Tract.[289] No opposition seems to have come this time from the Nagas.

CONCLUSION

Thus a survey of the British relations with the North-East Frontier tribes leads one to conclude that the first concern of the British was to dislodge the tribes from the Assam plains where they had established themselves before the advent of the British in Assam. Gradually the rights and privileges of the tribal people over the plains of Assam were abrogated by following a policy of what may be called in the words of Col. Henry Hopkinson, the Commissioner of Assam, "Gold" and "Steel". This means that they were to be conciliated by granting 'gold' or cash payment in lieu of the customary '*posa*' of the Ahom regime; but when they declined to accept the new terms of the new rulers, 'steel', that is to say, armed force, was to be employed to compel them to accept the offer. Till 1910, the British Government was quite unwilling to burden itself with the responsibility of administering the tribes of the Frontier; they followed a policy of what is called "let alone", that is, to leave the tirbes to themselves. But if they (tribes) violated the terms of engagements imposed on them by the British Government, punishments were meted out to them. After 1910, beginning with 'loose political control', direct control and administration were imposed on the tribes, and their territories were tagged to the province of Assam. But then the tribes were lagging so much behind the people of the plains as a result of neglect for such a long time that the Government of Assam had no alternative except to write to the Government of India in 1931: "what is needed for future is a policy of development and unification on lines suited to the genius of the hill people."[290]

REFERENCES

1. (Buragohain) Padmeswar Sing, *Ahom Buranji*, transcript No. 109, vol. IX, p. 569.
2. Revenue Proceedings, 11 August, 1834, No. 5.
3. A. Mackenzie, *History*, p. 6.
4. Foreign Proceedings, March 1885, No. 5.
5. *Ibid.*
6. *Ibid.*
7. *Ibid.*
8. *Ibid.*
9. L. Devi, *Ahom Tribal Relations*, p. 199.
10. *Ibid.*
11. Foreign Political (India), 12 September 1838, Nos. 64-85.
12. *Ibid.*
13. *Ibid.*
14. Foreign Political (India), 12 September 1838, No. 48.
15. *Ibid.*, 18 July 1836, Nos. 76-78.
16. C.U. Aitchison, A Collection of *Treaties, Engagements and Sanads*, Related to India and Neighbouring Countries, Vol. I, p. 143.
17. A. Mackenzie, *History*, p. 17.
18. *Ibid.*
19. *Ibid.*
20. *Ibid.*
21. *Ibid.*
22. *Ibid.*
23. *Ibid.*
24. Political Proceedings (Bengal), October 1864, Nos. 18-21.
25. Foreign Proceedings (Assam), March 1885, No. 40.
26. *Ibid.*
27. *Ibid.*
28. L. Devi, *op. cit.*, p. 199.
29. A. Mackenzie, *Memorandum on the North-East Frontier of Bengal*,

henceforth referred to as Memorandum., p. 5.

30. Foreign Political (India), 20 Februrary 1834, Nos. 23-24.
31. *Ibid.*
32. *Ibid.*
33. Foreign Proceedings (Assam), November 1875, Nos 3-4.
34. Foreign Proceedings (Assam), March 1885, No. 40.
35. J.A.M. Mills' Reprot, p. xcv.
36. Foreign Proceedings (Assam), March 1885, No. 40.
37. Foreign Proceedings (Assam), March 1885, No. 40.
38. *Ibid.*
39. Lakhimpur Deputy Commissioner's Collection, No. XVII of 1915-16, F. 7.
40. Foreign Proceedings (Assam), November 1875, Nos. 3-4.
41. File No. 309 of 1873, Sl. 15 (Bengal Papers) in Assam Archives.
42. Foreign Proceedings (Assam), April 1878, Nos. 8-12; July 1878, No.1.
43. *Ibid.*
44. Political Proceeding (Assam), December 1914, Nos. 1-37.
45. Proceedings of Governor's Secretariat, Tribal Affairs Deptt., June 1940, Nos. 535-626.
46. *Ibid.*
47. Revenue Proceedings (Bengal), 21 August 1834, No. 5.
48. H. Barua, *op. cit.*, p. 40; Singh P., *op. cit.*, p. 569.
49. David Scott, son of Archibald Scott was born in August, 1786 in England. He joined the East India Company's service and served as a Judge and Magistrate between 1812-1813 at Purnea (Bihar) and Rangpur and became Commissioner in 1823 in the latter place. In 1824 he was appointed Agent to the Governor-General on the North-East Frontier and Commissioner of Revenue and Circuit in the districts of Assam, North-East Rangpur, Shirpur and Sylhet. He encouraged the Christian missionaries in the Garo hills. He escaped the massacre of April 4-5 of 1831 of Nungklow and established a Sanitarium at Cherrapunjee. He died on August 20, 1831. See C.E. Buckland, *Dictionary of Indian Biography*, pp. 378-79.
50. Political Proceedings (Bengal), 5 February 1825.
51. Foreign Proceedings (Assam), March 1885, No. 40.
52. *Ibid.*
53. *Ibid.*
54. Political Proceedings (Bengal), 13 March 1835, Nos. 7-8.
55. *Ibid.*
56. *Ibid.*
57. Political Proceedings (Bengal), 16 January 1838, Nos. 41-48.
58. *Ibid.*, 19 April 1841, Nos. 80-81; 27 September 1841, Nos. 95-96.
59. Foreign Proceedings (Assam), March 1885, No. 40.
60. *Ibid.*, In 1944, Capt. Gordon had granted Rs. 32 each to

Chengkolee, Singingkandor and Sarsoo and Rs. 24 to Narsoo; and in 1848 he further granted Rs. 40 to Srigi and Rs. 32 each to Barsoo, Kangsoon and Rs. 22 each to Pasoo, Deekoks and Dhenno.

61. Foreign Proceedings (Assam), March 1885, No. 40.
62. *Ibid.*
63. Political Proceedings (Assam), June 1880, Nos. 55-56.
64. Bengal Papers in Assam Archives, File No. 309 of 1873, Sl. 15.
65. *Ibid.*, April 1874, No. 11.
66. *Ibid.*, June 1874, Nos. 23-24.
67. A. Mackenzie, *History*, p. 26.
68. *Ibid.*
69. Foreign Proceedings (Assam), December 1884, Nos. 7-9.
70. Judicial Proceedings, File No. 1545 of 1883, Nos. 1-18.
71. Judicial Papers (Assam), File No. 116J of 1884, Nos. 1-26.
72. Judicial Papers (Assam), File No. 116J of 1884, Nos. 1-26.
73. *Ibid.*
74. *Ibid.*
75. *Ibid.*
76. Foreign Proceedings (Assam), March 1885, No. 34.
77. *Ibid.*
78. Foreign Proceedings (Assam), January 1888, No. 8.
79. Foreign Political (India), November 1897, Nos. 15-104.
80. Foreign Proceedings (Assam), July 1900, No. 40.
81. *Ibid.*
82. Political Proceedings (Assam), December 1914, Nos. 1-37.
83. Political Proceedings (Assam), December 1914, Nos. 1-37.
84. *Ibid.*
85. Administration Report, 1924-25.
86. *Ibid.*, 1938-39.
87. Bengal Papers in Assam Archives, File No. 309 of 1873, Sl. 15.
88. H. Barua, *op. cit.*, p. 40; P. Sing, *op. cit.*, p. 569.
89. Revenue Proceedings (Bengal), 11 August 1834, No. 5.
90. Foreign Political (India), 20 February 1834, Nos. 22-24.
91. Bengal Papers (Assam), F. No. 298 BG. of 1835.
92. Foreign Political (India), 20 February 1834, Nos. 22-24.
93. *Ibid.*
94. *Ibid.*, 18 July 1836, Nos. 76-78.
95. *Ibid.*
96. Political Proceedings, 8 May 1837, Nos. 62-63, 15 May 1837, Nos. 10-11.
97. Foreign Political Proceedings (India), 18 July 1836, Nos. 76-78.
98. *Ibid.*
99. A. Mackenzie, *History*, p. 28.
100. *Ibid.*

101. Foreign Political (India), 20 February 1834, Nos. 23-24.
102. Lakhimpur Deputy Commissioner's Collection, No. XII, F. 7, 1884.
103. *Ibid.*
104. *Ibid.*, February, 1870, Nos. 1-2.
105. Political Proceedings (Bengal), June 1871, No. 28.
106. *Ibid.*, May 1877, No. 11.
107. *Ibid.*
108. Foreign Proceedings (Assam), June 1888.
109. *Ibid.*, March 1888, Nos. 11-24.
110. *Ibid.*, May 1899, Nos. 24-25.
111. *Ibid.*, March 1900, Nos. 18-24.
112. *Ibid.*, March 1900, Nos. 18-24.
113. *Ibid.*, March 1900, Nos. 18-24; April 1899, Nos. 1-7; May 1899, Nos. 24-26.
114. Political Proceedings (Assam), August 1910, No. 25.
115. *Ibid.*, February 1911, Nos. 77-84; March 1911, Nos. 5-70.
116. Political Proceedings (East Bengal and Assam), March 1912, Nos. 149-97.
117. Political Proceedings (Assam), December 1914, Nos. 1-37.
118. R. Reid, *History of the Frontier Areas Bordering on Assam*, from 1883-1941.
119. Political Proceedings (Assam), June 1926, Nos. 587-603.
120. Administration Report, 1924-25.
121. R. Reid, *op. cit.*, p. 294.
122. *Ibid.*
123. *Ibid.*
124. Administration Report, 1938-39.
125. A. Mackenzie, *History*, p. 35.
126. *Ibid.*
127. H. Barua, *op. cit.*, p. 40; P. Sing, *op. cit.*, p. 569.
128. Political Proceedings (EBA), May 1906, Nos. 1-11.
129. A. Mackenzie, *History*, p. 36.
130. *Ibid.*
131. Lakhimpur Deputy Commissioner's Collection, No. XII, F. 7, 1884.
132. Foreign Secret Proceedings, 26 February 1830, Nos. 5-6.
133. *Ibid.*, 7 May 1830, Nos. 47-48.
134. Political Proceedings (Bengal), 16 March 1840, No. 112.
135. *Ibid.*, 28 April 1848, Nos. 104-06.
136. A. Mackenzie, *History*, p. 36.
137. *Ibid.*
138. Political Proceedings (Bengal), June 23, 1849, Nos. 23-29.
139. Revenue Proceedings (Bengal), 12 March 1851, Nos. 61-62.
140. *Ibid.*
141. Judicial Proceedings (Bengal), 19 August 1858, Nos. 262-89.

142. *Ibid.*
143. *Ibid.*
144. *Ibid.*, 25 January 1859, Nos. 88-100.
145. *Ibid.*, August 1860, Nos. 417-19.
146. Judicial Proceedings (Bengal), August 1860, Nos. 417-19.
147. *Ibid.*
148. Judicial Proceedings (Bengal), January 1862, Nos. 305-08.
149. *Ibid.*, May 1865, Nos. 119-21.
150. *Ibid.*, October, 1862, No. 176.
151. *Ibid.*, January 1863, Nos. 310-11.
152. *Ibid.*
153. *Ibid.*
154. Judicial Proceedings (Bengal), March 1863, No. 248.
155. C.U. Aitchison, *op. cit.*, p. 299.
156. Judicial Proceedings (Bengal), May 1865, Nos. 119-21.
157. *Ibid.*, November 1863, No. 166.
158. *Ibid.*, June 1866, Nos. 6-7.
159. A. Mackenzie, *History*, p. 42.
160. Foreign Proceedings (Assam), January 1878, No. 7.
161. *Ibid.*, October 1878, No. 12.
162. *Ibid.*, No. 6.
163. Foreign Proceedings (Assam), November 1878, No. 14.
164. *Ibid.*, September 1887, Nos. 35-38; June 1916, No. 37.
165. Foreign Proceedings (Assam), January 1880, Nos. 4-5.
166. Lakhimpur Deputy Commissioner's Collection, No. XII of 1904-08, F. 6.
167. Foreign Proceedings (Assam), February 1885, Nos. 2-6.
168. Lakhimpur Deputy Commissioner's Collection, No. XII of 1906, F. 6.
169. Foreign Proceedings (Assam), September 1887, Nos. 35-38.
170. *Ibid.*, June 1890, No. 15.
171. Foreign Proceedings (Assam), July 1894, Nos. 34-371.
172. *Ibid.*
173. *Ibid.*
174. R. Reid, *op. cit.*, p. 199.
175. Foreign Proceedings (Assam), January 1901, Nos. 37-40.
176. *Ibid.*, 177.
177. Lakhimpur Deputy Commissioner's Collection, No. XV of 1908-10, F. 32.
178. *Ibid.*, No. XII of 1907-08, F. 59.
179. Political Proceedings (Assam), March 1912, Nos. 149-197.
180. *Ibid.*, June 1912, Nos. 140-200.
181. *Ibid.*
182. *Ibid.*, December 1914, Nos. 19-54.

183. Administration Report of the Central and Eastern Section, 1917-18.
184. Proceedings of the Governor's Secretariat, Tribal Affairs Deptt., June 1940, Nos. 535-626.
185. G. Barua, *Ahom Buranji*, pp. 231-33.
186. H. Barua, *op. cit.*, p. 185.
187. A. Mackenzie, *History*, p. 47.
188. Secret Proceedings, 29 April 1825, No. 2.
189. Bengal Papers, 23.
190. Political Proceedings (Bengal), 6 March 1837, No. 67.
191. *Ibid.*
192. Foreign Proceedings (Assam), July 1899, Nos 32-49.
193. Judicial Proceedings (Bengal), 16 July 1857, Nos. 168-72.
194. *Ibid.*, 10 September 1857, Nos. 120-23.
195. *Ibid.*, 31 December 1857, Nos. 182-84; 25 February 1861, Nos. 351-60.
196. *Ibid.*, 16 July 1857, Nos. 168-72.
197. Political Proceedings (Bengal), February 1866, Nos. 11-15.
198. *Ibid.*, May 1868, Nos. 56-57.
199. A. Mackenzie, *History*, p. 52.
200. *Ibid.*
201. *Ibid.*
202. Foreign Proceedings (Assam), January 1907, Nos. 13-70.
203. *Ibid.*, August 1900, Nos. 46-60.
204. *Ibid.*
205. *Ibid.*, July 1899, Nos. 32-49.
206. Political Proceedings (East Bengal and Assam), January 1907, Nos. 13-70.
207. *Ibid.*, March 1912, Nos. 47-148.
208. Political Proceedings (Assam), April 1921, Nos. 243-68.
209. *Ibid.*, June 1934, Nos 1300-29.
210. Administration Report, 1937-38.
211. *Ibid.*, 1939-40.
212. G. Barua, *op. cit.*, p. 364-65.
213. S.K. Bhuyan, *Tungkhungia Buranji*, p. 120.
214. Political Proceedings (Bengal), 13 March 1835, Nos. 1-8.
215. Political Consultations (India), 15 May 1837, Nos. 12-13.
216. Foreign Political (India), 18 April 1838, Nos. 56-57.
217. *Ibid.*, 15 May 1837, Nos. 12-13.
218. Political Proceedings (Bengal), 24 November 1835, No. 11.
219. *Ibid.*, 13 March 1835, Nos. 1-8.
220. *Ibid.*, 20 February 1839, Nos. 105-10.
221. *Ibid.*
222. *Ibid.*, 20 January 1844, No. 61.
223. Foreign Political Proceedings (India), 20 January 1844, Nos. 61-66.
224. Foreign Political Proceedings (Assam), June 1917, Nos. 5-6.

225. *Ibid.*, November 1916, Nos. 3-5.
226. *Ibid.*, June 1917, Nos. 5-6.
227. S.K. Bhuyan, *op. cit.*, pp. 150-207.
228. A. Mackenzie, *History*, p. 62.
229. *Ibid.*, p. 63.
230. *Ibid.*
231. *Ibid.*
232. *Ibid.*, p. 64.
233. *Ibid.*
234. *Ibid.*
235. *Ibid.*
236. Political Proceedings (Bengal), 7 May 1830, Nos. 7-8.
237. A. Mackenzie, *History*, p. 66.
238. Political Proceedings (Bengal), September 25/26 1835, Nos. 1-48.
239. *Ibid.*, 6 March, 1837, Nos. 33-34.
240. A. Mackenzie, *History*, p. 67.
241. *Ibid.*, p. 68.
242. Political Proceedings (Bengal), 4 April 1838, Nos. 103-04.
243. *Ibid.*, 27 January 1841, Nos. 59-60.
244. *Ibid.*
245. *Ibid.*, 7 August 1841, Nos. 187-89.
246. *Ibid.*, 1 February 1843, Nos. 162-63.
247. A. Mackenzie, *History*, p. 69.
248. *Ibid.*, p. 70.
249. *Ibid.*, 9 March 1844, No. 142; 28 April 1848, Nos. 103-04.
250. *Ibid.*
251. *Ibid.*, March 1844, Nos. 89-91.
252. Assam Secretariat, File No. 547J of 1887.
253. *Ibid.*, File No. 613J of 1888.
254. Political Proceedings (East Bengal and Assam), May 1910, Nos. 13-40.
255. *Ibid* (Assam), December 1914, Nos. 1-3.
256. Administration Report, 1917-18.
257. *Ibid.*
258. H. Barua, *op. cit.*, pp. 11-12.
259. *Ibid.*
260. A. Mackenzie, *History*, p. 91.
261. *Ibid.*
262. *Ibid.*, 24 November 1835, Nos. 32-33.
263. Political Proceedings (Bengal), 10 April 1837, Nos. 120-23.
264. *Ibid.*, 8 May 1837, Nos. 64-66.
265. A. Mackenzie, *History*, p. 89.
266. Revenue Proceedings (Bengal), 8 August 1842, Nos. 125-26.
267. A. Mackenzie, *History*, p. 95.
268. A.J.M. Mills' Report, p. ixxxiv.
269. February 1870, Nos. 110-11.
270. A. Mackenzie, *History*, p. 99.

271. Political Proceedings (Assam), August 1874, No. 18.
272. *Ibid.*, April 1874, No. 14.
273. A. Mackenzie, *History*, p. 99.
274. *Ibid.*
275. Lakhimpur Deputy Commissioner's Collection, No. XII of 1888, No. 10.
276. *Ibid.*
277. Lakhimpur Deputy Commissioner's Collection, No. XII F. 8, 1904-08.
278. Lakhimpur Deputy Commissioner's Collection, No. XII of 1904-08; Political Report of 1904-05.
279. *Ibid.*
280. *Ibid.*, Collection IX-5 of 1836, sl. 1.
281. *Ibid.*, Collection IX-2 of 1937, sl. 1.
282. *Ibid.*, Collection No. XII of 1905, F. 1.
283. *Ibid.*, Collection XVII of 1915-16, F. 19.
284. Political Proceedings (East Bengal and Assam), April 1910, Nos. 13-40.
285. Lakhimpur Deputy Commissioner's Collection, No. IX of 1937, F. 10.
286. *Ibid.*, Collection IX of 1939, F. 15.
287. *Ibid.*, Collection IX of 1935, F. 2.
288. *Ibid.*, Collection No. IX of 1936, F. 1.
289. Administrative Jurisdiction, p. 1.
290. Political Proceedings (Assam), September 1931, No. 135.

3

THE INNER LINE, THE OUTER LINE AND THE MCMAHON LINE

DRAWING OF BOUNDARY

The British came to Assam during the Anglo-Burmese War of 1824-26 and occupied it as a conquered territory. The treaty of Yandabu (1826) did not define the boundary of Assam; it simply stipulated that the Burmese would not interfere in Assam and its dependencies.[1] The Ahom kings whose place the British stepped in did not possess any map to show the boundary of their kingdom, nor did they possess any documentary records giving descriptions of their frontiers. Therefore, the new rulers of Assam did not know the bounds of their newly acquired territories.

The study of the British relations with the hill tribes shows that the extent of the territory of Assam and the hills was not known definitely. The hill tribes, whether dependent on Assam or independent of any political master, claimed tributary payment not on the basis of lands the peasants cultivated but on the very ground of their living in the certain areas.[2] Whether the villages from which the hill chiefs collected levies were within Assam or had been taken possession of by them during the troublesome days of war cannot be definitely ascertained.[3] Then again, these hill tribes in many cases were still in a nomadic state; they were moving from place to place in pursuit of their livelihood.[4]

Yet another problem of the relation of the hill tribes with

the Ahom princes remains. The Ahom prince Pratap Singh had granted the right of *posa* to the Bhutias, Akas (Hrussos), Nishis and Adis. But whether these tribes were independent of or subordinate to the Ahoms cannot be categorically said. We know that during the reign of Gauri Singh an army was sent to punish the Nishis and many were brought down as captives.[5] If we assume that the Nishis were vassals of the Ahom kings (which is of course, not portable) then also we face another problem, that of the boundary of the Nishi territory.[6] The same problem arises in regard to the territories of the other hill tribes, *e.g.*, the Bhutias, Akas (Hrussos) and Adis. Indeed, we do not know the extent of the territories of the different tribes of the North-East Frontier.

The attention of the British was drawn at first towards the boundary between Assam and Burma and between manipur and Burma. Till the second Anglo-Burmese war the British were anxious to check the Burmese invasion of Assam and, therefore, they came to an agreement with regard to the boundary between Assam and Manipur on the one hand and Burma and Manipur on the other hand. The Burmese claim upon the territories west of the Patkai range extending to Upper Assam and Joypur was turned down, but the Kubo Valley was restored to the Burmese giving a compensation the ruler of Manipur. The British stressed upon the watershed of the Patkai range as the boundary between Assam and Burma and held fast to this contention till Burma was absorbed in the British Empire after the third Anglo-Burmese war.[7] The boundary between Assam and Burma, however, was not demarcated; in 1967 the Government of India and Burma entered into an agreement regarding the border between the two countries.[8]

The question of settling the boundary in the north-west between Assam and Bhutan was taken up after the annexation of the Duars to British India. At the time of annexation of the Duars, the boundary between Bhutan and Assam was not defined or demarcated. The Bhutia chiefs sometimes came down and laid claims upon the British territories; at least in some cases they claimed jurisdiction within the British area. The British authorities now decided to settle the boundary problem and delegated Lt. Col. Graham, the Deputy Commissioner of Darrang, to demarcate the boundary between Assam and Bhutan. He completed the task in 1872-73, but he went up to the river Deoshan, beyond the boundary of Assam and Bhutan, in the Nishi hills.[9] The boundary between Assam and Bhutan was agreed upon by the Bhutia and English authorities, but the boundary beyond was not an international boundary as the tribes living there were neither paramount nor vassals of any sovereign master.[10] Therefore, the boundary of Assam in the north on the side of Tibet remained to be agreed upon between the two countries.

It has been observed in the preceding chapter that the British authorities had resumed the territories of the different tribes on the foot of their hills on condition of paying them some blackmail. The tribes withdrew within the hills but then where the territory of the hill tribes began was not known. Lt. Col Graham had demarcated the southern boundary of those tribes who came down and agreed to accept the line as the dividing line between Assam and their territories. But the question of jurisdiction of the British authorities was not settled. E.J. Monahan, the Secretary to the Chief Commissioner of Assam, wrote to the Government of India that the Boundary Commissioner Lt. Col. Graham had demarcated the boundary of Assam up to the river Baroe but the boundary beyond Deoshan could not be regarded as valid as no treaty was entered into in this regard. He observed, "the agreement which we have with the Bhutias of Towang, who are dependent on Tibet, and with the independent Bhutias and Akas, do not provide for any delimitation of the territory nor have we any such agreement with the Dafla tribes further east. There exist some treaties with some of the Abor tribes which distinctly mention that British territory extends to the foot of the hills. The Chief Commissioner has ascertained that the frontage of the Abor territory covered by their agreements extends from a point near Mesaki on the west to Nizamghat on the Dibong on the east. After crossing the Brahmaputra, it follows approximately the Daphabum range to the south and then turning south-west follows the crest to Patkai range as far as the north-east corner of Manipur territory. But the Chief Commissioner can find no definite authority for the adoption of Daphabum range and the crest of the Patkai range as the 'outer line' of British India."[11]

THE INNER LINE

The problem of the boundary was further complicated by the specification of the Inner Line from 1875. By the beginning of the seventies of the nineteenth century, the economy of Assam had become promising and trade and industry had made a good start. Tea, petroleum, coal, rubber and wood became flourishing industries and elephant-catching and ivory were engaging growing attention. Besides, the revenue of the Assam valley increased so as to provide for good surplus and huge fallow lands could yield more if tenants were invited to take them up. But the economy depended upon the Administration's capacity to maintain law and order in the province. All the districts of the Assam valley bordered on some hills inhabited by the tribes. The unrestricted intercourse between the people who had come for commerce and who knew very little about the tribes led to many disputes and sometimes these took violent dimensions.[12] Moreover, the tribes driven into the hills sometimes had to fall upon the plains to draw their supplies. The problem of regulation of the intercourse between the tribes and ryots and businessmen of the Assam plains, therefore, drew the attention of the Administration. The hill tribes problem forced them to create a barrier between the hills and the plains which would reduce contact and consequently friction between the civilised valley-dwellers and the primitive hill tribes. This was done by a Regulation in 1873.[13]

Regulation I of 1873, called a "Regulation for the peace

and Good Government of certain districts on the Eastern Frontier," commonly known as the Inner Line Regulation of 1873, authorised the Local Government, with the previous approval of the Governor-General in Council, to prescribe and from time to time alter, a line, to be called the 'Inner Line', in each or any of the districts of Assam.[14] The term 'Inner Line', however, originated from the suggestion of Arthur Hobhouse who observed in his draft for the Regulation of 1873 that the line to be prescribed under the Regulation might be called 'Inner Line'.[15] The Local Government was also empowered to prohibit all British subjects, or any class of British subjects, or any person residing in or passing through such districts, from going beyond such Line without a pass under the hand and seal of the executive officer or such officer as might be authorised to grant such pass. The Local Government, however, was given the power to suspend or vary this prohibition from time to time. Any person who went beyond the Inner Line fixed according to the above process, without a pass, was liable to conviction before a Magistrate of first or second class and to a fine not exceeding Rs. 100 for the first offence; for each subsequent offence there could be a fine not exceeding Rs. 500 or simple or rigorous imprisonment for a term not exceeding three months or both.[16]

The object of the Inner Line Regulation was to keep outside the boundary all "tracts over which semi-savage tribes wandered or in which they lived", for their free intercourse with the people of the plains might lead to complications. It was clearly expressed that Government of India would not be responsible for life and property of the people beyond such Line and, if necessary, people might not be allowed to go beyond the Line. The Government of India had suggested to the Government of Bengal that while prescribing such Line, they should see that the Line corresponded to the natural features of the country, and if there was no such feature it was to coincide with obligatory points like crossing of a road. The place where a road crossed the Line was to be clearly shown in maps, and if the area where it ran had not been mapped, arrangement should be made for topographical survey as well. If any tea garden was there on the frontier, that should be brought within the Line, if possible, for avoiding possible complications.[17] Commerce beyond the Inner Line could be carried on pass basis, that is, people desirous of capturing elephants, cutting wood, collecting forest products like rubber could carry on their trade in the tribal area getting pass from the government, but they would be subject to payment of tolls to the tribes inhabiting the region where such trade was to be carried on.[18]

Some conclusions may be drawn from an examination of the provisions of the Inner Line Regulation of 1873. In the first place, the British government defined a boundary up to which it would exercise its authority and uphold law and order; it would decline responsibility beyond, and there the tribes would be left to themselves. Secondly, it did not mention whether the tribes living beyond the Inner Line were under its political control; nor did it accept any paramount power of exercising control over them. Finally, free intercourse of the people of British India with the tribes was restricted, but no restriction upon the movement of the tribes was imposed. The tribes were allowed to fish and hunt on both sides of the Inner Line.[19] People from within the administered districts of Assam were allowed to go within the Inner Line and even beyond with pass, but the businessmen had to pay blackmail or tolls to the tribes for collection of wood or other forest products from the territories which were regarded as outside the so called boundary of Assam.[20] The Miju Mishmis even collected tolls from the Hindu pilgrims visiting the Parasuram Kund as it was regarded lying outside the administered area.[21]

For the first time, the Inner Line was notified for the Lakhimpur district on 3 September 1875, applying Regulation I of 1873.[22] The Deputy Commissioner of Lakhimpur, Major W.S. Clarke, submitted his final proposal, after revising his original proposal of 1873, on 22 May

1875.[23] In his original proposal of December 1873 for the south-eastern and eastern part of the Inner Line of the Lakhimpur district he had proposed to include within the Line the three tea gardens of Taurack, Hukanjuri and Namsang which were held by M/s Minto & Company on a lease from the Namsangia Naga Chief and which were considered to be outside British territory; those were intended to be brought within the British jurisdiction on agreement by the Government from the Nagas and then leased to Messers Minto & Company. But then the Line would cut off a tongue of the hilly country lying between the Disang (Dilli) and Namsang rivers. The Line running down the Namsang river to its mouth, or its confluence with the Boori Dihing, would go up the course of the Boori Dihing as far as the mouth of the Makumpani, which ran southward from the hills into the Dihing; it would then deviate from the natural boundary, but it was supposed to be the most practicable line. The Line was then to run down the course of the Tirap to where it fell into the Boori Dihing, and then be marked by the Boori Dihing to where the Kherampani fell into it, then up the Kherampani to the Noa Dihing, and along that stream to the Brahmaputra.[24]

To the north the Line should take the course of the Rajghur Ali, from the Darrang boundary to the Sisi river; thence by as direct a line as practicable to the Dimu guard. Thence it should be marked by a frontier path as straight as circumstances might allow as far as the Poba military guard; thence by a frontier path running along the line of the Brahmaputra to Lallimukh; thence by a line to Dibongmukh by the Debong to the Debong guard; thence by the path communicating between the Debong and the Dikrang guards; thence, by the general line of the frontier guards, to the revenue survey masonry pillar on the Brahmaputra.[25]

But the Chief Commissioner of Assam instructed Major Clarke to redraw his proposal keeping in view that the boundary should be as far as practicable coterminous with the revenue survey, and the boundary between ordinary and political jurisdiction should be consistent.[26] It was practically impossible to suggest a line through a natural line in a country unsurveyed, practically uninhabited and covered by dense jungle. Therefore, in his revised proposal, Clarke suggested small modifications. The Line which he finally drew up would take the course of the Dihing, in the south-eastern section, as it was a good natural boundary though it kept outside the Inner Line the coal-fields of Tirap and Namdang, situated in the neighbourhood of peaceful and small Naga villages. The tea gardens of Namsang, Hukanjuri and Taurack, however, were brought within the Inner Line as an agreement with the Namsangia chief was being processed to bring the latter under direct agreement with the government, and arrangement for revenue survey was provided for. The tea gardens of Joyhing and Harmati were also brought within the Inner Line. In the original proposal the Line was to adhere to the boundary of the ordinary jurisdiction, and deviation from such boundary was proposed under the orders of the Commissioner. The new line thus would pass from Dimu guard to the Debong river; the revenue survey boundary, and the boundary between ordinary and political jurisdiction, ran from Dimu to Boori Sooti, and down the Sooti to the Brahmaputra, and then along the right bank of the Brahmaputra to the mouth of the Debong.[27]

The revised proposal of Major Clarke was forwarded and recommended to the Government of India by the Chief Commissioner of Assam and the Government of India notified the Line on 3 September 1875 in the *Gazetteer of India*. The Line as notified ran as follows :[28]

> Commencing on the south-east of the district at the Desang (Dilli), from the Taurack garden, on the Desang river, along the path leading to Hukanjuri garden on the Namsang river; thence along the Namsang river, to its junction with the Boori Dihing along the course of the Boori Dihing to where the Kheramapani runs into it; thence along the Kherampani to its junction with the

Noa Dihing; along the Noa Dihing to where it joins the Brahmaputra.

North of the Brahmaputra, commencing from the Darrang boundary, along the Rajgurh Ali to where it meets the Dihing to where it is met on its other or left bank by the Rajgurh Ali, to the Rangadi; thence including within the line the Joyhing tea-garden, along the Rajgurh Ali, so far as it is practicable; and thence along the base of the Abor Miri hills to the Sisi river; and thence to be marked by as straight a line as may be practicable to the Dimu guard; thence by a frontier path, taken as straight as practicable, to the Poba guard; and from thence by a frontier path to Lallimukh, where the Lalli falls into the Brahmaputra; thence along the Brahmaputra river to Debongmukh, along the Debong to the Debong gurad; thence by the path connecting the Debong and Dikrang guards; thence along the general line of frontier guards and the boundary of the revenue survey to the revenue survey masonry pillar on the Brahmaputra, and thence by the Brahmaputra to Noadihingmukh, the termination of the Inner Line on the east.

The drawing of the Inner Line of the Darrang district did not prove as difficult as the case was with the Lakhimpur Inner Line. The boundary of the district and the hill tribes had already been demarcated by Col. Graham in 1873 along the Daflagurh which was a continuation of the Rajgurh Ali of Lakhimpur. The Deputy Commissioner proposed the same line, stretching it a little between boundary pillar No. 160 and the Daflagurh so as to include within the Inner Line the tea garden of Singlijan which was held under wast land grant No. 18 in Darrang district. The Line commenced from the eastern boundary of the district of Kamrup, that is, from pillar No. 98 on the Bor Nado, and then followed in an easterly direction the southern boundaries of Bhutan (including the tracts of Kuriapara and Charduar Bhutia), and of the Aka and Dafla Hills, as defined by the revenue survey in the years 1872-73-74-75, and demarcated by pillars Nos. 98 to 160, inclusive. From pillar No. 160 the Line ran in a south-easterly direction to the point where the Balum river cut the northern boundary of the Singlijan tea waste land grant No. 18. Thence the line followed the eastern boundary of the Singlijan grant No. 18 to the point where the boundary cut the Daflagurh. Thence the Line followed the Daflagurh to a point on the More Sessa river being the north-westerly extremity of the Inner Line of the Lakhimpur district, as notified on 30 September 1875 in the *Gazetteer of India*.[29] The Line was notified on 8 March 1876.[30]

THE OUTER LINE

The origin of the term Outer Line, unlike that of the Inner Line, is vague and could not be traced. A note of the Froeign Department, Political Branch, goes like this : "The limits of the district were at first thrown very far forward, too far to enable us to exercise jurisdiction all the way up to them; so it became necessary to draw a line up to which we intend to work. This was the Inner Line. The limits of the district as originally proposed became the Outer Line....."[31] So the Inner Line passed through the British territory and marked the boundary of the ordinary and political jurisdictions of the district officers. But the Outer Line was purposely kept undefined so as to enable them to bring any tract of territory within the jurisdiction of the district officers as and when necessary. "The Outer Line is purposely left indefinite, so that we can advance the Inner Line to any extent circumstances may render necessary."[32] So far as the international border is concerned, the British authorities did not care at all till the advent of the Chinese across Rima in 1910.

Thus the Inner Line was the line up to which the British officers exercised regular jurisdiction. Between that Inner Line and the originally accepted boundary of Assam which in course of time began to be called Outer Line, the British government claimed some sort of sovereignty, but did not exercise any regular jurisdiction except some sort of personal influence. Beyond it lay the territories of the tribes over which they did not acknowledge any paramount power. The limits of this Outer Line were purposely kept undefined and indefinite so that the Line could be advanced to any extent that circumstances might render necessary. The Lt. Governor of Eastern Bengal and Assam, Sir Lancelot Hare, wrote to the Government of India that the boundary of the Lakhimpur district was wholly undefined and unknown till 1875 and it was impossible to say how far the British jurisdiction extended.[33] While proposing the Inner Line in 1873 the Deputy Commissioner of Lakhimpur tried to include all the existing lands granted under the Waste Land Grant Rules and proposed a line beyond which British jurisdiction should not be extended at that time. But he made it clear in his notes that over all territories beyond that Line the British authority would be indefinite but sufficient for all purposes, and there could be no dispute as to British authority beyond the Inner Line. He did not, of course, like to propose any Outer Line.[34]

The issue of the Outer Line was very nicely put in Lord Hardinge's despatch of December 22, 1910. He wrote, "I think I hardly brought out with sufficient distinctness one important consideration which should induce us to press forward beyond the limits by which under a self-denying ordinance our frontier is at present limited. We only now claim suzerainty up to the foot of the hills. We have an Inner Line and an Outer Line. Up to the Inner Line we administer in the ordinary way. Between the Inner Line and the Outer Line we only administer politically. That is our Political Officers exercise very loose jurisdiction, and to prevent troubles with frontier tribes passes are required for our subjects who want to cross the Inner Line. The counrty between the two lines is very sparsely inhabited and is mostly dense jungle."[35]

In fact the jurisdiction of the Chief Commissionership of

Assam was never defined specifically nor was it ever demarcated. The Inner Line which was specified from time to time in different districts by applying Regulation I of 1873 did not in any way solve the problem of the boundary. The Inner Line was jurisdictional, and not a territorial limit. Godfrey, the Deputy Commissioner of Lakhimpur, wrote: "I don't know that the limits of the Chief Commissionership have ever been specified so that we know precisely what the area within which the acts of the Governor General in Council are in force. I have been inclined to think that the Inner Line marked the boundary of our regular jurisdiction, that is, our courts of law.... but the Inner Line Regulation is not one that defines jurisdiction. The Chief Commissionership of Assam extends up to the borders of China and Tibet and Burma."[36] He further writes, "We have, of course, got an admitted political control over the border tribes which emanate from, and is dependent upon, our being possessed of superior force, and so we command obedience to such orders as may be passed by our officers in their political capacity : it has accordingly been my opinion that the Deputy Commissioner has beyond the Inner Line a general political authority resting upon force, but no law as such can be enforced upon the inhabitants of those tracts."[37]

The relations of the British Government with the border tribes bear out the reality of the situation. We have seen that though the British authority did not penetrate into the territories of the Bhutias of the present Kameng district, the British pursued the Aka (Hrusse), Nishi, Adi, Mishmi, Khampti and Singpho tribes as and when necessary. Troops were sent beyond the Outer Line and the Government exacted fines, arrested criminals, destroyed villages of the tribes and were thus free to deal with them. The Dalai Lama and his ministers gave the Government of India to understand that these tribes were under the British by their consent.[38] Of course, the government always shrunk from the responsibility of administering these tribal tracts as it was expensive. Several officers advocated the imposition as direct administration on these hill tracts. Col. Hopkinson clearly wrote to the Government of India that by the anexation of Assam the British Government had undertaken an obligation to administer and civilise these tribes.[39] But the Government scrupulously avoided the responsibility.

The issue of the delineation of the border and assertion of paramountcy over the border tribes became imperative after the appearance of the Chinese on the other side of the border. The Chinese general Chao Exh-feng having consolidated his imperial power in Szechuan and Sikiang province of China made thrust into Tibet through the eastern marshes. A report of Chinese concentration beyond the Abor hills was reported as early as 1908. Then a fresh force appeared beyond the Mishmi hills in 1910. Though the recommendations of the Local Government for bringing the frontier tribes under administration on humanitarian and logical grounds could be flouted for pecuniary considerations, the prospect of a Chinese thrust into the valley of the Brahmaputra, full of British capitalist enterprise, could not be ignored. The hill of the tribes under Chinese control, influence or occupation would render the plains below vulnerable, and if the Dragon was to be resisted at all that should be done before it crossed the hills and came down to the plains. The unspecified and undemarcated nature of the North-East Frontier boundary made the title over the range of the Eastern Himalayas disputed. Therefore, the whole frontier policy came under fresh examination and orientation.

The Political Officer at Sadiya, on receiving the information of the Chinese crossing the border, sent a message to the Government and sought permission to declare that the Mishmis were under the political control of the British Government. As a matter of fact, the Mishmis looked towards the British as their masters and from time to time sought permission to settle on the plain land below their hills. The British officers also had from time to time gone to the Mishmi Hills and taken prosoners from among the offending tribes. Yet the Administration had avoided responsibility for the Mishmis. So when Kugno, the Mishmi Chief, approached the Assistant Political Officer and reported that the Chinese had asked them to construct a bridle path down the valley through their hills, the latter sought permission from the Government to declare that Mishmis were under British control. The Lt. Governor of Eastern Bengal and Assam saw wisdom in his report and recommended to the Government of India the proposal of the Assistant Political Officer, though the Commissioner of the Assam Valley districts had declared in 1907 that the Mishmis were never under the control of the government.[40] The Government of India, though much concerned at the advent of the Chinese, was hesitant.

Meanwhile the Chinese had withdrawn, the Tibetans had declared their independence of China, and China herself was in the throes of a revolutionary upsurge. Williamson, who visited the Mishmi Hills along the Lohit valley and proceeded up to Walong, recommended to open up the hills to Walong by constructing a bridle path along the Lohit valley and to appoint for each of the tribes in the Mishmi and Adi Hills some influential man as British agent to report on the developments on the borders and look after the upkeep of the proposed bridle tracks. He recommended the name of the Mishmi men who were to be appointed and the Government accepted his proposal.[41]

But the unsettled state of the boundary could no longer be neglected. Younghusband had laid emphasis on the settlement of the boundary between India and Tibet.[42] The success of the Russians in Mongolia and reports of their activities in Tibet further highlighted the problems of the frontier. It was also apprehended that China under a Republican Government would be more powerful and aggressive than under the Manchus. The Political Officer at Kalimpong, Charles Bell, in his report on the developments in Tibet spelled out the consequences of the rise of the Chinese power and suggested the settlement of the India-Tibet boundary and bringing of the border tribes within the Indian side of the frontier under the jurisdiction of the British

Government.[43]

Bell clearly pointed out that the Government of India could no longer avoid the problem of the North-East Frontier. The military reports on the North-East Frontier made it clear that the Government of India never apprehended the slightest chance of invasion of Assam by a civilised military power and consequently no strategic plan, no defence arrangement and no organisation whatsoever were ever provided to repel such an invasion. As it would not be possible to keep China out of Tibet, it would be of vital importance to keep China and other powers out of the narrow strip of territory between India and Tibet.[44]

The natural corollary of such a policy as contemplated by Bell was that the Government of India should maintain inviolate the territory that intervened between Assam and Tibet. Two things, he thought, would be essential to implement this policy. First, China should not be allowed to enter into the territory. Secondly, no Indian or British vested interest should be allowed inside the territory as far as possible. But he did not advocate the assumption by the Government of the responsibility of internal administration of the territory of the tribes at all. The reason for not allowing the Indian or British vested interests in the region was that by allowing such interests to grow up in the zone, the Government would assume some sort of obligation to protect them. Again, such a course would destroy the buffer which the Government of India should maintain between the two countries and create those difficulties which the Government wanted to remove. Moreover, the management of tribal affairs by the tribes themselves was very much prized by the tribal people. A guarantee that there would be no interference in the internal affairs would win the hearts of the tribal communities as in the case of Bhutan.[45]

Bell in his letter cited the reports of the growing public concern for the developments in the North-East Frontier. He quoted from the newspaper *Englishman* of August 1910 which wrote that while the "Secretary of State for Foreign

Affairs and the Secretary of State for India were content with philosophising along the lines of radical thought" .... the growing pressure on North-East subjected India to serious dangers." "There is a vast region of forests, hills and rolling downs inhabited by the Nishis, Mishings, Adis and Mishmis through which access can be had into the Assam valley without too much difficulty. It will not be long before Chinese activities and ambition manifest themselves in that region at present practically unregarded by us.[46]

Bell had gathered intelligence from the Tibetan ministers in Darjeeling that they regarded the northern and north-eastern tribes of the Assam frontiers as under British suzerainty rather than under Chinese or Tibetan subjection. They thought that the tribes had been conquered by the British. He apprehended that the Chinese would not be content with such a view as they were making claims of suzerainty and sovereignty where ever possible. Therefore, explorations, survey, cultivation of friendship with the tribal chiefs and arrangements of political control over the area which were claimed by the British were imperative. Control through the Deputy Commissioners of the Assam valley districts over the tribal territories would not be sufficient. He held that separate Political Officers who would serve for a long period should be appointed.[47]

The lines of action proposed by the Political Officer, Charles Bell, were similar to those recommended by the General Staff of the Army regarding military policy on the North-East Frontier from the Bhutan border to the west of Burma as set forth in their Memorandum. It admitted that under an improved administration or in alliance with some Western country, China might in future become a formidable military power, and she appeared to have wished to regain effective control over her dominions bordering on India. They were afraid that China might wish to recover Burma which she considered as a Chinese province and which they thought, had been forcibly taken away from her. In case of the Chinese move to India, she would exert pressure on the

North-East Frontier and with a view to carrying out that policy, she must first open out some of the undeveloped territory in her possession up to the Indian border. (This was surprisingly found to be true in 1962). They apprehended that this could be done either by working through Tibet towards Nepal but more likely through Uunan towards Burma and Assam, as the latter seemed to offer greater advantage and less difficulties.[48]

Under such circumstances, the Army General Staff recommended that the first concern of the Indian Government should be to obtain such a frontier as would render incursion into India by the Chinese as difficult as possible. For that purpose, the mountainous region and the almost impassable mountains on the North-East of Assam and Burma would offer the greatest advantage. The natural mountain frontier, they suggested, was the watershed of the Brahmaputra and Irrawaddy valleys extending from Bhutan in the west to the Salween-Irrawaddy divide. The Memorandum recommended extension of the Government's hold and control over the tribes inhabiting the region and effective occupation of the valley of the Zyul-chu as far as the Chinese outpost near Rima. If the Government of India did not do that, the Chinese would gradually occupy these valleys and with the aid of the industrious population obtain in time a base of supplies on this side of the watershed which would greatly facilitate their further advance into India. The Memorandum also recommended to inform China that the Indian frontier lay across the natural line of the Himalayas from the border of Bhutan to Burma. It further suggested the setting up of Military Intelligence posts all along the Frontier.[49]

The Staff Memorandum on strategic grounds, opposed the proposal of railway link with China through the Mishmi Hills from Sadiya to Batang in the Chinese province of Szechuan or any plan of connecting China through Upper Burma as these would ultimately facilitate the movement of the Chinese troops.[50]

Meanwhile another development had occurred which to

some extent influenced the course of action in regard to the frontier to be followed as per suggestion of Charles Bell, the General Staff of the Army and the Government of Eastern Bengal and Assam. Noel Williamson, who had crossed the Outer Line and penetrated into the interior of the Adi Hills contrary to the orders of the government, was murdered together with his companion Dr. Gregorson. This revealed the enmity of the Adis towards the British which again meant the possibility of easy Chinese penetration into the Adi Hills, through the Khams province of Tibet across Tum-La and Shoka-La. Therefore, with a view to punishing the offending Adi hills to delineate the boundary between India and China-Tibet, an expedition was sent to Adi hills. Almost simultaneously, teams were sent to the Mishmi and Nishi hills for survey and exploration.[51]

Meanwhile the Government of Lord Minto had addressed a letter to the Secretary of State urging the settlement of the India-Tibetan border. They suggested that a "representation should be made at Peking pointing out that disorders on our border would not be viewed with indifference by us" and "subject to further information being obtained in regard to the nature and extent of the territories of the tribes and their position *vis-a-vis* China and Tibet, etc., that the external boundary should run, approximately from the east of the wedge-shaped portion of Tibetan territory known as the Towang district which runs down to the British frontier north of Odalguri in a north-easterly direction to latitude 29° longitude 94°, thence along latitude 29° to longitude 96°, thence in a south-easterly direction the Zayul Chu valley to the Zayul Chu-Irrawaddy watershed, and then along that watershed until it joins Irrawaddy-Salween watershed."[52]

The results of the surveys and explorations carried on by the 'Abor expedition', 'the Mishmi Mission' and the 'Miri Mission' were the basis of the recommendations of the Political Officers of the Western Section and the Central and Eastern Sections, G.A. Nevill and W.C.M. Dundas respectively, as well as the Chief of the General Staff. All unanimously recommended that the boundary between the two countries should be the water parting of the Sanpo (Brahmaputra) and the Subansiri and their tributaries which were co-terminus with the traditional, customary and geographical boundaries between India and Tibet. The Chief of the General Staff pointed out that the results of the survey of the 'Miri Mission' were unsatisfactory and could not be the basis of a proposal for fixing a boundary between the two countries. But then the results of the survey could be combined with the data collected from the traders and other sources and on the basis of that he suggested that the high snow mountain range between Longitude 94°, Latitude 28°25" to Longitude 93°, Latitude 28°20" without break, with peaks rising from 13000 to 16000 feet, could be a well-defined boundary between India and Tibet beyond the Western Section of the North-East Frontier.[53] It may be pointed out here that this line was later on pushed back further towards the north-west to include the Tawang tracts after the explorations and surveys conducted by Bailey and Nevill in 1913-14, as pointed out by Lamb.[54] For the Central and Eastern Sections of the North-East Frontier, the Chief of Staff suggested the Pemakai range and the Dibong and the Lohit watersheds, together with their tributaries respectively, as the boundary between India and Tibet.[55]

Recommendations of G.A. Nevill for the Western Section of the North-East Frontier Boundary between India and Tibet was the Miri Section boundary suggested by the Chief of the General Staff. Nevill suggested a line south of Se La and he was supported by W.C.M. Dundas.[56] Both of them suggested the line south of Se La as shown in the map of Alaister Lamb. The line recommended by nevill commenced from Dho Shong La on the headwaters of the Siyom in the neighbourhood of Lungu La to the mountain range Sha Gam La through the peaks, 19423, 18056, 18813, 17279, 19026, 21276, 20950, 21488 and 20860 to Saila pass (Se La) and then following mountain range to 13550 to Bhutan border.[57]

For the boundary between the Central and Eastern

Sections of the North-East Frontier (the Abor and Mishmi Section of the General Staff Note) and Tibet, W.C.M. Dundas recommended a line, beginning from the tri-junction of India, burma and China at Talok La in the west, through the Dichu to its confluence with the Lohit : thence down the Lohit to the confluence of the Tor Chu : thence up the Tor Chu to its lowest sources : thence in a north-westerly direction along the range which forms the watershed between the Rong Thod Chu and the rivers flowing into Assam, that is to say, the Dou, Delei, Tiding, Ithun, Tangon, Dri, and tributaries past the Glei Dakhru, Hadigra, Dakhru, Kaya and Aguia passes to peak 19557 at Latitude 29°27" approximately : thence along the same range in south-westerly direction to and the head of the Andhra and its tributaries and past Yonggypla Andhra La to peak 13838 at the source of the southern tributary of the Chimdru Chu : thence north along the subsidiary feature forming the watershed between the Chimdru Chu and the smaller streams training into the Dihong as far as the confluence of the Chimdru Chu : thence up the Dihong to the confluence of the Nyalam Chu (also called the Nyalam Thangpo) : thence up the Nyalam chu to its source below the Nam La on the main Himalayan range : thence in south-westerly direction along the main range which was the watershed between the Taang Po and the rivers flowing into the Dihong past the Doshang La, Deyan La, Lushe La and Lungma La.[58]

The Line suggested by Dundas included some villages established in recent times by some Tibetan Monbas (Menbas). Therefore, he proposed an alternative line if the government wanted to exclude the Memba tracts. The line commencing from "peak No. 13838 in a westerly direction round the source of the Nyigong (also known as the Yen-sangchu) and down to the spur between Korbo and Mongku villages to the Dihong; up in Dihong to the confluence of the Nugong; thence up that stream to the Deyanla on this main Himalayan range, past the Damnyala, Lushela Nungmala and around the headwaters of the Siyom, the point where it was suggested that the boundary between Tibet and the W. Sati of the North-East Frontier should begin."[59]

Meanwhile Chao had occupied Lhasa but failed to subjugate Tibet. Active resistance to the Chinese continued in the south-east while in Lhasa the people resisted the Chinese in every way they could. The Tibetan National Assembly adopted a sullen and sometimes hostile attitude towards the Chinese forces.[60] The Dalai Lama in exile in India tried to obtain British and even Russian help against the Chinese, but to no effect.[61] But before the Chinese could come to any conclusion on the Tibetan issue, the Emperor and the Manchu dynasty were swept away by the Chinese Revolution of 1911. The effect of the Revolution was immediately felt in Tibet. The Chinese garrison in Lhasa mutinied and broke up into unruly mobs. The Tibetans rose against the disorganised Chinese and with a zeal of hatred and vengeance slaughtered thousands of them.[62] The Dalai Lama returned to reassert his authority in Tibet and declared his independence of China.[63] The Mongols had also declared their independence similarly, and concluded a convention of mutual help and co-operation for meeting internal and external dangers with Russia which was confirmed by the Russo-Chinese agreement of 1913. This was followed by a Mongol-Tibet treaty.[64]

On the other hand the Anglo-Tibetan Treaty of 1904 concluded after the Younghusband Mission was made ineffective by the Anglo-Chinese Adhesion Agreement of 1906 and the Anglo-Russian Convention of 1907. "A disorganised Tibet has already proved a direct menace to India and to our broader imperial interests", writes Henry McMahon.[65] The Japanese subjects were in intimate relations with the high authorities in Lhasa. Russian consular students were receiving training in Kumbum Monastery on the Tibetan frontier; a Russian Buriat and a Japanese were training the Tibetan troops.[66] The collapse of Chinese power and the prospect of Russian intervention and intrigue changed the whole situation. The Mongol-Tibet treaty and the Urga

Convention gave the Russians an indirect but real basis of intervention in Tibetan affairs. The chance of Tibet undergoing the fate of Outer Mongolia was imminent.[67]

The British were in a dilemma. They could either convert Tibet into a thinly veiled British protectorate as was the case with Nepal, Bhutan and Sikkim as requested by the Dalai Lama when he was in India.[68] But the British had declined the offer for two reasons. It would have extended the boundary by 2000 miles or so, enclosing 500,000 square miles of territory mostly high ranges and unpopulated, lacking utterly in communication, and brought her face to face with China and Russia. It would also have given the Russians a chance to modify the Anglo-Russian Convention of 1907 and to put forward inconvenient demands. Secondly, the British could have helped Tibet to be an independent country. But it was quite certain that Tibet could not stand alone without the help of any foreign power and would fall an easy victim to Chinese aggression. There was also a risk of Tibet throwing herself into the arms of the Russians which it was the primary aim of the British policy to resist and eliminate. Therefore, a message was given to the Dalai Lama on his return to Tibet that the Government of India desired him to regain internal autonomy under the Chinese suzerainty.[69] A third alternative was to allow China to re-conquer Tibet and constitute it into a Chinese province. But that would have left the possobility of intrigues and incursions into British territories in India and Burma.

Therefore, neither China's policy of considering Tibet as a province nor the Dalai Lama's rejection of Chinese suzerainty suited the British. They wanted to keep the fiction of China's position of suzerain as the Russians had done in Outer Mongolia because it provided China with some legal primacy while depriving her of any effective control.[70] Therefore, on 17 August 1912 they proposed to the new Republic of China that Tibet's status be negotiated on the basis of the situation which had existed before the Younghusband Mission.[71] The Chinese were disturbed by the success of the Russians in Mongolia and the weakness of their own Government; further the prospect of direct British negotiation with Tibet ultimately force them after much reluctance not only to negotiate Tibet's status with the British but to accept a representative of Lhasa as a co-equal plenipotentiary in the negotiations.[72] The acceptance of an equal representative was in fact an important part of the British diplomatic plan. It was calculated that Tibet's full participation in the negotiations would constitute evidence of its autonomy.

MACMAHON LINE

The conference began at Simla, the summer capital of India on 6 October 1913. Sir Henry McMahon was the British plenipotentiary and was assisted by Charles A. Bell who had a thorough knowledge of the Tibetan affairs and the Indo-Tibetan border. China was represented by Ivan Chen. Tibet sent Lonchen Shatra, a leading minister of the Government of the Dalai Lama.[73] The Tibetan concern at the conference was to get an admission of their independence which they had declared after the eviction of the Chinese troops and officials. They wanted the cancellation of the Anglo-Chinese Convention of 1906; they also desired to have a fresh Trade Regulation. At the same time, they proposed a re-definition of the Sino-Tibetan frontier so as to include all Tibetan people within the Tibetan boundary. Lonchen Shatra put forward a stupendous mass of materials in support of his claims : revenue records; list of houses, officials and headmen; charters, agreements and other materials relating to disputed districts.[74] In reply, Iban Chen in utter panic ignored all historical records and practices and emphasized only conquest of Tibet by Chingiz Khan and the last victory of Chao in support of his claims. In recognition of the claim to sovereignty over Tibet, Ivan Chen demanded the right to station an Amban with 2000 troops in Tibet and to control military and foreign affairs of the country. As for the frontier, the Chinese claimed a line only some sixty miles east of Lhasa.[75]

Under the circumstances both Iban Chen and Lonchen Shatra requested McMahon to suggest some definite solution of the problem, which they would refer to their governments without delay. McMahon had anticipated this impasse; he had already worked out in consultation with London a solution which was likely to afford satisfaction to the contending parties and at the same time accord with Indian interest. This solution envisaged the division of Tibet into two zones, to be called Inner and Outer Tibet (as viewed from China), on the lines of Inner and Outer Mongolia created by Russians. Outer Tibet was to be the wider area to the east of the historic Yangtse frontier, over which the Tibetan Government had for many centuries exercised complete jurisdiction. Here, the Chinese were not to send their troops, nor station any civil or military personnel, nor establish any colonies. But as a symbol of their suzerainty, they might install at Lhasa an Amban to look after the Chinese interests. Inner Tibet was to be the broad peripheral area of Tibet extending in the north to the Atlya Tagh range and in the east to the old provincial borders of Kansu and Szechuan in which the population was mainly Tibetan by race and religion. China would have full administrative authority over this zone, subject to the provision that it could not be made a Chinese province and, in the selection and appointment of high priests of the monasteries control was to be vested in the Lhasa authorities. McMahon spelt out this solution in the form of a draft convention and the proposed boundaries of Outer and Inner Tibet were shown on the accompanying map.[76]

Both the parties were dissatisfied with this solution; but the atmosphere was one of strain and anxiety, and it was considered desirable to avoid an immediate break down. All the three plenipotentiaries accepted the draft convention prepared by McMahon and initialled the revised convention on 27 April, 1914.[77] The map signed by both the Chinese and

Tibetan representatives was initialled by McMahon who congratulated the delegates on the excellent work they had done.[78] The Chinese Government, however, disallowed the action of its plenipotentiary on 29 April and declined to recognise the settlement.[79]

Simultaneously with the tripartite negotiations, two other bipartite negotiations were conducted between Great Britain and Tibet during the Simla Conference. The first related to the delineation of a boundary alignment between India and Tibet to the north of Assam, and the second to a new Trade Agreement between these two countries.[80] On the Indian side, C.A. Bell, the Political Officer of Sikkim, was entrusted with a task of conducting negotiations with Lonchen Shatra on the border issue. The broad principle followed in the delineation of the Indo-Tibetan border was the principle of watershed usually followed in demarcating borders in inaccessible mountainous regions, which was followed in suggesting the boundary of the North-East Frontier by the Chief of the General Staff, Nevill and Dundas.[81] In determining the Sikkim-Tibet frontier in 1890, the crest of the mountain range separating the waters flowing into the Sikkim Tista and its affluents from the waters flowing into the Tibetan Mochu and northward into other rivers of Tibet was the determinant.[82] The Same principle of watershed was accepted as the basis of demarcating the border between Inner Tibet and Outer Tibet by Ivan Chen.[83]

Although watershed was generally kept in view in determining the alignment, a multiplicity of factors—historical, ethnic, geographical and strategic—were also considered. While anxious to secure a frontier which would be consistent with India's strategic requirements, Henry McMahon and Charles Bell tried to exclude what was undisputedly Tibetan territory. Moreover, in Subansiri region, the two holy places of Tibetan pilgrimage, Tso Sharpo and Tsari Sharpo, together with the village of Migyitun, wherefrom the pilgrimage started, were kept north of the McMahon Line to enable the Tibetan pilgrims[84] smooth and unrestricted entry into those places disregarding the watershed principle. Therefore, though based principally on watershed, the boundary line as it emerged in the Simla Agreement was drawn "on a combination of ridge, watershed and high crest," as aptly pointed out by Ekelen.[85]

To protect the Tibetan private ownership in some estates south of the McMahon Line, Lochen Shatra said to Bell: "The Potala Trung-Yik Chenpo and the Loseling college of Drepung monastery each get 10 Dotse (1Dotse - Rs. 84) from Tawang for the right to send Agents to manage the land of the Tawang monastery, which right they farm out to them considered as the right of private individuals. The Lebrang and Nyetsang get a share of about Rs. 500 together, out of the subsidy paid by the British Government annually for the Kuriapara Duar. This, Lonchen requests, may be continued to be paid to them. The families of Shewo and Sam-drup Po-trang have also private estates in Tawang which, he requests that they may be allowed to retain. The Tawang monastery, established by the 5th Dalai Lama, has got about 300 monks, although its official strength is about 500. This monastery has got private estates at Dhirang and Takla Jongs which he requests that they may be allowed to retain with the monastery's other income." Charles Bell agreed that "all proprietory rights (Dak-top) of the individual Tibetans on the British side of the frontier will be retained by those who at present enjoy them.[86]

The Tibetan Government, on reference by Lonchen Shatra, agreed to the transfer without prejudice. So the agreement drawn up to Simla was agreed to by Lonchen Shatra.[87] The Chinese were not invited to take part in the discussions about the Indo-Tibetan frontier and their specific acceptance was not sought; but they were provided with information about it. The Indo-Tibetan boundary alignment, on a reduced scale, was shown in the map showing the boundaries of Inner Tibet and Outer Tibet, which was enclosed with the Simla Convention and was duly initialled by all the three plenipotentiaries.[88]

The boundary line, which was named in India as the McMahon Line after the name of the Indian plenipotentiary at the conference, as it emerged from the Indo-Tibetan Boundary Agreement of 1914, runs over a distance of 820 miles of which 640 miles are between India and Tibet from the tri-junction of Bhutan, Tibet and the Kameng district of the present Arunchal Pradesh of India through the crest of the Himalayas to the Diphuk Pass (Talok-La) to the north-west of Burma where India, Burma and Tibet meet. Commencing from a point to the east of Bhutan at 92°40" E, 27°48" N, it crosses the Namjang river and follows the eastern range of the Great Himalayas, which is also the watershed between the Chayul Chu in Tibet and the Kameng, Kamla and Kru rivers in India, and then proceeds east and north-east and crosses the Subansiri river and then the Tsari river just south of Migyitun. From this point it takes a north-eastern direction, crosses the Tunga pass (approximately Longitude 94°10" E and Latitude 28°59" N), continues eastward again, crosses the Dihang (Siang) and ascends the watershed between Chimdru Chu and Rongta Chu in Tibet and the Dibang and its tributaries and India. Thereafter it runs south to a point, just below Latitude 28°30" and just west of Longitude 96°30", continues in easterly direction, crosses the Lohit river a few miles to the north of Kahas and a few miles to the south of Rima and joins the tri-junction of India, Burma and Tibetan boundaries near the Diphuk or Talok pass.[89]

With regard to the inclusion of Tawang and Walong inside the Indian side of the border, there were disputes and authorities expressed different views. Alaister Lamb holds the view that although the British did not recognise any paramount power over the north-eastern tribes, Tawang was undoubtedly Tibetan territory.[90] Again, he says that the Indo-Tibetan Agreement involved a nominal transfer of territory from Tibet to India.[91] As for the situation and inclusion of Walong, the Government of India at first was hesitant, but subsequently it was found to be outside the Tibetan province of Zayul Chu till the advent of the Chnese and inside the Indian side of the frontier, from watershed, geographical and historical points of view. Walong is situated on the left bank of the Lohit which forms the Indo-Tibetan boundary there. The area was at one time inhabited by the Mishmis but later on abandoned by them. In 1914, the area was largely uninhabited, but the Mishmi occupation of the region was still testified by the Muju names of the places, hills flats and rivers.

W.C.M. Dundas wrote to the Chief Commissioner regarding Walong:

> There was no question about this strip of land until the Chinese came and arbitrarily fixed their bondary at Menilkrai.
>
> Sati is the last Miju village on the right bank of the Lohit, and Sama the first old established Tibetan village. Almost midway between the two is one Tibetan house at Walong which in the past was allowed to remain through the forbearance of the Mijus to whom this family of Tibetans was useful, as a halting place on the journey to Rima, and also because they kept and pastured the Mijus cattle, beyond Walong north of the Namti and between that stream and the Kraoti. There are remains of terraced fields which shows that there was once a Tibetan village on the site. These people, it is said, were driven north by disease, and also on account of continual attacks by Mijus who once raided as far as Rima itself, besieging that place. The absence of Miju habitations is accounted for by the fact that there is no soil suitable for Jhum cultivation. That Mujus jhumed the land years ago and occupied it, I have no doubt. The appearance of the land gives colour to this belief. All the cultivable patches are denuded of trees and covered with short san grass, while the steep slopes are thick with pine forests, proving to my thinking that the barer flats are the sites of Miju cultivation, which have been abandoned as, owing to the

> lack of timber, the soil cannot recover enough even to be jhumed again.
>
> The names of places, hills, flats and streams are Miju and these are the names used by Tibetans who have none of their own for the Yepuk, Namti, Kraoti, Dunai, etc. The first Tibetan name met on the right bank of the Lohit, proceeding north, is Tor Chu. Sama has neither cultivation nor any claims to land south of that stream.
>
> As a matter of fact the whole area is uninhabited (except for one house of Walong) from Sati stream to the Tor Chu and is a kind of Tom Tiddlers ground, belonging actually to the Mijus who, however, for many years have had no use for it.
>
> I went into this question carefully when I was in charge of the Mishmi Mission. Just the one visit of the Chinese to Menlikrai and the planting there of their flags which indicate no boundary line, and the notification has given rise to the belief that the land above as far as the Tor Chu cannot be claimed by us.
>
> Across the Tor Chu, it is very different; Sama and Singor are undoubtedly Tibetan and very long established communities.
>
> For the left bank of the Lohit, I have proposed the Dri Ti as our boundary with Tibet. The last Miju village is Wati, and the first old established Tibetan village Kahao (or Kahap). In between, there is one Tibetan house at Tine (or Tinai) opposite Walong, and two at Dong about 1½ miles further north. The arguments given above all apply even to the Miju names of all places including the Kri Ti which is pure Miju. Kahao village has no cultivation or land south of the Kri Ti.[92]

Ivan Chen held that the Tibetan Government did not possess any control over the Zayul which he held, was inhabited by independent tribes called Miris, Mishings, Adi, Abors and Mishmis.

Tawang, it has been held, was an undisputed Tibetan

territory. This part of territory is separated from the Tibetan plateau by a range of rugged mountains averaging 16000 feet in height and is known as Monyul or low country by the Tibetans.[93] The people of the tract are known as Mompas who, it has been shown by T.S. Murty, who was Political Officer in the NEFA, are racially, linguistically and culturally different from the main stream of the Tibetan population.[94] But it cannot be gainsaid that the Tawang monastery is an off-shoot of the Drepung monastery of Lhasa and was founded in the 5th century as a daughter institution of the same. It was, however, an independent institution. Pandit Nain Sing of the Trigonometrical Survey of India, who visited the monastery in 1874-75, on his way back to Assam from Lhasa found that the affairs of the Tawang district were managed by a sort of Parliament termed Kato, which assembled in public to manage business and administer justice. The Kato was composed entirely of Lamas, chief officials of the principal monastery. "The Tawang monastery", he says, "is entirely independent of the Dzongpon (of Tsona) and of the Lhasa Government."[95] Almost 50 years later, G.A. Nevill, who visited Tawang in 1914, stated the same thing.[96] It is significant to note that Lonchen Shatra told Bell at Simla about the temporal authority of the Tawang monastery in the area and existence of private estates only. Be that as it may, the McMahon Line was first published by Charles Bell in his book on Tibet in 1924. The Government of India soon after the Simla Conference was engaged in the First World War and Sir Henry McMahon was transferred to Egypt. It was not before 1929 that the Map was incorporated in the volume of Aitchison's work entitled *Treaties, Engagements and Sanads* etc. Thereafter it was published in 1962 by the Government of India after the Sino-Indian border clashes of 1962.[97]

After the delineation of the North-East Frontier in the Simla Conference of 1914, the Government of India took effective measures to exercise control over the area stretching up to the McMahon Line. By a notification dated

25 September 1924, the Frontier Tracts were constituted into three political charges: (i) Central and Eastern Sections consisting of the hills inhabitated by the Nagas, Khamptis, and Singphos; (ii) the Lakhimpur Frontier Tract, and (iii) the Western Section. The first was to be administered by three Assistant Political Officers at Sadiya; the second and the third were left under the Assistant Political Officer of Charduar. By another Notification, the Assam Frontier Tract Regulation of 1880 was promulgated in these tracts; it was amended insubsequent years.[98] But control over outlying areas was extended only gradually over the years as we have already noted in studying the relations of the tribes with the government.

Government of India equated the frontier with a buffer as it was believed by McMahon. He held that frontier or buffer meant a tract of neutral territory separating two potentially antagonistic neighbours; but a boundary was specific line, either delimited by precise map description or demarcated by ground surveys. To him, it was the frontier buffer zone which had the greatest importance, and the boundary was comparatively less significant, particularly when it ran through uninhabitable mountain or desert terrain. Hence, the delay in establishing administration and control over the border region.[99]

The position of the North-East Frontier was well expressed in the words of a well-known Foreign Secretary of the Government of India, Sir Olaf Caroe: "In the early days of British rule, the external frontiers of India were conceived as lying at the limits of the territory of India where the British writ ran. But on the North-East, as on the belt known as the North-West Frontier, there lay beyond the limits of administered territory an agglomeration of tribes owning no master. In such cases, it became the practice of the early British administration to exercise in the region beyond the administered border what was known as a loose political control. Trans-border agencies were set up, but it was not until later that the need was felt to show the tribes so politically controlled as excluded from the neighbouring states and included in India."[100]

INDO-CHINESE BORDER CONTROVERSY

After 1954, when relations between India and China began to be strained on the score of the so-called border incidents and when the Chinese troops began to violate the North-East Frontier of India from January 1959, Prime Minister J.L. Nehru addressed a letter to the Chinese Prime Minister Chou Enlai. Good humouring the Chinese Prime Minister on the progress made by China in agricultural developments, he pointed out that the Chinese Prime Minister had regcognised the North-East boundary of India during his last visit to India though he did not approve of the method the British had adopted in settling the issue.[101] The letters that followed from the Chinese Prime Minister and the memoranda that came from the Chinese Government thereafter regarding the Indo-Tibetan border alleged that the McMahon Line was a product of the British policy of aggression against the Tibetan region of China; juridically too the Line could not be regarded as valid as it was discussed only secretly between India and Tibet behind the back of China, and the question had never been formally raised at the Simla Conference. Moreover, the Boundary Agreement was agreed between India and Tibet by a secret exchange of notes between Lonchen Shatra and Charles Bell, and China never ratified the Simla Convention of 1914.[102] Further Chinese arguments ran as follows:

(i) "Tibet is part of Chinese territory. China has full sovereignty over Tibet". The Chinese represen-tative made it clear on 30 October 1913 that Tibet was an integral part of Chinese territory. Tibet had no right to conclude treaties with foreign countries independently of the Chinese Central Government, unless authorised by and consented to by the Chinese Central Government.[103]

(ii) The treaties of 1842, 1856 and 1904 which Tibet had concluded with Kashmir, Nepal and India respectively were all entered into with the prior or *ex-post facto* approval of the Chinese Central Government.[104] The Boundary Agreement of 1 March 1914, the Simla Convention of July 1914 and the Trade Regulation of 1914 were illegal as China had never ratified them. The Anglo-Tibetan negotiations of 1921-27 were of a local nature.[105] But the delimitation of the Indo-Tibetan boundary was a problem concerning a major internal administrative division of China, and since the McMahon Line was widely at variance with the traditional customary boundary, Great Britain was not competent to change it unilaterly.[106]

(iii) "The Chinese Government holds that the so-called McMahon Line is wholly illegal ... it is known to the world that the Simla Convention itself is void of legal validity." China made it clear in three statements made in 1914 on 21 April, 3 July and 7 July that the Convention could not be recognised by her.[107]

(iv) The Simla conference did not deal with the question of Sino-Indian (Indo-Tibetan) boundary, "the Simla Conference only discussed the boundary between so-called Outer and Inner Tibet, it never discussed the boundary between China and India." No such discussions were reported to the Chinese representative as well. The only map that was presented to the Conference showing the Indo-Tibetan boundary showed all of Tibet's external boundaries and not those with India alone. Even this map was not referred to in the Agreement of March 1914 and the Convention of July 1914.[108]

(v) The Simla Conference of 1914 was a part of the British plan to separate Tibet from China, make Tibet an independent State, and bring it completely under the British control. The aggressive intentions of

Britain towards Tibet were given out in Lord Curzon's letter dated 11 June 1901 addressed to the Secretary of State for India and in the Memorandum of the British Government proposing a tripartite conference.[109] China expressed her regret and dissatisfaction with it. These aggressive intentions of Britain were recognised by Prime Minister Nehru also in his statement of 30 March 1959.

(vi) On 15 April 1914, the Chinese representative objected to Tibet being given an equal status with China in the preamble to the draft Simla Convention. As such, the question of China accepting Tibet's equal status did not arise.[110] The communication from Great Britain to China, dated 26 June 1914, should not be regarded as indicating acceptance by China of Tibet's status since it was a position forced on China by Great Britain.[111] On 17 March 1959, Prime Minister Nehru said in the Lok Sabha that no country had recognised the independent of Tibet.

(vii) "Besides even the local authorities of Tibet did not regard as reasonable the so-called McMahon Line..." as can be seen from a letter dated 18 April 1945 to the Political Officer, Sikkim, regarding withdrawal of British troops from Kalkatang and Walong.[112]

(viii) The equivocal nature of the Simla Agreement of 25 March 1914 can be seen from the fact that the British Government did not dare publish–till 1929–either the letters or the map constituting a part of the Agreement.[113]

The Government of India to refute the Chinese allegations put forward the following points:

(i) Tibet was competent to settle her own boundaries with India and Chinese adherence or recognition of the Anglo-Tibetan Boundary Agreement of March 1914 or the Anglo-Tibetan Convention of July 1914 was not relevant to the formalisation of the Indo-Tibetan boundary. Tibet had signed treaties with Kashmir in 1852 and Nepal in 1842 and 1856. The Chinese had themselves agreed that Tibet was competent to conclude the Non-aggression pact in 1853. The treaty-making power of Tibet, as different from that of China, is evident in China's inability to enforce the Anglo-Chinese Convention of 1894 concerning Tibetan trade. This Convention had accepted the treaty-making power of Tibet by including the Anglo-Tibetan Convention of 1904 in the Anglo-Chinese Convention of 1906 and by abrogating the Nepal-Tibet Treaty of 1856 by the Sino-Nepalese Treaty of 1956. Extra-territorial rights, as in the Treaty of 1856, can be conferred only by sovereign nations. The Tibet Trade Regulations of 1914, signed independently of China, were also operative till their abrogation in 1954.[114] Tibet's competence to settle her own boundary with India, without consulting China, was further evident from the negotiations on her southern border which Tibet held with India in 1921, 1924 and 1926.[115]

(ii) Long before the Simla Conference, Sino-Tibetan relations had virtually ceased to exist. The Tibetans had issued a declaration of independence and resisted China's attempts to re-establish her authority. During 1940-44, Tibet even refused the combined request of China, Britain and America to allow Indian military supplies for China to pass through Tibet. The fact that in 1950 the Chinese Government considered it necessary to 'liberate' the Tibet region was further proof that areas contiguous with the Indian frontier were parts of Tibet and the power to confirm the boundaries of Tibet rested with the Tibetan Government at Lhasa.[116]

(iii) The British Memorandum of 17 August 1912 had envisaged Tibet taking part in the Simla Conference as an equal partner with China. This was reiterated, among other occasions, on 25 May, on 28 July and 25 Autust, 1913.[117] China also recognised Tibet's right to participate on equal basis in the Simla Conference as "the Chinese representative accepted the credentials of the Tibetan representative as being in order." One of the causes for convening the Simla Conference was the Chinese Government's anxiety to re-establish its relation with Tibet.[118]

(iv) The Chinese were not intimidated into joining the Simla Conference. "The Foreign Minister of China wrote to the British representative on the 7th August 1913 that the Chinese plenipotentiary would proceed to India to open negotiations for a treaty jointly with the Tibetan and British plenipotentiaries." China was willing and eager to commence negotiations with Tibet. It is clear from the proceedings of the Conference that China took full and wholehearted part in the proceedings.[119]

(v) During the preliminaries to the Simla Conferences, discussions were held on relations not only between Tibet and China but also between Tibet and India. The proceedings of the Simla Conference leading to the Indo-Tibetan Boundary Agreement of March 1914 and the Convention of July 1914 were attended by India, China and Tibet in November 1913 in Delhi.[120] The British representative pointed out that the territorial limits of Tibet should be defined before her political status could be discussed. As a result, the Indo-Tibetan frontiers in the eastern region were shown in maps presented to the Conference on 17 February 1914 and 22 April 1914. If the Indo-Tibetan boundary shown in these maps was not discussed at the plenary session among all the three representatives, it was because the problem concerned India and Tibet only and not China. "The Chinese representative at the Simla Conference was fully aware of the McMahon Line boundary between India and Tibet."[121]

(vi) The Simla Agreement and the Simla Convention of 1914 were not kept as secrets. The boundary line accepted in those agreements was the same as that shown in several maps presented at the Simla Conference. The Agreement and the Convention were published in the very first edition of Aitchison's book which was issued after the Conference in 1929 (the last preceding edition was published in 1909) and also in Indian official maps. The British War Office map published in 1907 shows almost the entire area within India. "Sir Francis Younghusband's volume *India and Tibet* published in London in 1910 shows the Tribal area in India; and so does the map in Sir Charles Bell's book *Tibet–Past and Present* (Oxford 1924)."[122]

(vii) Under International Law, failure of ratification by one of the parties to a multilateral treaty cannot affect its binding force on other parties or the validity of the obligations assumed by them.[123] Throughout the proceedings of the Simla Conference and in the subsequent diplomatic communications from China on 30 May 1914, no objection was made by China to the boundaries between India and Tibet as shown in the maps presented to the Conference. China "suggested some modifications of the Simla Convention with a view to reaching a final settlement. These modifications related only to the boundaries between Inner Tibet and China and Inner Tibet and Outer Tibet."[124]

(viii) The Tibetan Foreign Office wrote to the Indian Government on 18 April 1945 reiterating its continuing adherence to the Boundary Agreements of 1914.[125]

(ix) The Indian Government announced publicly on several occasions during 1946-50 that it regarded

> China as continuing to accept the validity of the McMahon Line.[126]

Chinese Government and the Government of India regarding India taking over the former British responsibilities in Tibet shows that the then Government of China accepted the validity of the arrangements made in 1914 and since enforced. The present Chinese Government was the successor to the governments in power in Tibet during 1914-50. It was, therefore, bound to accept the obligations imposed on Tibet by Agreement of 1914. The present Chinese Government was similarly the successor of Nationalist Government of China, and it was not entitled to repudiate the actions of the Nationalist Government just because these did not suit its present purpose.[127]

The Simla Agreement only formalised the natural, customary, traditional boundary in this sector and did not set up a new boundary. The water parting formed by the crest of the Himalayas is the natural frontier which was accepted for centuries as the boundary by the peoples on both sides. The tribes inhabiting the area south of McMahon Line–the Mompas, Akas, Daflas, Miris, Abors and Mishmis– are of the same stock as the other hill tribes of Assam and have no kinship with the Tibetans.[128]

It is evident from what we have seen in the foregoing paragraphs that the Indo-Tibetan border had remained unsettled till the advent of the Chinese across the traditional boundary of India in Tibet. The East India Company's Government was anxious first to stop the aggression into the Bengal Presidency through the north-east, and in quest of security for their newly founded empire in Bengal they had to come to Assam. First Assam was acquired not primarily for any material benefit other than the security of Bengal. But with the discovery of minerals and tea bushes the valley of the Brahamaputra assumed a new importance. To provide security to the tea plantations and the coal mines and oil fields which developed along the foothills, it was found necessary to keep away the hill tribes inhabiting the frontiers, for the Company's Government was reluctant to assume responsibility for them. Hence, the Inner Line.

The tribes of the frontier were kept aloof and no paramountcy was established over them excluding third-party influence over them as no such party posed any threat to British interest. The Outer Line was thus kept in abeyance and it was purposely left indefinite, unsettled and undemarcated. The British Crown which assumed the responsibility of Indian administration after the Sepoy Mutiny initially followed the same policy as did the Company's Government. But the Chinese invasion of Tibet in 1901 now opened the possibility of third-party influence over the frontier tribes. Therefore, it was now necessary to establish paramountcy over the tribes and settle the border. With a view to gaining knowledge of the territory, survey and explorations were undertaken and carried on between 1911-14.

Finally, it was now necessary to get approval of the border on the north-east from the countries beyond. Revolts in Tibet and China provided opportunity; and the Chinese and the Tibetans also wanted to formalise their relations with foreign powers following the revolutions in their respective countries. A Conference was convened in Simla where, during the negotiations between the Chinese and the Tibetans, the Indo-Tibetan boundary was settled: the McMahon Line was fixed by a Boundary Agreement between India and Tibet on 24/25 March 1914. The alignment of the border followed the principle of watershed usually followed in mountainous terrain, but ethnic, historic and strategic considerations were also given due weight. The Sino-Indian border clashes followed in 1962. The unilateral cease-fire in the midst of their success by the Chinese and their withdrawal beyond the McMahon Line from all areas except Che Dong and Longju which the Chinese hold are south of that McMahon Line confirm India's North-East Frontier along the McMahon Line.

REFERENCES

1. C.U. Aitchison, *op. cit.*, vol. 1.
2. A. Mackenzie, *History*, p. 27.
3. *Ibid.*
4. C. Von. Furer—Haimendorf, *op. cit.*, pp. 4-5.
5. W. Robinson, *op. cit.*, p. 354.
6. C. Von. Furer—Haimendorf, *op. cit.*, pp. 4-5.
7. Bengal Papers in Assam Archives, F. no. 308 of 1870, sl. 12.
8. All India Report, 1967.
9. Bengal Papers in Assam Archives, F. no. 309 of 1873, sl. 15.
10. Foreign Proceedings (Assam), December 1903, No. 14.
11. *Ibid.*
12. Bengal Papers in Assam Archives, F. no. 293/521 of 1873, sl. 10.
13. *Ibid.*
14. *Ibid.*
15. Foreign External Proceedings (India), October 1884, Nos. 366-75.
16. Bengal Papers in Assam Archives, F. no. 521 of 1873.
17. *Ibid*, F. No. 293, 1873, sl. 10.
18. Foreign External Proceedings (India), October 1884, Nos. 366-75.
19. Foreign Proceedings (Assam), January 1904, No. 5.
20. *Ibid.*, No. 7.
21. Assam State Archives (Bengal Papers), F. no. 652, 1874, sl. 1.
22. Foreign External Proceedings (India), October 1884, Nos. 366-75.
23. Foreign Proceedings (Assam), April 1874, No. 14.
24. *Ibid.*
25. *Ibid.*
26. *Ibid.*
27. *Ibid.*
28. *Ibid.*
29. *Ibid.*, February 1875, No. 1.
30. Assam Administration Report, 1874-76, Part II B, para 8.
31. Foreign External Proceedings (India), October 1884, No. 366-75.
32. *Ibid.*
33. *Ibid.*
34. Foreign Political Proceedings (India), December 1873, Nos. 42-43.
35. R. Reid, *op. cit.*, p. 7.
36. Foreign Proceedings (Assam), July 1886, No. 5.
37. *Ibid.*, December 1903, No. 14.
38. Foreign Political Proceedings (India), May 1912, No. 202.
39. *Ibid.*, March 1886, No. 25.
40. Political Proceedings (East Bengal and Assam), 10 August 1910, No. 4.
41. Lakhimpur Deputy Commissioner's Collection, No. x, F. 16 of 1909.
42. F. Younghusband, *India and Tibet*, p. 488.
43. Foreign Proceedings (India), Secret 'E', January 1911, No. 211-240.

44. *Ibid.*, No. 233.
45. *Ibid.*
46. *Ibid.*
47. *Ibid.*
48. *Ibid.*, Nos. 5, 211-40.
49. *Ibid.*
50. *Ibid.*
51. Foreign Proceedings (India), Secret 'E', May 1912, Nos. 210-337.
52. Political Proceedings (East Bengal and Assam), March 1912, Nos. 149-97.
53. Foreign Political Proceedings (India), November 1912, No. 619.
54. A. Lamb, *The McMahon Line : Study in the Relations between India, China and Tibet,* p. 537.
55. Foreign Political Proceedings (India), November 1912, No. 619.
56. Political Proceedings (Assam), May 1914, No. 74.
57. *Ibid.*, No. 70.
58. *Ibid.*, No. 74.
59. *Ibid.*
60. Foreign Political (Secret) Proceedings (India), October 1914, Nos. 134-396.
61. *Ibid.*
62. *Ibid.*
63. *Ibid.*
64. *Ibid.*
65. *Ibid.*, May 1915, Nos. 36-50.
66. *Ibid.*
67. *Ibid.*
68. F. Younghusband, *op. cit.*, p. 395.
69. Foreign Political (Secret) Proceedings (India), October 1914, Nos. 134-396.
70. *Ibid.*
71. *Ibid.*
72. H.E. Richardson, *op. cit.*, p. 107.
73. Foreign Political (Secret) Proceedings (India), October 1914, Nos. 134-396.
74. *Ibid.*
75. *Ibid.*
76. *Ibid.*
77. *Ibid.*
78. *Ibid.*
79. *Ibid.*
80. *Ibid.*
81. Foreign Political Proceedings (India), November 1912, Nos. 599-690.
82. Krishna K. Rao, "The Sino-Indian Boundary Question and International Law" Reprinted by the Ministry of External Affairs,

New Delhi, 1963, from *International and Comparative Law Quarterly*, pp. 31-33.

83. Foreign Political (Secret) Proceedings (India), October 1914, Nos. 134-396.
84. *Ibid.*
85. P.C. Chakravarty, *Evolution of India's Northern Borders*, p. 75.
86. *Ibid.*, p. 84.
87. Foreign Political (Secret) Proceedings (India), October 1914, Nos. 134-396.
88. *Ibid.*
89. P.C. Charkravarty, *op. cit.*, pp. 77-78.
90. A. Lamb, *op. cit.*, p. 310.
91. *Ibid.*, p. 349.
92. Political Proceedings (Assam), May 1914, No. 66.
93. T.S. Murty, *op. cit.*, pp. 527-28.
94. *Ibid.*
95. Survey of India Records, vol. VIII, Part I, p. 178.
96. Political Proceedings (Assam), December 1914, Nos. 1-37.
97. White Paper, vol. II, p. 47.
98. Political Proceedings (Assam), April 1914, Nos. 1-16.
99. Foreign Political (Secret) Pròceedings (India), May 1915, Nos. 36-50.
100. P.C. Chakravarty, *India-China Relations*, p. 149.
101. White Paper, vol. I, p. 49.
102. *Ibid.*, vol. I, p. 53.
103. *Ibid.*, vol. IV, p. 14.
104. *Ibid.*
105. *Ibid.*, vol. IV, p. 9.
106. *Ibid.*
107. *Ibid.*, vol. III, pp. 63-64
108. *Ibid.*
109. *Ibid.*
110. *Ibid.*
111. *Ibid.*
112. *Ibid.*
113. *Ibid.*
114. S.P. Sharma, *The India-China Border Dispute : An Indian Perspective.*
115. White Paper, vol. III, p. 94.
116. Report of the Officials of the Government of India and the People's Republic of China on the Boundary Question, p. 17.
117. *Ibid.*, Part III, p. 112.
118. White Paper, vol. III, p. 95.
119. *Ibid.*, vol. II, p. 38.
120. Report of the Officials of the Government of India and the People's Republic of China on the Boundary Question, p. 112.

121. White Paper, vol. II, p. 38.
122. *Ibid.*, vol. II, pp. 39-41.
123. *Ibid.*, "Oppenheim points out that, according to the principle of restransit cum Saononere, treaties of the extinct State concerning the boundary lines, repairing of the main roads, navigation on rivers and the like, remain valid and all rights and obligations accruing from such treaties of the extinct state devolve on the absorbing State". A Appadorai, "Bases of India's Title on the North-East Frontier" *International Studies*, vol. I, No. 4, p. 370.
124. *Ibid.*, vol II, pp. 38-39.
125. Report of the Officials, etc., p. 115.
126. *Ibid.*, p. 16.
127. *Ibid.*, p. 18.
128. White Paper, Vol. II, p. 40.

4

ADMINISTRATION OF THE NORTH-EAST FRONTIER

After the annexation of Assam in 1826 the immediate task of the British was to provide for an administrative set-up for the new province as the Ahom system of government had collapsed completely during the Burmese depredations. In April 1826, a kind of dyarchy was brought into existence; David Scott was appointed Political Agent to the Governor-General and was entrusted with the management of the newly acquired territories while Col. Richards was entrusted with the administration of civil and criminal justice. The Political Agent, however, was forbidden to interfere with purely military affairs though he was to conduct negotiations with the border tribes and native princes of the region.[1] In 1828, when martial law was withdrawn from Assam, David Scott became the Commissioner of Assam as well as the Political Agent to the Governor-General for the North-East Frontier. In the letter capacity, he was entrusted with the management of the border tribes and conduct negotiations with them.[2]

SADIYA AGENCY

Meanwhile an Agency was extablished at Sadiya to conduct negotiations with the chiefs of the Moamarias of Mattack, the Khamptis of Sadiya and the Singphos of Upper Assam.[3] In 1832, the Supreme Government took the decision to restore an Ahom prince in Upper Assam and Purandar Singh was selected to rule tributary king. The Political Agency of Sadiya was empowered to conduct negotiation with the Ahom prince.[4] Lower Assam was retained within the British territories. In 1835, the territory of Lower Assam was divided into three districts each of which was put under a Senior Assiatant to the Commissioner whose title was later on changed to that of Principal Assistant to the Commissioner.[5] But for the management of the border and to conduct negotiations with the border tribes, the district officers were given the title of Assistant Agent to the Commissioner of Assam, as the Commissioner had the title of Agent to the Governor-General for North-East Frontier.[6] After the annexation of Upper Assam to the British territories, it may be recalled, Capt. Vetch, the district officer of Darrang, had initiated the negotiations with the tribes on the Darrang frontier for payment in cash or kind to the tribes stopping the system of direct collection by the tribes themselves.[7]

The district officer, entitled Assistant Agent to the Governor-General, maintained relations with the border tribes. It was the district officers who had to punish the tribes for violating the terms of their engagement with the British. When a punitive expedition was authorised to chastise any offending tribe, usually the district officer accompanied the expeditionary force as Political Officer and obtained satisfaction for the offence committed by the tribe of its member or members.[8] These Agents presented the annual *posa* to the tribes and heard theri complaints and kept the higher authorities informed of what was happening in the hills, collecting information through the Kotokis.[9]

Intelligence Service

As for intelligence service, in the North-East Frontier the British did not bother very much except for a short period after the Anglo-Burmese War of 1824-26. For sometime, the spectre of a Burmese invasion haunted them and a Political

Agency was, therefore, setup, as already mentioned, at Sadiya. "Their duties consisted chiefly in keeping a watchful eye on the proceedings, journeying and communications with the tribes beyond the frontier, of all the clans, especially those situated near the Burmese frontier, and gaining through them intelligence, as early and accurate as possible, of all movements in Upper Burma."[10]

To oversee the proceedings and report on the movement of the tribes some watchers and interpreters were appointed in the Agency establishment at Sadiya. In the middle of the nineteenth century, when Mills submitted his report, on Jamadar, a Shan Interpreter and seven Harkaras were retained in the Agency which continued to function under the district officer of Dibrugarh, when the Political Agent was withdrawn from Sadiya. All these officers were natives of Assam. The post of the Muharrir, that is the clerk, was held by a Khampti Chief, the post of Jamadar was filled up by an Assamese gentleman who was the head of the Doanies of Makum and knew frontier languages; the seven Harkaras were all local people who were well-versed in frontier tactics.[11] After the news of combined Mishmi and Singpho rebellion proved to be a mere rumour in 1866, the Agency establishment was subordinated to the police establishment of Sadiya.[12]

The duties of the Political Agent, however, consisted chiefly of the management of the Singpho and Khampti tribes who acknowledged the British supremacy and engaged to refer their inter-tribal disputes to the British officer. These tribes, by agreement, had bound themselves to obey all orders issued to them through the Political Agent and bring all heinous crimes for settlement to the Political Agent as they were not subject to the ordinary jurisdiction of the Magistrate of the Lakhimpur district. The Political Agent was required to mediate in their quarrels, keep peace between rival clans, and investigate into heinous crimes like murder and dacoity originating amongst these clans as also all complaints against them by other parties, whether British subjects or foreigners.[13]

Except at Sadiya, at no other place any regular intelligence establishment or agency was provided for. The states beyond the frontiers of Assam, Tibet and China were not considered powerful and were themselves in decaying condition in the nineteenth century. Therefore, no possibility of invasion of Assam after the Second Anglo-Burmese War loomed large over the frontiers. The petty tribes of the frontier hills committed only petty raids for which no intelligence was thought necessary. But after the Bhutia raid of 1849, one Jamadar and 10 Chowkidars were appointed for watch and ward on the Darrang frontier : the Deputy Commissioner wanted to retain them permanently as he thought that by travelling on Duars and Mahals of Darrang they could provide useful intelligence regarding the border tribes.[14]

RULE IN ASSAM

With the consolidation of the British rule in Assam, the hands of the district officers of the Assam Commission were full with work. Assam was a Non-Regulation province; personal care and attention was more necessary for good administration here than in the Regulation provinces. Over and above their executive duties, the officers of the administration were also judges and registrars in Assam; as such they were required not only to maintain law and order in their respective jurisdictions, but as District Magistrates they were required to dispose of civil and criminal cases, register the transfer of land and try revenue cases.[15] It was now found necessary to have some sort of agency to maintain relation with the frontier tribes. Therefore, the office of native political agents called Kotokis was now revived to assist the district officers to conduct relation with the hill tribes of the frontiers.

KOTOKIS

The office of the Kotokis had its origin in the Ahom period.

The Ahom kings appointed political officers to open negotiation with neighbouring princes and sometimes sent ambassadors to the courts of the Mughals. These political officers and ambassadors were styled as Kotokis. Usually high caste Brahmins, well-versed in the Shastras, intelligent, smart, with unusual common sense, were appointed to such offices. Naturally the respect they commanded was commensurate with their high office and bearings.[16]

The Kotokis who manned the frontier service were established throughout North Lakhimpur in connection with the Nishis, 'Chang Meeres', Adis and other hill tribes in that quarter. There were Kotokis–one each–for 'Banskota Daflas' and Chaiduar Dufla clans'.[17] After the Aka (Hrusso) expedition of 1882, Capt. Maxwell who had the expedition recommended the appointment of Kotokis in relation to the Akas (Hrusso) in the Darrang frontier as well. On the recommendation of the Deputy Commissioner of Darrang, two Kotokis for the Hazarikhawa Akas (Hrussos) and two for the 'Kapachars' were appointed.[18] The Bhutias of Tawang conducted their intercourse directly with the Deputy Commissioner, but the Bhutias of Rupa came through the Mauzadar of Orang and the Charduar Bhutias had two Kotokis. There were some eleven Kotokis for the Adi tribes known as Panibatia, Tarbatia, Charak and 'Ghasi Merees'.[19] Kotokis were employed to carry on intercourse between the government and the hill tribes; a *parwana* of appointment was issued and a register giving details of the man who held the post together with his address was maintained at the headquarters.[20]

The duties of the Kotokis, wrote Capt. H.S. Biver, were to proceed to the hills on any occasion when required to do so in connection with the tribes and to render aid in furnishing information on the tribes and in interpreting any matter, as also to attend upon the Deputy Commissioner when he proceeded to the country bordering on the hills of the tribe to which they were attached.[21] Though the Kotokis were appointed by Government, they were also in close connection with the tribe for which they were appointed and accompanied them when the tribesmen came down to the plains. The government remunerated them by the grant of revenue-free land and paid them a paltry salary; they sometimes received some remuneration from the tribe as well. The Charduar Bhutias paid their Kotoki Rs. 10 per annum and stayed with him whenever they came down to the plains.[22]

But the Kotokis who began to be appointed for service in the frontier were practically a misnomer or a caricature of the Kotokis of the Ahom regime. No educational qualification was required for holding the appointment. The Kotokis were remunerated by allowing them to enjoy twelve *bighas* of revenue-free land for doing the hard and risky job of carrying on transactions with the 'savage tribes' of the perilous hills or were paid a paltry sum of 5 to 15 rupees per annum.[23] Intelligent people who commanded respect in society for their acccomplishments and wealth did not usually come forward to undertake the job.

INTELLIGENT AT FRONTIERS

In 1903, after the Adi and Mishmi raids at the close of the preceding century, the Chief Commissioner of Assam opened the question of intelligence on the frontiers. He issued a circular to the Deputy Commissioners of Assam asking them to submit their opinions on the agency of intelligence to be employed for keeping themselves informed of the attitude of the tribesmen of the frontier, as also on the possibility of utilising effectively the Kotokis in the frontier service.[24]

The Deputy Commissioner of Darrang and Sibsagar suggested the abolition of these offices as useless but the Deputy Commissioner of Lakhimpur considered it useful.[25] Appreciation of the services of the Kotokis and recognition of their usefulness were brought to the notice of the local administration by P.G. Militus, the then Commissioner of the Assam valley districts. He wrote, "our Kotokis, if inefficient, are at any rate a cheap agency, and their inefficiency is, I think, to a great extent, due to bad system."[26] In 1884, the Deputy Commissioner of the Darrang district had suggested that the Kotokis be required to visit the hills they served at least once a year, preferably in the winter, and submit reports to the Deputy Commissioner.[27] As early as 1874, the officiating Superintendent of Police, Goad, had recommended to place the Kotokis under the Inspector of Police.[28] Nothing was done to give effect to these recommendations.

It is worth noting that Assam was a non-regulation province from the very beginning and it was only in 1837 that a system of code, drawn up in the spirit of Bengal Regulations, was prepared for a simple form of administration of the province.[29] The system continued to provide the basis of law in Assam, which was regarded as a Frontier province, till the end of the Sepoy Mutiny; the Civil Procedure Code (Act VIII) and the Criminal Procedure Code (Act XXV of 1861) were introduced in Assam on 26 April 1860 and in January 1862 respectively. In 1861, the designation of the district and subdivisional officers was changed, henceforth they were termed Deputy Commissioner and Assistant Commissioners and Extra-Assistant Commissioners instead of Principal Assistant, Senior Assistants and Junior Assistants respectively.[30] The officers of the Assam Commission consisted of chiefly the military officers of the Indian army who were deputed to civil service. Only some percentage of the vacancies were reserved for the Indian Civil Service, the rest being a monopoly of the Indian Army personnel. The first Commissioner was a civilian, but he had an Assistant from the Army. The Principal Assistant and Junior Assistants were selected from the military personnel.

The province was surrounded on all sides by hill tribes whom the British wanted to keep at arms length. This was done by deploying army under the civil authority. The duty of the civil administrators in such a province involved political intercourse tempered by armed force. The judicious employment of the army for civil purposes necessitated some knowledge of military tactics. Therefore, it was no wonder that the civil offices of the province, like the headship of districts and subdivisions, were filled up by army personnel on deputation to civil service. At the time of amalgamation of Assam with Eastern Bengal one-fourth of the membership of the Assam Commission was reserved for army personnel; one Commissionership and 8 posts of district officers were open to them.[31]

But for the administration of the hills of the frontier the English did not employ any officer. They wanted to leave them (tribes) 'alone' but wanted to keep themselves abreast of the intentions or movements of the tribes.[32] Therefore, they provided for a hedge of outposts manned by units of Indian Army. At certain points, which were cross-roads of tribal movement, some intelligence establishment was set up. To convey the government policies and orders to the tribes as well as to act as guides and interpreters of the tribes some native agents termed Kotokis were attached to each tribe along the frontier.[33]

DEFENCE OF PLAINS

For the defence of the plains below the North-East Frontier hills, a chain of outposts were established. These posts, for the most part, governed the principal routes along which the tribal people moved or made inroads in the plains in the past.[34] The posts were held by the armed police and military guards. The army was employed because the police had an undue dread of the tribes and the army again lacked knowledge of the land, people and language of the tribes they had to guard against.[35] Therefore, the armed police who had knowledge of the territory of the tribes and their languages were employed in guarding the frontier along with the detachments of the army. In the event of a determined attack an outpost of a few persons could do little or nothing to protect the country around it; indeed, they could hardly defend the ground it stood on. But in case of a prowling enemy, the outpost was of much use, as the fear of being caught by a patrol or cut up on their return journey when burdened with plunder prevented raids on villages and robbery in the plains.[36] Behind the outposts, strong reserve was garrisoned and as and when called for they marched towards the frontiers. In 1861, at Kuriapara there were 70 men of miliatary force to guard against possible attack of the Bhutias; at Balipara some 40 military personnel were stationed in dry season to guard against raids of the Hrussos, besides a reserve of 176 for general purpose.[37] To guard against the Nishis, a chain of posts along the frontiers were provided. Thus in1874, guard posts were set up at Behali, Singlijan, Ghera, Gohpur, Katori, Barpathar, Ooahat, Sellonibari and at Joyhing.[38] To guard against the Adis and Mishmis posts were set up at Dimoh, Pobah, Sesei, Dibong, Dikrang, Disoi, Difoo and Sohpura; besides a reserve at Sadiya consisting of 210 military personnel and 69 armed police was quartered. These posts at Sadiya, Sesori, Dibong and Poba were held by the army and the rest were left with the armed police.[39]

Army

After marital law was withdrawn in 1828, British soldiers began to be withdrawn from Assam leaving the defence of the Brahmaputra valley to the Rungpore Light Infantry, named the Assam Light Infantry after three years of service in Assam and of the Surma Valley to the Sylhet Light Infantry.[40] Another corps of Sebundy troops was raised in 1835 to defend the Sadiya frontier. This was reorganised as the Second Assam Light Infantry in 1842.[41] But the defence of the frontier against the tribal incursions required a stronger force. In the Surma valley another corps known as the Cachar Levy was raised to defend the Cachar and Manipur frontier, and in Assam in 1840 a force known as the Jorhat Militia was raised.[42] Yet the regular army had to be quartered in Dibrugarh for defence of the Sadiya frontier against attack of the frontier tribes. In 1861, there was in Dibrugarh one European Artillery 100 strong and another Eurasian Light Infantry 100 strong, besides one Company of Native Local Artillery of 100 men. Besides, the 46th Regiment of Light Infantry was located at Dibrugarh with detachments at Sibsagar and the 47th Regiment of Native Infantry was stationed at Gauhati with detachments at Nowgong, Goalpara and Darrang. A total of 2300 men were thus employed in defence of the frontier.[43]

Military Police

But the cost of the army was too high to be borne for defending the frontiers against possible attacks of petty and disorganised frontier tribes who practically possessed no fire arms. Therefore, the goverment considered the question of withdrawal of troops from Assam leaving the defence to the police. Lt. Col. A. H. Paterson, who was Inspector General of Police, Lower Provinces, recommended the withdrawal of military contingents leaving the defence of the Assam frontiers to a corps of 1860 Military Police to be organised for the purpose.[44] Lt. Col. Agnew, Commissioner of Assam, had proposed in 1871 to employ one Regiment of Native Infantry and a wing of regular troops with 300 Armed Police for the defence of the frontiers. And yet a third proposal of organising two local corps of pioneers, each 700 strong, for the defence was mooted by reducing the number of the Armed Police.[45]

But the expediency of leaving the defence of the frontiers entierly to the military police was doubted. As early as 1861 Col. Henry Hopkinson, the then Commissioner of Assam, had suggested the disbandment of the three Native Regiments together with 400 Armed Police employed for the defence of the frontier and recommended to raise a force to be equipped specially for the peculiar duty in the frontiers under British officers. He, of course would not agree to the withdrawal of the army altogether from the frontiers.[46] In 1862, the Police Commissioner had recommended to abolish the Military Police and organise Armed Police for the defence of the frontiers.[47] But Capt. J. R. Pughe, officiating Inspector General of Military Police, Lower Provinces, held that those who would be employed in defence of the frontiers would discharge quasi-military duties and as such it was inadvisable to abolish the Military Police.[48]

In 1873, the Bengal Government deputed Barker of the Bengal Police to recommend measures for frontier defence. He recommended to employ a separate force to be called Frontier Police, altogether separate from the Civil Police, for frontier duty. Accordingly, forces designated as the Surma Valley Frontier Police and Lakhimpur Armed Police Battalions were organised for the defence of the Surma Valley and the Assam valley respectively.[49] On the creation of a Chief Commissionership, the issue of raising a separate force for gaurding against the tribal incursions into Assam and punishing the raiders was again taken up. Consequently, as recommended by the Chief Commissioner of Assam, Keating, battalions of Military Police were raised in 1878 disbanding the Surma Valley Frontier Police and the Lakhimpur Armed Police battalions.[50] Units of these battalions were assigned to the border posts and a reseve was kept in readiness at the district headquaters to march to the frontier.

The year 1882 witnessed a further reorganisation. Sir Charles Elliot,[51] Chief Commissioner, recommended to form the Military Police into an essentially military body, altogether separate from the Civil Police. In the new organisation that was raised, the members of the force were drilled and equipped as soldiers, bore military designations and made into an armed force. The battalions were put under European officers of the Indian Army who had distinguished service records. The terms of service in the new force were assimilated with those of the Indian Army.[52]

During the First World War, the Indian Army was altogether withdrawn from Assam, leaving the defence of the frontiers to the Military Police. The designation of the Military Police was changed into Assam Rifles in 1919, as the police appellation seemed to be unpopular among the members of the corps.[53] The relations of the Assam Rifles with the Gorkha Regiment of the Indian Army had become so intimate that in 1924 the relations between the two were formalised by affiliating the battalions of the Assam Rifles with the Gorkha Regiments of the Indian Army.[54]

Recruits of the frontier forces of Military Police came largely from the Gorkhas recruited from Jalpaiguri and Darjeeling in Bengal and the battalions were put under the command of European officers of the Indian Army and the Bengal Police who were selected for their special qualifications and previous experience.[55] In 1905, the expediency of mixed enlistment, as in Burma, of servicemen of the Bttalions was mooted. But S.B. Chatterton expressed the opinion that mixed enlistment was not desirable for the recruitment of personnel of the Military Police as the Gorkhas were the best for service in the frontiers; they were rice-eaters and rice was available locally in sufficient quantity.[56] However, the Military Police force was originally regulated by the Police Act of 1861. But in 1882 the Assam Frontier Police Regulation was passed for enforcement of discipline and to assimilate the terms of the service with those prevailing in the Native Army–as already referred to. In 1890 and 1912, the terms were further modified; in 1919 the Assam Rifles Act was passed to govern their services without altering their status as a civil force while assimilating the form with the Indian Army.[57]

It is significant to note that for the tribal hills of the frontiers no police force was ever raised. In the sixties and seventies an attempt was made to provide guns to youngmen of some tribes to guard their own villages against the possible attack on them by the tribes of the interior hills. A little cash payment was also sanctioned.[58] But gradually the system fell into disuse and in the twentieth century we hear no more of those frontier wardens. The responsibility of watch and ward was regarded as a local responsibility and as in the Assam valley, no rural police operated in the frontier hills.[59] The village headmen maintained law and order in their respective hills.

The Military Police and the Assam Rifles, together with the Army, were employed mainly to check the tribesmen's propensity to raid the plains. The border posts indirectly influenced the villages in the vicinity. Any violence in the neighbourhood would have raised an alarm in the post and possibility of punitive expedition helped maintenance of law and order in the tribal villages. Moreover, the frontier force which discharged its duties with indefatigable energy and ruthless discipline and did not shrink from any kind of manual labour set examples before the tribes and this acted as a civilising agency in the frontiers.[60]

Reference has already been made in the preceding chapters to the Chief Commissioners of Assam.[61] The objects of separation of Assam from the Bengal Presidency was to provide security by invigorating the system of administration of the province.[62] The Jaintia rebellions of 1860 and 1862, the Bhutia raids of 1849, the necessity of waste land grant without survey to the European tea planters, the problem of immigrant labour for plantation and mining industries, construction of roads along the strategically important routes, distribution of armed forces in different strategically important places most economically–all these required an officer of sufficiently high rank on the spot to give quick decision and sanction. But the most important need was to formulate and follow an essentially uniform policy towards the extensive frontiers inhabited by savage tribes. The urgency of the last factor brought home the need for change in the system of administration of Assam. The Government of Bengal which was incharge of a very extensive area and a very large population, admitted the necessity of some relief.[63]

SEPARATION FROM BENGAL PRESIDENCY

APPOINTMENT OF CHIEF COMMISSIONER

The Governor-General in Council considered the issues involved and decided to separate the frontier province of

Assam from the Bengal Presidency; it was to be put under a Chief Commissioner who would be under the direct control and authority of the Government of India. But Sir William Grey, a member of the Governor-General's Council, differed as to the course of action to be taken to strengthen the Assam administration, though he too admitted the necessity of relieving the one-man Government of Bengal which could scarcely do justice to its heavy work and at the same time look after 1000 miles of frontiers. He suggested to provide the Lieutenant-Governor of Bengal with an Executive Council and leave the administrative departments of Assam independent of the central administration of Bengal, as Sind was administered from Bombay. Sir Henry Durand, another member of the Governor-General's Council, expressed doubt as to the effciency of the proposed setup of Chief Commissionership. He pointed out, "Assam is so much connected with Bengal that it seems very inexpedient to separate it from that government, even though a Chief Commissioner be appointed as a panacea, which will not do much to restore its prospects unless the Bengal Government work cordially with him; and it is more likely to do so when under its own authority than if detached from it."[64]

But the Viceroy argues, "the object, I take it, is to strengthen the new administration and to bring it to a more forward state. The Government of India has far greater resources than the Government of Bengal command, both for assistance and encouragement. The new Chief Commissioner would be the man on whose personal exertion success would mainly depend, whoever be selected, he will assuredly prefer being under the Government of India and will thereby be in better heart and spirit."[65] Therefore, the Governor General addressed a despatch to the Secretary of State for India proposing creation of a Chief Commissionership for Assam.

Administration under a Chief Commissioner was more personal than formal. As such, when newly acquired territories required an administration, a Chief Commissionership served as a convenient and useful machinery. Generally such a territory was governed in a rough and simple fashion by an executive partly civilian and partly military. The executive government accommodated all that was good in the indigenous institutions and in the local usages of the country in admininstering the territory. The head of the administration took quick decision on any issue depending upon the exigency of the situation.[66] Therefore, the Secretary of State for India observed, "I cannot doubt that when strength and directness of power are required in any subordinate administration, it is best to place that administration immediately under the Supreme Government so that it may, as directly as possible, enjoy the support and carry the authority of the Governor-General in Council. Assam and the eastern districts seem to be eminently a case requiring such an administration."[67] Receiving the approval of the Secretary of State for India, the Government of India constituted Assam into a Chief Commissionership on 7 February, 1874.[68]

The title of Chief Commissioner was first used in 1853 when John Lawrence was appointed head of the executive government in the Punjab in substitution of the Board of Administrators under a President. It was to distinguish the head of the Administration from the Financial and Judicial Commissioners who were also appointed at the same time. In earlier years, the title given to such a delegate entrusted with administrative functions in a new territory was Commissioner. For instance, Mountstuart Elphinstone was given this designation when he was appointed to administer the territories of the Deccan conquered from the Peshwa in 1818.[69] The Act of 1854, however, provided for the creation of Chief Commissionerships. It authorised the Governor-General in Council to take immediate authority and management by proclamation any territory and provide for its administration. But the title Chief Commissioner was not recognised by any Act of Parliament and as such the territories committed to the charge of a Chief Commissioner were theoretically under the immediate authority and management of the Governor-General in Council. Therefore, in official terminology, a Chief Commissionership was regarded as a Local Administration rather than a Local Government.[70]

DECLARATION OF SCHEDULED DISTRICTS

To provide for a simpler form of administration in the new province of Assam, the districts of Kamrup, Darrang, Nowgong, Sibsagar, Lakhimpur, Garo Hills, Khasi and Jaintia Hills, Naga Hills and Cachar were declared Scheduled Districts on 1 January 1873, Goalpara on 15 December 1873, and Sylhet on 1 August 1874, as per resolutions of the Secretary of State in Council dated 15 September 1873 and 4 June 1874 respectively.[71] It was realised that the whole or parts of those districts were inhabited by hill tribes who lived unsophisticated life and were not fit for administration through the regular judicial and administrative set-up; the regulation and laws passed from time to time in the Legislatures of India were too sophisticated for them. Q.Vict. Act XXXIII, Chap. 2, known as an act to make better provisions for making laws and regulations for certain parts of India and for certain other purposes thereto, authorised to Local Administration to propose to the Governor-General in Council draft of any Regulation, together with the reasons thereof, for the peace and good government of the territories of the Scheduled Districts. Such drafts, when approved of by the Governor-General in Council and after it had received the assent of the Governor-General, were to be notified in the Local Gazette and the *Gazette of India* when it would have the force of law in the Scheduled Districts, or parts of the Scheduled Districts as proposed.[72] Special rules for the administration of justice, both civil and criminal, had already been provided for under provisions of this Act in the Garo, Khasi, Jaintia and Naga Hills; these were reissued under the provisions of the Scheduled District Act.[73] Now these were supposed to be extended to the fringes of the Darrang,

Lakhimpur, Sibsagar and Nowgong districts on whose borders lived the hill tribes of the frontiers.

The problem of tribal administration had caught the attention of the Government of India after the rising of the Hos of Singbhum in 1831, the Khonds in 1846 and the Santhals in 1885. Measures to provide for a simpler form of administration for the tribal territories by regulations in which the tribal customs and conventions could be accommodated for settling the disputes had begun to be considered by the Government of India.[74] The results of application of special rules for the administration of justice in the Hill Districts of Assam under Q. Vict. Act XXXIII, Chap. 2 had been found satisfactory. Therefore, to give the Local Administration more powers to deal with the problem of tribal administration, a new Act known as the Scheduled Districts Act was passed by the Government of India in 1874.[75] This Act empowered the Chief Commissioner of Assam to extend to the frontier tracts, for peace and good government, with the previous sanction of the Governor-General in Council, any Act or part thereof passed by the Legislature of any provincial or of the Central Government, by notification in the Local Gazette. Under Section 2 of the said Act, the Chief Commissioner had the power to propose to the Governor-General in Council the draft of any Regulation for the peace and good government of the frontier tracts, which when approved by the Governor-General in Council had the force of law after notification in the Local Gazette. The same Act authorised the Chief Commissioner, under Section 6, Clause C, to define by what authority and jurisdiction, powers and duties incidental to the operation of any enactment for the time being in force in the frontiers would be exercised and performed.[76]

Meanwhile the Inner Line Regulation was passed in 1873 and the Deputy Commissioners were asked by the Chief Commissioner to propose the Inner Line of their respective districts. The Deputy Commissioner of Lakhimpur, Col. Clarke, while submitting his proposal in respect of his district, stated that the frontier of his district was inhabited by tribesmen, whom it would be inadvisable to administer as people in other parts of the district, which were inhabited by more advanced plains people. The Chief Commissioner wrote to the Government of India that he would prepare the draft of a set of rules for the administration of justice in the frontier tracts which, if approved by the Governor-General in Council, would provided the basis of administration of justice in the frontier. He was advised to consult the rules in force in the Hill Districts of Assam for formulating his proposal.[77] Col. Clarke had drawn up the proposal, but, as he was subsequently transferred from Dibrugarh, Col. Graham, who succeeded him, submitted the proposal in 1876 to the Chief Commissioner.[78] The rules were further modified by the Chief Commissioner and then submitted to the Governor-General in Council for their approval.

The object of the rules was to provide an outline pattern of rules applicable ordinarily to all tracts of the frontier districts allowing exemption to 'semi-barbarous' or 'barbarous people' over whom British control had been extended, from the operation of regular system of procedure prescribed by the Civil and Criminal Procedure Codes, to which they would become subject on the inclusion of their country within the British limits. The end in view was to be attained by issuing a notification under Section 2 of the Scheduled Districts Act of 1874 declaring that the Civil and Criminal Procedure Codes were not to be in force in those tracts, and then under Sections 6 (a) and 6 (b) of the said Act declaring by what authority the administration of the tracts was to be conducted and under what rules of procedure, as soon as any tract had been brought within its scope.[79]

But it was necessary to detract the areas of the existing regulation districts which were inhabited by tribal people who were to be exempted form the operation of Regulations and Acts, and define the boundary of the tracts separating them from the adjoining districts and repeal the Act and Regulations operating in them, and again provide for their proper administration. The proposal had already been made by the Chief Commissioner to the Governor-General while proposing the Inner Line of his province.[80] After the specification of the Inner Line, it now became imperative to detract the tribal areas and provide for their administration. Therefore, the Chief Commissioner now submitted to the Governor-General in Council the drafrt of the Regulation which would authorise him to remove certain frontier tracts "inhabited or frequented by the barbarous or semi-civilised tribes" and repeal the operation of the enactments existing therein and provide for their proper administration. This draft was approved by the Governor-General in Council and assented to by the Governor-General and notified in the Gazette of India on 24 January 1880 and in the Assam Gazette on 31 January 1880.[81]

The Regulation, known as the Assam Frontier Tract Regulation or Regulation II of 1880, authorised the Chief Commissioner, under Section I, to specify the boundaries of the tracts by which they were to be separated from the regulation districts and define the authorities which would administer them under which Rules or Acts. Section II of the Regulation empowered him to remove or introduce Acts or Regulations for their proper administration.[82] The Chief Commissioner, by notification on 27 August 1884, withdrew the following Acts from the frontier tracts : the Court Fees Act, 1874; the Registration Act, 1877; the Indian Stamp Act, 1899; the Transfer of Properties Acts; the Criminal Procedure Code; and the Civil Procedure Code.[83] On the same date on which the boundary of the Lakhimpur Frontier Tract was defined, that is to say, on 22 August 1884, rules for the administration of justice in the Lakhimpur Frontier Tract were passed by the Chief Commissioner.[84]

But by defining boundary of the frontier tract, the existing responsibilities in regard to extending British control over tribes hitherto not interfered with were in no way increased. The rules for the administration of justice in the Dibrugarh Frontier Tracts were formulated in such a way that the main principal of the system of administration was to leave the primary responsibility for reporting and preventing crimes on the village authorities, if any such authority existed, or any such authorities created where they did not exist, and to invest those authorities with power of disposing of petty cases among themselves, leaving the remainder to the discretion of the Political Officers.[85]

The Rules for the Administration of Justice, 1884, empowered the Deputy Commissioners of the frontier districts to nominate local authorities, subject to confirmation of the Chief Commissioner, and assign them their functions and define the limits within which they should perform their duties. The Regulation had provision to vest ordinary duties of police and justice, both criminal and civil, in the local authorities who would deal with petty cases according to the existing local customs and convention. The more serious criminal cases and civil suits involving bigger amounts were to be dealt with by Deputy Commissioner or his Assistants in their political capacity, as also the cases involving the European British subjects or plains people. No legal formalities were to be observed by the tribal local authorities nor would legal advice from professional lawyers be allowed in their courts. The High Court of Judicature in Calcutta which had jurisdiction over the Assam Valley districts was denied jurisdiction over the frontier tracts, the Chief Commissioner being the highest court of appeal in the territory.[86]

ACTS EXTENDED AND ENACTMENTS

The following Acts were extended to the new charges and used for due administration of the frontier tracts: the Indian Penal Code, 1860 (XLV of 1860); the Indian Police Act, 1861 (XI of 1861); the Indian Arms Act, 1878 (XI of 1878); the Assam Land and Revenue Regulation, 1886 (I of 1886) with the exception of Sections 3-5; the Assam Forest Regulation, 1891 (VII of 1891); the Whipping Act, 1909 (IV of 1909); the Eastern Bengal and Assam Military Police Act, 1912 (III of 1912). The Chief Commissioner explained to the Governor-General the reason for the extension of the above Acts. He wrote that the Assam Land and Revenue Regulation was necessary in the frontier tracts for repealing any Regulation that might exist there : the Police Act was necessary for enforcing due discipline among the Police in the frontier tracts; Forest and Elephant Preservation Acts were necessary to protect the forests and elephants in the region; and finally, the Penal Code, the Arms Act and the Whipping Act were necessary for proper administration of new charges.[87]

There were two sets of enactments in force in the frontier tracts–all Acts of the Governor-General in Council which extended *proprio-vigore* to the whole of British India and the operation of which had not been barred under section 2 of Assam Frontier Tract Regulation of 1880 or delcared not to be in force under Section 3 of the Scheduled District Act of 1874, and secondly Acts and Regulations either passed specifically for a certain locality or definitely declared in force or extended with or without modification under sections 3 and 5 of Act XIVof 1874. In case of amending Acts, again there were three different classes. In cases of all Acts applying *proprio-vigore* to the whole of British India at the time of passing of the Scheduled District Act of 1874, and not barred under the provisions of the Assam Frontier Tract Regulation of 1880 or the Scheduled District Act of 1874, were automatically in force in the Scheduled Districts, unless definitely barred either by the amending Act itself or by action under the Assam Frontier Tract Regulation or the Scheduled District Act. In case of Acts not extending to the whole of British India at that time and not declared to apply under section 3 of the Scheduled District Act amending Acts or separate measures which were extended under section 5 of that Act were only operative. Thirdly, in the case of Acts which though originally applicable to the whole of British India had been barred under Regulation II of 1880, or the

Scheduled District Act, amending Acts would not come in force unless and until they were specially extended.[88]

Though the Assam Frontier Tract Regulation and Rules for the administration of justice were passed, no agency was provided for the administration of the new region. But in the late seventies and early eighties, the need for an officer who would serve in the frontier tract for a longer period was felt. The simple and rude frontier tribes better knew the man whom they dealt with; the Deputy Commissioners, to whom was committed the charge of frontier administration and political relations with the hills tribes, did not stay in the district for a long period. The good relation that developed between a particular district officer and the tribes lapsed after the district officer was transferred. The new-comer lacked experience of frontier tribes and there was no continuity in frontier policy. The officers came on loan to Assam from the Bengal Government and looked for the day when they would go back from Assam. Therefore frontier administration lacked in continuity and understanding of the problems.

ASSISTANT POLITICAL OFFICER APPOINTED

In view of the above-mentioned facts, Sir Charles Elliot, while reviewing the results of the advance of outpost on Nizamghat on the left bank of the Dibang river in the Adi hills, proposed to appoint an Assistant to the Deputy Commissioner of Dibrugarh on the border of whose district lay the extensive Dibrugarh Frontier Tract and the frontier hills of the Adis whom the British regarded at that time as most stubborn and troublesome. He pointed out that an officer, if intelligent in his instinct, quick in his sympathies and a good linguist, might in due course of two or three years attain influence on the frontier and might from that vantage position use any opportunity that might occur of opening friendly communication with the tribes and impress upon them the advantage of regular commerce between the plains and their country. His suggestion was to put a man from police service in charge of frontier relations who would serve for a longer time than any Deputy Commissioner and thus would bring the personal factor in frontier politics.[89]

The first duty of the Assistant Political Officer, Sir Charles Elliot proposed, would be to make himself thoroughly acquainted with the history of relations between the Government and the hill tribes and gain all information that he might acquire from other local authorities; he would become personally acquainted with the leading members of the tribes, their chiefs and Kotokis,and by frequent tour in their territories establish as far as possible friendly and cordial relations with them, he would learn the local languages so as to enable him to speak with the tribesmen without the aid of interpreters and become a past master in border politics which would be his special sphere; and he would acquire as much knowledge as possible to arrive at right judgement and provide sound opinions on questions in relations to borders.[90] But Elliot did not propose to put the Assistant directlly under him; he proposed to keep him under the Deputy Commissioner of Lakhimpur, as his subordinate and special adviser on frontier affairs.

In 1882, Jacks Francis Needham of the Bengal Police was appointed as Assistant Political Officer at Sadiya on the suggestion of Elliot. The Agency establishment, consisting of a clerk, an interpreter and the Karkaras of Sadiya, was now put under him. Though apparently the Assiatant was appointed to cultivate good relations with the Adis in particular and all other tribes in general by touring the hills inhabited by them, he was saddled with much administrative business. The administration of the Frontier Tracts was now his headache and he was responsible for the arrangement of frontier outposts, their location and supplies and patrolling of the borders of the administrative districts. Moreover, he was assigned criminal work in and around Sadiya, maintain law and order in that territory and look the collection of revenue in the settled villages within the frontier tracts.[91]

Needham served for 23 years as Assistant Political Officer and was succeeded by Noel Williamson in 1905.[92] During his long tenure of service in the Sadiya Frontier Tract (named after the headquarter of the Dibrugarh Frontier Tract) he had succeeded in establishing an image of the government before the tribes and tried vigorously to achieve the objective of the government. The government policy was that of minimum of interference in the tribal life; it aimed at impressing upon the tribesmen the uselessness of raids on the British territory and at making them look upon the British as their master. By his extensive tours and punitive expeditions, Needham had bred in the hill tribes of the frontier a sense of looking towards the British as their master. In 1910, when the Chinese contigent appeared across Rima, the Mishmis reported to the British not only the advent of the Chinese but rejected the orders of the Chinese, assuming themselves to be under the British paramountcy.[93]

During the term of Needham, the utilisation of the village authorities in the administration of the frontier tracts was not attempted. The administration was busy with preventing the tribesmen from violating the law within the British territory; they were asked not to take the law into their own hands in case of any offence being committed against them or anybody running away from their territory after doing wrong to seek asylum. To prevent the tribesmen's raids in the villages within easy march of the tribes beyond the Inner Line, a tract of territory, 10 miles in width from the Inner Line on both sides, was kept as no-man's land where no settlement was usually allowed.[94] The people who ran away from the tribal territory beyond the Inner Line were kept in detention for sometime for verifying the innocence of the person migrating into British territory; and in case of run-away slaves a ransom was usually paid to the owner of the slave who was allowed to purchase his freedom by earning money.[95] If any tribesman or tribe violated the British law for settlement of dispute, the man or the tribes' leaders were taken into custody and tried according to the Rules for the

Administration of Justice in the Frontier Tracts.[96]

Noel Williamson wanted to bring the frontier tracts and the hills beyond the Inner Line under the immediate and direct control of the Government as has already been noted.[97] He envisaged the gradual extension of a system of taxation in the hill areas in recognition of the British authority over the tribes. Further, he wanted to utilise the indigenous tribal institutions for the administration of the frontier hills.[98] The investment with authority of the village headman under the Rules for the Administration of Justice was initiated, and[99] by his tours and display of force Williamson wanted to impress upon the tribes British paramountcy over them. He wanted first to bring under control and authority the Adis who held a position of preeminance among the hill tribes, for if the Adis were brought under subservience, the other tirbes would be easily brought to terms.[100]

DIVISION OF FRONTIER IN THREE TRACTS

The Chief Commissioner of Assam proposed to the Government of India the division of the frontier tracts which after the Simla Conference was supposed to extend up to the international border, i.e., the McMahon Line into three sections as recommended by General Bower. The three new charges would be known respectively as : (i) Central and Eastern Sections, North-East Frontier Tract; (ii) Western Section, North-East Frontier Tract; and (iii) Lakhimpur Frontier Tract. The Inner boundary suggested for the Central and Eastern Sections ran along the existing Dibrugarh Frontier Tract, but it was stretched a little further south of the existing boundary to accommodate a strip of country south of the existing Dibrugarh Frontier Tract to include lands inhabited entirely by the Mishings, as also Saikhowa which was the Bazar for the frontier tribes, though it icluded five small villages inhabited by the Assamese people. The boundary of the Western Section of the North-East Frontier Tract would run from the river Subansiri which was the boundary between the Central and Eastern Sections and the Western Section. The Inner boundary of this section was also stretched a little within the district boundary to include some lands inhabited by hillmen and to bring them within the jurisdiction of the Political Officers. The Lakhimpur Frontier Tract was so defined as to leave within the regular jurisdiction of the Deputy Commissioner of Lakhimpur the areas in which exploration of coal and oil were being worked and through which the tea railway line of Assam Railways and Trading Company ran, giving him at the same time jurisdiction, under the Assam Frontier Tract Regulation of 1880, over the less civilised area over which the Assam Oil Company prospected for oil.[101]

Draft Notification extending to these territories, the Assam Frontier Tract Regulation of 1880 by the Governor-General of India in Council, and repealing all enactments in force except the Assam Frontier Tract Regulation of 1880, together with the Scheduled District Act of 1870, were placed before the Government of India. These were accepted. The Governments of India and Assam notified these changes, and now emerged new charges in the Frontier Administration of India in 1914 with provisions for peace and good government in them.[102]

The effect of these notifications was to extend the British authority over the frontier hills beyond the previous Lakhimpur Frontier Tracts and it was now necessary to provide personnel for its proper management. For this purpose, W.C.M. Dundas of Bengal Police, who was on Special Duty on the North-East Frontier with three Assistants, was appointed as Political Officer of the Central and Eastern Sections of the North-East Frontier. Dundas had accompanied the Dibang valley promenade as Political Officer in 1912 and made recommendations for management of the new territory.[103] G.A. Nevill of Bengal Police, on Special Duty in the North-East Frontier, who also had taken part in the exploratory promenade as Political Officer in 1912, was also enlisted for appointment as Political Officer of the new charge of the Western Section.[104] The third Section, of course, was left in charge of the Deputy Commissioner of Lakhimpur, who had jurisdiction over the district of Lakhimpur on whose border this Section stood.[105]

The management of the frontier hills meant, of course, exercise of 'loose political control' over areas to be gradually brought under administrative control. Though the Assam Frontier Tract Regulation of 1880 was extended to the hills following the precedent of 1898 when under Regulation II of that year the Lushai Hills were placed, under the jurisdiction of the Chief Commissioner of Assam, the Administration did not at a time bring the hills under immediate authority. It planned to advance gradually into the interior hills, step by step.[106] In exercise of the powers conferred by Section I of the Assam Frontier Tract Regulation of 1880, the Governor-General in Council extended to the new charges Rules for Administration of Justice as they were in force in the Frontier Tracts.[107]

Administrative Structure of Tracts

The Political Officers were provided with establishment for administrative control over the frontier tribes step by step from hill to hill and from hills to the borders. The Central and Eastern Sections were supposed to have three sub-divisions and Dundas was provided with two Assistant Superintendents of Police, T.E. Forze and T.P.M.O. Callaghan, and one Extra Assistant Commissioner, W.T.H. Ballantine, as Assistant Political Officers to be appointed in Adi Hills, Mishmi Hills and Sadiya respectively to assist him in controlling and administering the territory. But Nevill was not given any Assistant, as it was expected that the control area in the north-western hills of his charge would not be established in near future, as the First Great War had ensued and border affairs had temporarily lost their importance in the sight of the government.[108]

The duties of the respective office-bearers of the

Frontier Service may be noted for understanding the administration of the frontier. The duty of the Political Officer in the former Frontier Tract was to administer justice as per Rules for the Administration of Justice in the Frontier Tracts, maintain law and order, collect revenue and poll-tax from the tribal villages which were gradually brought under assessment, supervise the local authorities which were now invested with powers under the Frontier Tract Regulation, and arrange posting of the Assam Rifles men and patrols.[109]

The Political Officer had the power to expel anybody from his jurisdiction if he cosidered the presence of such a person prejudicial for the peace and security of his charge. A system of poll-tax began to be levied gradually on the hill tribes, who were exempted so long from taxation. The Political Officer was responsible for its collection.[110] In the even of fighting occurring or being imminent, the officer commanding the escort would take charge of the operation and would be responsible to take measures necessary to ensure the success and safety of the force.[111] The Political Officers were to hold an annual Durbar where they would present *posa* to the tribes, hear their grievances and explain to them the policy of the government.[112]

But to ensure the achievement of the above objective in tracts like the frontier hills it was impossible for the Political Officer with one or two Assistants to carry on the administration. It was wellnigh impossible for the officer to go round the entire area even once in the whole year. Therefore, the services of the Political Jamadars, Harkaras and Kotokis were very important. The Kotokis, now under the Political Officer, were on regular duty and toured the area under him and brought to his notice any breach of rule of peace, and in many cases they attended the meetings of the tribal council which settled disputes. The Political Jamadar did the same job where there was no Kotoki on regular employ. In the Lakhmipur Frontier Tract, the Political Officer disposed of petty cases, both civil and criminal, bringing to the Deputy Commissioner only the serious ones for trial in regular process[113] and he was responsible for collection of poll-tax through the village heads.[114] The Political Jamadar of Margherita held the post almost hereditarily and the tribal people having disputes to settle came to him in the first instance, as if he was the man to satisfy them.[115] The Harkaras served a very useful purpose where there was regular civil police to help the administration in summoning the offenders and bringing them for trial. The Harkaras carried the order of the officers from place to place and served as a check on bad characters.[116]

EXPERIMENTS IN ADMINISTRATION

The Agencies which served to bring the tribes under government influence were administrative posts, trading posts and Military or Armed Police posts which were set up in different parts of the frontier hills. An administrative post was set up with a suitable unit of Military Police or detachment of army and a medical dispensary. While the Political Officer was the symbol of government authority, the Military Police served as a deterrent to any rising or revolt. But the medical dispensaries in the administrative posts served the tribesmen besides treating the administrative and military personnel. These centres relieved the suffering of the tribal people unaccustomed to any sort of medical treatment and thereby won their hearts, preparing them to eagerly welcome the government.[117] Nevill, the Political Officer of the Western Section, repeatedly recommended the extension of administration posts with armed guards and medical dispensaries in the area under his charge.[118] Besides, such an administrative post was expected to have some schools and chapels for community worship which had civilising influence over the tribesmen. The shops in the administrative posts facilitated the marketing of the tribal people and that also endeared the government posts to them.

As a matter of fact, facilities of commerce had a greater effect on the tribes to bring them under the government. The tour diary of the Chief Commissioner of Assam shows that he was very eager to advance trading posts through the Adi hills into the interior with schooling facilities to impress the people and bring them under the influence and control of the government. A trading post consisted of some private shops which would exchange goods with the tribesmen or sell these to them at government-fixed price.[119] The tribes of the interior so long were barred by those on the borders to come for trade into the plains. But when the trading facilities were extended gradually into the interior, people realised their usefulness and welcomed the government. The Chief Commissioner wrote in his tour diary that for opening up the country and advancing trading posts within it was necessary to construct roads linking the interior. For the purpose, a corps of Sappers and Miners were employed to serve under the Political Officers permanently and a plan of advancing gradually into the interior was also chalked out.[120]

He wrote, "as the road is made, I would move the Balek post further and further west until a position is found which would meet all the political considerations in the control area between Pasighat and the Subansiri, and remove the blocks to trade which now exist.... Trade is but one aspect of the case. It is equally important to get near the people over whom we are to exercise loose political control." Later he wrote to the Government of India, "No sort of control can be exercised over the tribes unless the country is gradually opened out. The Chief Commissioner... solicits permission only to the gradual extension of the bridle path and the gradual move forward of the trading post in the direction of Riga as well as to move the Balek outpost to Mishing."[121] Agricultural demonstrations in trading outposts educated the tribesmen. Medical benefits and educational facilities attached to the trading posts brought the people under government influence.[122]

An Armed Police or Military post in the frontier not only demonstrated the government authority in the area of its location but the enterprise of the personnel of the force had much educative effect on the people. The forces were employed in building roads and cultivating rice in the terraces or in plain lands in wet-rice cultivation. The examples of the force were followed by the tribal people which benefited them; friendship also developed between the forces and the tribesmen. Besides, in big posts there were medical facilities which were made available to the tribal people. With the extension of political control over the Mishmis an armed police post was established at Walong. The members of the force were supposed to produce rice for their consumption and thus demonstrate to the people improved methods of cultivation.[123]

The British Government had, prior to the Simla Conference, scrupulously avoided all responsibility of administration in the frontier hills which were kept beyond the Inner Line. But after that it ushered in an era of activity to endear British authority to the tribal people. Agricultural demonstration, medical benefits and schooling facilities began to be gradually extended in the frontier territory. The Administration tried to provide primary schools and dispensaries with the administrative and trading posts. Agricultural demonstrators were employed to educate the tribal people in the improved methods of cultivation; improved varieties of seeds were supplied in some areas to impress upon the simple tribal folk. But the measures were belated; as the World Wars intervened between their withdrawal from India and the Simla Conference and the freedom movement in India gained momentum during the intervening period, the resources made available for welfare purposes were too meagre to have any significant impact.

Notwithstanding the above factors, the British administrators appreciating the immensity of the problems of the frontier administration carried on experiments till practically the end of their period in the frontier territory. The names of the Western and Central and Eastern Sections of the frontier administration were changed in 1919 and they were henceforth known as Balipara and Sadiya Frontier

Tracts respectively.[124] The Frontier Tracts were kept under the charge of the government when reforms were introduced in 1920 in the new Governor's province of Assam.

The authors of the Mont-Ford Reforms emphasised the necessity to protect the backward tribes in the Frontier Tracts and recommended to keep them outside the purview of the reforms.[125] The Government of India Act, 1919, accommodated the recommendation to safeguard the interest of the backward tribes.[126] Therefore, the Governor of Assam continued to administer the frontier tracts with the Political Officers and their Assistants, as the Chief Commissioners had done when the new province of Assam had come into force.

The Indian Statutory or Simon Commission also emphasised the need to keep the frontier hills outside the jurisdiction of the provincial government and, as demanded by the Government of Assam, it also recommended to keep the frontier territories as "Excluded Areas" where Indian Ministers would have no say or control.[127] The Government of India Act, 1935, provided in sections 91-92 for a different sort of administration for the frontier tracts. It provided for creation of "Excluded Areas" by the Secretary of State under section 91(2), and alter or define the boundary of such Areas. The administration of the said tracts under section 91(3) was vested in the Governor of the province at his "discretion" as a delegate of the Governor General. Under Section 92(1), the Indian Legislature had no power to legislate for these areas unless requested by the Governor, and Section 92(2) provided for special regulations to be framed by the Governor for the peace and good government of the Areas; it also empowered him to extend to the Areas any Act of the Indian or any provincial legislature with or without modifications.[128] By an order of 3 March 1936, the frontier tracts were declared to be "Excluded Areas".[129] In 1937, the frontier tracts were put under the Governor's Secretariat and a new department termed as "Tribal Affairs Department" was created under a separate Secretary and the Chief Secretary was relieved of the frontier affairs. No provision was made to return or nominate representatives from the Areas to sit either in the Provincial or the Central Legislature to take care of their interests. The frontier tracts continued to be administered under the provisions of the Assam Frontier Tracts Regulation, 1880, and the Scheduled District Act, 1874, as they were administered before the introduction of the Reforms in 1920 and 1937.

During the Second Great War, when the Japanese made an attempt to penetrate into India through Manipur and the Naga hills and China was cut off from the world through the sea, the British felt an urge to speed up the direct administrative control over the tribal hills on the frontier. For that purpose, an Adviser to the Governor of Assam was appointed in 1943. The rank of the Adviser was that of a Senior Secretary to the Government and he was supposed to carry on the administration and development of the hill areas of the North-East Frontier under the nominal authority of the Governor who had many preoccupations and had very little time to devote to the tribal affairs.[130] J.P. Mills, who had much experience of tribal administration, was given charge of the Adviser's portfolio.[131]

Meanwhile the importance of the low-lying hills leading to Burma across the Patkai through the Pangsu pass increased as a result of opening a metalled road to connect China through Burma. For giving more attention to the area, portions of the Sadiya Frontier Tract and the Lakhimpur Frontier Tract were combined to be put under a separate Political Officer in 1943.[132] The charge was named as Tirap Frontier Tract. Towards the close of the Great War, the British once again felt the necessity to advance towards Tawang up to the McMahon Line and, therefore, the Balipara Frontier Tract was bifurcated in 1946 into the Sela Sub-Agency and Subansiri Area.[133]

Thus, it appears from a study of the growth of the administration of the North-East Frontier that the East India Company's Government cared very little to provide a system of administration for the frontier territory, for their concern was to provide for a system or security for the province of Bengal. With the purpose in view, they came to Assam and ultimately annexed it to the Bengal Presidency.

The transfer of authority to the Crown did not immediately bring in a change in the mode of administration of the frontier. But gradually, in the interest of the security of the Indian Empire, the frontier territory had to be demarcated and a system of administration of the hitherto neglected territory began to be devised. As the diverse tribes lived savage and semi-barbarous life, a rough and ready system of administration was created by special provisions like the Assam Frontier Tract Regulation, 1880, Scheduled Districts Act, 1874, and later by providing safeguards in Government of India Acts, 1919 and 1935. The British realised the necessity of developing the area, and small charges under Political Officers began to be created. During the Second Great War, an Adviser to the Governor for fast development of the region was appointed as the Governor and the General Administration were too busy to pay much attention to tribal territories. Before the fruition of the belated measures, the British had to withdraw from India, leaving the burden of developing the system of administration to its logical culmination to the free Indian Government.

REFERENCES

1. Political and Secret Consultations, 2 July 1824, No. 16.
2. *Ibid.*, 5 April 1825, No. 24.
3. A.J.M. Mills' Report, p. lxxxiv.
4. *Ibid.*
5. Assam Administration Report, 1920-21, para 75.
6. Letters of the Distrct Officers appended to Mills' Report (1854), show it.
7. Foreign Proceedings (India), July 1838, No. 84-85.
8. Political Proceedings (Assam), December 1911, No. 1.
9. *Ibid.*
10. Mills' Report, p. lxxxiv.
11. *Ibid.*, p. lxxxvi.

12. Political Proceedings (Bengal), July 1866, No. 70.
13. Mills' Report, p. lxxxiv.
14. Political Proceedings (Bengal), 8 March 1843, No. 147.
15. John Butler, *Travels and Adventures in the Province of Assam*, p. 5.
16. H. Barua, *op. cit*, p. 36.
17. Judicial Proceedings (Bengal), December 1861, No. 195.
18. Foreign Proceedings (Assam), August 1884, No. 6.
19. Political Proceedings (Assam), April 1905, No. 76.
20. Foreign Proceedings (Assam), August 1884, No. 6.
21. Judicial Proceedings (Bengal), December 1862, No. 195.
22. Political Proceedings (Assam), April 1905, No. 70.
23. Lakhimpur Deputy Commissioner's Collection, No. XII, F. 7, 1904-08.
24. Political Proceedings (Assam), April 1905, No. 59.
25. *Ibid.*, No. 64.
26. *Ibid.*, No. 71.
27. Foreign Proceedings (Assam), August 1884, No. 5.
28. *Ibid.*, March 1874, No. 20.
29. Assam Administration Report, 1920-21, para 75.
30. Assam Administration Report, 1874-76, Part IIA, para 112 & 114.
31. Eastern Bengal and Assam Administration Report, 1905-06, Part IIA, para 120.
32. Mills' Report, p. lxxxiv.
33. Foreign Proceedings (Assam), April 1905, No. 59-93.
34. *Ibid.*, March 1885, No. 24.
35. *Ibid.*, January 1880, No. 1.
36. *Ibid.*, March 1885, No. 24.
37. Police Proceedings (Bengal), December 1861, No. 180.
38. Foreign Proceedings (Assam), November 1874, No. 1. The post at Behali consisted of 10 soldiers, Singlijan, 20, Ghera 12, Gohpur 12, Katroi 12, Barpathar 20, Ooahat 15, Sellonibari 15 and Joyhing 19.
39. *Ibid.*, January 1880, No. 1.
40. L.W. Shakespeare, *History of the Assam Rifles*, p. 6.
41. *Ibid.*, p. 7.
42. *Ibid.*, p. 8.
43. Police Proceedings (Bengal), July 1861, No. 252.
44. Police Proceedings (Bengal), October 1870, No. 137.
45. *Ibid.*
46. *Ibid.*, December 1861, No. 179.
47. *Ibid.*, September 1861, No. 340.
48. *Ibid.*
49. Home Public Proceedings (India), March 1876, No. 33-37.
50. *Imperial Gazatteer*, Vol. IV, p. 101.
51. Sir Charles Alfred Elliot, son of Rev. H.V. Elliot of Brighton was born in December 1835. He was educated at Harrow and Trinity

College, Cambridge. He secured Indian Civil Service by open competition and arrived in India in November, 1886. He served in North-West Frontier Province between 1870-77, in Mysore as Famine Commissioner in 1877 and became CSI in 1878. He was Secretary to the Famine Commission of 1878 and Census Commissioner of 1878. In 1881 Sir Elliot was appointed as the Chief Commissioner of Assam and served in the Frontier Province for five years. Subsequently he held the post of President of the Committee for the retrenchment of public expenditure, 1886. He was a member of the Supreme Council between 1887-90 and in 1890 he became the Lt. Governor of Bengal; he served the province for five years. Sir Elliot laboured with ability and energy in all charges and became an expert in Settlement, Famine, Finance and Education. *See* Buckland, *op. cit.*, p. 136.

52. Home Public Proceedings (India), August 1883, No. 86.
53. Judicial Proceedings (Assam), 1917, No. 53--54.
54. L.E. Rose, *North-East Frontier Agency of India*, p. 58.
55. Home Public Proceedings (India), December 1884, No. 11.
56. Lakhimpur Deputy Commissioner's Collection, No. XII, F. 58, 1904-06.
57. Judicial Proceedings (Assam), 1917, No. 53-54.
58. *Ibid.*, (Bengal), December 1857, Nos. 182-84.
59. L.E. Rose, *op. cit*, p. 62.
60. Shakespeare, *op. cit*, p. VI.
61. See, p. 69, 134.
62. Foreign Secret Proceedings (India), 1871, No. 37-39.
63. *Ibid.*
64. *Ibid.*
65. *Ibid.*
66. W.J. Kaye, *The Administration of the East India Company*, p. 433.
67. Home Public Proceedings (India), October 1873, No. 517.
68. *Ibid.*, February 1874, No. 165. Also *Gazette of India*, 1874, No. 6.
69. *Imperial Gazetteer*, vol. IV, p. 32.
70. Report on the Constitutional Reforms (1919), para 42. Also Ilbert, *The Government of India*, pp. 92-94.
71. Assam Administration Report, 1874-75, part IIA, para 144.
72. *Ibid.*, para 143.
73. *Ibid.*, 1882-83, para 103.
74. (Col.) P.N. Luthra, *Constitutional and Administrative Growth of NEFA*, p. 18.
75. *Ibid.*
76. *Ibid.*, p. 48-49.
77. Foreign Political Proceedings (India), October 1884, No. 366-75.
78. Foreign Proceedings (Assam), April 1884, No. 5.
79. *Ibid.*
80. Foreign Political Proceedings (India), October 1884, No. 366-75.

81. Foreign Proceedings (Assam), April 1884, No. 1.
82. *Ibid.*
83. *Ibid.*, July 1879, No. 4.
84. Judicial Department (Assam), File No. 134J of 1884.
85. Foreign Proceedings (Assam), April 1884, No. 5.
86. Judicial Department (Assam), File No. 134J, Sl. 21, 1884.
87. Political Proceedings (Assam), December 1914, Nos. 14-50.
88. Lakhimpur Deputy Commissioner's Collection, No. XIV, F. 40, 1910-12.
89. Deputy Commissioner's Collection, No. XII, F. 6 of 1906.
90. *Ibid.*
91. R. Reid, *op. cit*, p. 184.
92. Lakhimpur Deputy Commissioner's Collection, No. XIV, of 1910-11, F. 3.
93. *Ibid.*
94. Foreign Proceedings (Assam), March 1874, No. 16.
95. *Ibid.*, No. XVII, F. 17 of 1916-17; Also Collection XII, F. 6 of 1904-08.
96. See p. 101.
97. Deputy Commissioner's Collection, No. XIV, F. 32 of 1909-10.
98. *Ibid.*, Collection No. XII, F. 26 of 1904-08.
99. *Ibid.*, Collection No. XIV, F. 18 of 1909.
100. *Ibid.*, Collection No. XII, F. 26 of 1904-08.
101. Political Proceedings (Assam), April 1914, No. 2.
102. Political Proceedings (Assam), January 1914, No. 25.
103. Political Proceedings (Assam), May 1913, Nos. 1-15.
104. *Ibid.*
105. Political Proceedings (Assam), April 1914, No. 2.
106. Policial Proceedings (Assam), January 1914, No. 25. Also Administration Report, 1937-39.
107. Deputy Commissioner's Collection, No. XVII of 1916-17, F. 11.
108. Political Proceedings (Assam), May 1913, Nos. 1-15. Hitherto there were three political establishment at Dibrugarh, North Lakhimpur and Sadiya; there were two Interpreters, 4 Political Jamadars, 1 Hill Kotoki and five Harkaras under the Deputy Commissioner at Dibrugarh, 1 Political Jamadar and 2 Harkaras at North Lakhimpur under the Sub-divisional Officer 1, and 1 Mishmi Interpreter, 1 Harkara and two Chaprasis at Sadiya under the Political Officer at Sadiya. But now the Frontier Tract was divided into three charges and the Deputy Commissioner of Lakhimpur had only to deal with some Singpho and Naga tribes of the newly created Lakhimpur Frontier Tract. He retained one Political Jamadar at Margherita and two Interpreters at Margherita and Joypur respectively and three Harkaras, two for Margherita and one for Joypur, and two Harkaras at his Dibrugarh office. *See* Political Proceedings, May 1913, No. 8.

    By far the largest charge was supposed to be the Central and

Eastern Sections. Four clerks were appointed for the Office of the Political Officer and one Record Keeper was now appointed for his office. Two clerks were provided for two Assistant Political Officers' offices; two Political Jamadars for the Singphos and the Galong Abors respectively were provided for. Besides, there were two Tibetan Interpreters and two Interpreters for Mijus, 2 for Taraons, 2 for Chulikara Mishmis, 5 for Abors and one each for Khamptis and Singphos. As many as 10 Harkaras and 7 Chaprasis were provided for different offices. In the area under the Political Officer there were three big river crossings. Therefore 10 boatmen were employed; 6 for Sadiya, 2 for the Lohit valley and 2 for Pasighat or the Dibang. *See* Political Proceedings, May 1913, No. 19.

For establishment of Political Officer of the Western Section, one clerk, two Interpreters for Bhutia and Tibetan respectively, 1 Kotoki (for the Akas) and three Chaprasis and two Harkaras to serve in North Lakhimpur were sanctioned. But the Political Officer proposed to have three clerks, 2 Interpreters, 1 Kotoki for the whole year and 4 Kotokis for six months a year, 5 Chaprasis and one Chowkidar for his establishment. As the area under him was full of inaccessible forests having no regular track, he also wanted to have under him one elephant, two Mahuts and two grass-cutters for the elephant. Because of the war exigency, the clerks were not provided for the extra Harkaras and Chaprasis, but the elephant and Mahuts were provided for his service. *See* Political Proceedings, May 1913, No. 62-68.

109. R. Reid, *op. cit*, p. 183.
110. Political Proceedings, January 1914, No. 25.
111. Political Proceedings, December 1911, No. 1.
112. Political Proceedings, (East Bengal and Assam), February 1911, No. 77.
113. Lakhimpur Deputy Commissioner's Collection, No. IX of 1937, Sl. 1-7.
114. Political Proceedings (Assam), December 1914, No. 1-3. Also Collection XII of 1904-05, F. 1.
115. Administrative Jurisdictions, p. 1.
116. Lakhimpur Deputy Commissioner's Collection, No. XII, F. 10, 1904-08.
117. Annual Administration Report, Western Section, 1927-28.
118. *Ibid.*
119. Political Proceedings (Assam), July 1913, No. 56.
120. *Ibid.*
121. *Ibid.*, January 1915, No. 75.
122. *Ibid.*, July 1913, No. 56.
123. *Ibid.*, July 1914, No. 27.
124. Administrative Jurisdictions, p. 1.
125. Report on Indian Constitutional Reforms, p. 129.

126. Basu's *Constitutional Documents*, vol. I, p. 91.
127. Report of the Indian Statutory Commission, vol. II, pp. 108-10.
128. Basu's Constitutional Documents, vol. I, pp. 192-93.
129. *Assam Government Hand Book*, p. 1.
130. P.N. Luthra, *op. cit.*, p. 14.
131. *Ibid.*
132. Administrative Jurisdictions, p. 1.
133. *Ibid.*, p. 2.

5

BRITISH POLICY IN THE NORTH-EAST FRONTIER

Sir Alexander Mackenzie writes in his *Memorandum on the North-East Frontiers of Bengal* that "there has been always a decided policy towards those tribes (North-East Frontier tribes) must be evident".[1] That there had been a policy is undisputed, but it is not easy to trace its development. After the First Anglo-Burmese War, the British established themselves in the valley of the Brahmaputra expelling the Burmese from the country. As a result, they now faced a new problem, the problem of the hill tribes of the Assam Burma frontiers. A policy began to be formulated. It was not a static one. It had to be geared up to meet the exigencies in the frontiers. The essence of the policy was to control the tribal areas through the exercise of limited administrative authority.

The political aspect of the policy at its initial stage was to use the tribes on the eastern fringes, as a screen between the newly acquired territories and the Kingdom of Burma, was initiated.[2] With a view to using the Singpho tracts as a screen against the Burmese, treaties were concluded with the Singpho chiefs and the Khampti chiefs. The Moamaria tracts were also kept separate from the Upper Assam principality of Purandar Singh who was enthroned in 1832 and allowed to rule till 1838, with a view to securing ready supply of provisions for British troops passing through the region. But at Sadiya and Joypur, contingents of British Army were deployed to discharge watch and ward functions on the frontiers.

Meanwhile the study of the Ahom relations with the tribes to the west of Sadiya was undertaken and Bhutanese claims upon the Assam Duars were examined. It was found that the territories on the foothills were extremely rich; they contained valuable forests producing timber, rubber and ivory, and the fertile land in the area would produce surplus revenue if farmers could be helped to take up their cultivation.[3] Coal (1825) and petroleum (1825) were discovered in Upper Assam and tea bushes were found in the jungles nearby (in 1823). Tea was an important item of import of Great Britain from China and a very good amount of gold and silver bullions had to be exported from Great Britain to pay for the Chinese tea. The success of its cultivation in Assam in the later half of the century had a decisive effect on the Company's policy in the North-East Frontier. Moreover, the prospects of coal, mined since 1828, and petroleum, drilled from 1866, enhanced the value of Assam to the Company.

A study of the tribes revealed that, except towards the west, outside the eastern boundary of Bhutan there was no organised kingdom and the tribes there were not capable of resisting the British arms. But the attitude of the powers beyond the Chinese and Tibetan Governments had to be ascertained.[4] Therefore, to begin with, the tribes were called upon to forego their rights over the foothills and the adjacent plains as the lands were necessary for settlement of new ryots and tea plantations in lieu of payment by the British Government. Beginning with the Bhutias of Bhutan, a series of engagements were entered into with the tribes by which they undertook to surrender their rights in these territories in consideration of regular payment of compensation by the Company's Government.[5] The Government, however, did not intend to interfere in the affairs of the tribes who were to be left alone up in their hills.

Payment of 'Posa'

The payment of compensation in the form of *posa* or assignment of a part of revenue was a pre-British system. The Ahoms had introduced the system to reconcile the hill tribes living on the frontier of their kingdom.[6] "The *posa*", writes Mackenzie, "which under the Assam Government was paid to most of the hill tribes bordering on the plains was not, as has been sometimes imagined, an uncertain, ill-defined exaction depending entirely upon the capacity of the different hordes might descend to lay it; it was really a fixed, well-ascertained revenue payment on account of which a corresponding remission was made in the rent of the ryot satisfying it."[7] The Company's Government made a substantial change in the system which had existed under the Ahom rulers. It stopped the direct collection of the dues by the tribes themselves from the ryots, for it led sometimes to quarrels; instead, it began to pay them some cash, later called 'blackmail' collecting at the same time full dues from the ryots who were exempted from payment of dues to the tribesmen. This arrangement cut off direct contact between the ryots and the tribes.

Posa was payment in lieu of dues which the tribes were entitled to claim on the basis of customs recognised by the Ahom rulers. It was basically different from 'blackmail' which initially meant payment to prevent raids and implied that raiders had no recognised right of admission. 'Blackmail' had originated in Bengal in a different context under British rule.[8] The system of payment of 'blackmail' was a British policy which originated in a different context. The aborigines of the Rajmahal Hills in Presidency of Bengal had become a terror to the surrounding country and military expeditions had failed to subdue them. Thereupon the Government of Bengal had introduced the system of cash payment to the tribal chiefs of the region on condition of good behaviour and thereafter the tribes remained quiet and peaceful. The amount paid to the Rajmahal chiefs was larger than that paid to the tribes in the North-East Frontier which was meagre. Nevertheless, the principle was the same, *viz.*, protection of the plains against the ravages of tribal raiders, and it was expected to be as efficacious in the North-East Frontier as in the case of Bengal, for it was expected to impress upon the tribes in an indirect manner the consequences of the risk of their raid in the plains.[9]

Show of Force Against Violations

The consequences of non-compliance with the terms of engagements that different tribes had entered into with the British Government amounted, in some cases, to a 'blockade', that is, the closure of the markets of the plains to the offending tribe. A prohibitive order was issued to the effect that they would not be allowed to come down to the plains to purchase their necessaries; police patrol on the border of their hills was strengthened and watch was kept over their movement. In case of serious offences like murder or kidnapping of British subjects, a demand of surrender of the culprits to the British authority through the native political agent was served for the trial of the offenders under the government. If the demand was not complied with, an expedition to punish the offending tribes was despatched to the hills under a Political Officer with suitable armed forces. The expedition tried first through peaceful means and negotiation to arrest the offenders and realise a fine for non-compliance with the orders of the government and, in case of kidnapping, to secure the release of the persons kidnapped together with those connected with their capture. Sometimes, collective fines were imposed on the village of the offenders or on the tribe in case the culprits could not be arrested. In case the tribesmen resisted in any way the measures of the Administration to punish the guilty or adopted a hostile attitude, the whole village suffered. Fire was set to the houses of the village and all were burnt indiscriminately. The idea behind was to impress upon the whole tribe the dire consequences of the acts of a few guilty persons and to put the wrath of the whole community on the guilty, thus preventing in future the wild acts of its members.

This policy also has been traced back to the days of Ahom rule. The Ahom king Rudra Singh is said to have sent an expedition to the Nishi hills for the violence the Nishis had perpetrated on the plains and the officer in charge of the expedition is said to have brought a number of Nishis to the plains to serve under the government as a punishment.[10] S.K. Bhuyan has equated the Ahom policy to that of the British. He holds that it was a policy of "conciliation backed by a display of force."[11] But our study of the British relations with the frontier tribes shows that the British policy was different. The British law did not permit the molestation or destruction of property of an absconding criminal or his relations, but in th frontier for the supposd crime of a few sometimes the village and even the whole community suffered. It is uncertain as to how far the British Government followed the Ahom practice.

To begin with, the attitude of the tribes towards the British Government did not seem to have been hostile. The Khamptis and the Singphos had accepted the British overtures of friendship and Scott had succeeded in concluding the engagements he had in view. The attitude of the Adis was friendly till the middle of the century. Capt. Neufville wrote in 1830 that the Adis (Abors) were best disposed of all the tribes. The Nishis and the Akas (Hrussos) agreed to accept the money payment in the lieu of their right to collect their *posa* in the Duars. The so-called extra-Bhutan Bhutias (Mompas and Shedukpens) agreed to the British proposal of annual payment by the British Government for surrendering their right of direct collection in their Duars and thereafter never troubled the government or the people of the plains. But after the consolidation of British rule in Assam, the tribes became alive to the inherent dangers of the new system and became restive. The Khamptis were the first to revolt and were assisted by the Singphos. The might of the British arms suppressed the Khamptis attempt to regain their independence. The Khamptis were divided and dispersed over four tracts and brought under the direct control of the government.

The Adis attempt to assert their supremacy over their fellow-tribes, the Mishings (Miris) and over their land inhabited by the Assamese gold-washers, resulted in several raids and subsequent punitive British expeditions into their hills.[12] They had to acknowledge the supremacy of the British over the territories up to the foot-hills in an engagement in which the government promised to pay them regular annual subsidy for surrendering their claims over the lands up to the hills.[13] But the Adis discontent continued to mount; any attempt to interfere in their affairs was resented and opposed even after the government took upon itself the administration of the hills directly.[14]

The Akas and Nishis were giving trouble to the government till practically the end of British rule; their submission and the maintenance of peace depended upon the Administration's capacity to resist them. In the west, the Mompas and the Sherdukpens did not give the government practically any trouble till the end of their period in India. Perhaps they were not interfered with in any way by the British Government and they had an organised system of government of their own which enforced law and order in their hills where they had extensive territories. The Bhutias followed Buddhism which also instilled in them some sort of obedience, humility and regard for engagement.[15]

In the extreme east the Singphos and the Khamptis settled down to peaceful pursuits because they had learnt that the British were more ferocious and unscrupulous than themselves in avenging their raids. The Naga tribes of the Tirap district continued to commit petty thefts and loot for quite a long time as they began to be pushed up the hills with the extension of the tea plantations and the opening up coal mines.

The gradual increase of the tribal raids may be explained

by the sense of their feeling that life inside the hills was hard, and due to poverty and frustration they began raiding the plains below their hills. The government had gradually begun to substitute cash payment in lieu of articles and the money payment which was fixed in the then market price remained fixed althrough the British period.[16] Rather it was reduced in subsequent years. Representation for raising the *posa* met with scant attention and was in no case complied with. The refusal to raise the posa resulted in increase of raids which created a problem for the government as well as the people of the plains, for the government felt an obligation to provide protection to the ryots and the tea planters of the plains who had settled on the foot-hills and the businessmen and industrialists who carried on trade with the hill tribes.[17]

Outposts to Check Tribal Inroads

The government began to set up outposts along routes of the tribal movements to check the inroads of the tribes. But the nature of the terrain made such measures inadequate, for the tribes succeeded in attacking their prey by manoeuvring around the border posts. It may be noted that the Ahom king Kamaleswar Singh had created a number of such border forts to check the inroads of the Nishi tribes.[18] But how far the British were guided in their actions by Ahom precedents in setting up border posts cannot be ascertained. Col. Hopkinson, Commissioner of Assam, wrote as far back as 1862, "A military outpost in Assam is a protection against the hill tribes as an umbrella is against rain, but no more".[19]

Restriction on Plains People's Entry into Hills

Meanwhile the Inner Line Regulation was passed in 1873. It restricted the entry of the plains people into the tribal hills and thus minimised the contact between the hills and the plains as also the possibility of government action for the settlement of disputes between the plains and the hills people.

By passing the Inner Line Regulation and subsequent specification of the Inner Line along the foothills, the government undertook to protect the life and property of the British subjects up to the Inner Line, leaving the tribes beyond to themselves. But except in case of the Akas and the so-called Bhutias of the present Kameng district no restriction was put on the movement of the tribes either inside or outside the Inner Line.[20]

The British administrators were conscious of the fact that the wall they had created by promulgating the Inner Line between the hills and the plains would suffocate the tribes unless some holes were provided for the breathing of the inhabitants of the hills. Therefore, the government took initiative to bring the tribes to the annual fairs which were regularly held along the foothills. But it should be remembered that the term 'fair' as applied to the gatherings of these tribal people in the plains is practically a misnomer. The gathering lasted for over months. The government realised its importance and gave all sorts of encouragement. Government fund was spent to provide shelter, medical care, and proper police guard was provided for security purpose.[21]

Fairs and Popularising European Goods

The 'fairs' played a vital role in the economic life of the tribal people. At the onset of the British period in Assam, we find that the tribal people used to collect Assamese goods and sell their own in the plains market. At Udalguri, the Tibetan caravan sold their merchandise and purchased Assamese products. Some tribes, like the Akas and Nishis used to collect their dues from the plains in kind, that is, in Assamese products like cotton piece-goods, handkerchiefs, Mekhalachaddar, cotton-thread, dao, etc.[22] Even when the Company's Government began to pay them *posa* in cash, the tribal people used to purchase Assamese goods with the money which they now received from the government during the fair.

The British Government began from the very beginning to pursue a policy of popularising the British manufactures. When the government stopped the tribal rights to collect dues from the plains and began to pay them in cash, they used to present the tribal chiefs articles of British produce like wine, cigarette, broad-cloth, handkerchiefs made of cotton and silk, blankets, tobacoo-pipes, knives, etc.[23] The people accustomed to use these things now purchased like goods from the fairs as well. If we look at the items that the tribal people purchased from the fairs, these findings are corroborated. The report on the trade between Assam and the adjoining areas of 1890 shows that the tendency in trade indicated a steady increase in the demands for European cotton-piece goods, European cotton-twist and yarn, brass and copper, opium, salt and silk manufactures.[24]

In popularising the European goods and promoting their sale the fairs had vital importance. Tribal products, mainly raw materials, came down in the market and European goods poured into the tribal territories. A look into the list of articles brought down by the tribal people show that mainly they brought down raw materials, besides little bit of gold and silver, e.g., wool, yak-tail, musk, chillies, spices, wax madder, ivory, rubber, Mishmi-Teeta, mustard, etc.[25] Their purchases show that they bought mainly manufactured good, from later part of the last century, mainly European. The tribal people purchased from the fairs salt, mill-made cotton piece-goods, cotton yarn, opium, glass beads, metal and metal wares all imported from abroad.

Destruction of Tribal Craft and Industry

The British trade policy led to the destruction of tribal cottage industries and crafts. Salt manufacture and weaving were quite familiar with the tribesmen and salt was an important item of tribal export even at the beginning of British penetration into Assam. Hamilton's account bear testimony to it as also the report on trade in 1890.[26]

Pemberton writes that salt was produced at Sadiya and Borhat in good quantity.[27] But the imported salt, sold at cheap rate destroyed its production in the Hills. Weaving and spinning were respectful occupations in the tribal hills of the Frontiers.[28] But the influx of mill-made goods and yarn now discouraged spinning and weaving. Making of dyes from indigenous stuff was a common practice among many tribes. British imports replaced indigenous colours and at the colse of the last century it was given up practically.[29] Iron smelting and forging were known and the tribal people forged their own implements and weapons. But now a tendency developed to purchase manufactured tools from the plains. Craftmanship in metals and ivory of high standard were reported from the Khampti villages.[30] At the beginning of the twentieth century, they became things of history.

Exchange of Goods

Besides these fairs, trade between the plains and hills continued on a limited scale throughout the year. The tribesmen came down to the shops that were set up by the businessmen at some advance posts on the frontiers and the tribal people came to sell their goods and buy their necessaries from them. But such trade was considered hazardous by both the parties, for sometimes the tribal folk thought that they had been cheated and sometimes they looted the shops and murdered the traders. The government did not encourage trading in any and every place, for in case of trouble they were called upon to provide security and punish the offenders. For controlling the tribes, it was necessary that they should trade through particular marts where they could be subjected to control.[31] Sometimes the Government tried to set up stores for supplying the necessities of the tribes and E.T. Dalton had proposed, as early as 1852, to set up a *Gola* below the Adi hills to purchase their products. But such measures were never practically adopted.

Though the government attempt to open stores to provide the necessaries to the tribes did not materialise, some provisions were made by the Administration for the exchange of goods of the hills and plains. The government presented to the tribes at the time of payment of *posa* in cash on the occasion of the fairs some necessary items like broad cloth, handkerchief, cigarettes, wine, salt, etc., and received in turn tribal products like ginger, madder, Mishmi-Teeta, Dao, etc. A lost of articles for the year 1864 shows that the Deputy Commissioner of Lakhimpur presented to the Khampti, Singpho, Adi, Mishmi, Naga and Doania tribes articles worth Rs. 851-12-0 and received in return goods worth Rs. 364-9-0. Over and above this the Commissioner of Assam presented to the same chiefs goods worth Rs. 2,177-2-0 and received from them articles worth Rs. 551-8-0.[32] It may be mentioned here that the original Abore treaty provided for payment in kind and only in 1878 money payment began to be made. The Nishis were provided with some salt and wine in addition to the *posa* in cash.[33]

From the sixties of the nineteenth century, the officers of the Assam Commission became increasingly concerned at the increase of the tribal raids into the plains of Assam and the need of an officer of higher rank on the spot to give quick orders on issues involved was felt. To meet this requirement, Assam was separated from the Presidency of Bengal in 1874. The policy to be pursued in relation to the hill tribes was also examined. The Government of India asked the Bengal Government to prepare a report on the problem like that of J.A.M. Mills' Report of 1854 on Assam in general. The Memorandum on the North-East Frontier of Bengal Written by Alexander Mackenzie, Secretary to the Government of Bengal, came out as a result of the advice in 1869.

Consolidation and no Extension

While discussing the Cachar and Manipur frontier problems, the Deputy Commissioner of Cachar, J.W. Edgar, suggested that for the sake of concerted action, all the Frontier Officers should be brought under one officer who should function under the orders of the Government of Bengal. The Officer in charge of the Frontiers should move from place to place in the region and, receiving reports from the subordinates, dispose of cases as and when required. But the cardinal feature of the policy should be "to acknowledge no territory as ours, unless we are prepared to exercise jurisdiction over the inhabitants and to protect them if attacked.[34]

The leading points in the policy, which he advocated, may be sumed up as follows: (i) the determination not to acknowledge as British territory any area to which British jurisdiction did not extend; (ii) an equally settled determination not to attempt to obtain any control or nominal jurisdiction over tribes settled beyond the boundary so fixed; (iii) endeavours to induce the nearest tribes to settle in the uninhabited jungle between their villages and the administrative districts where cultivation ended; (iv) the tribes so settled to be treated as independent of British administration and not as protected by the government, but provision to be made for supply of fire arms and cash money on condition of their aiding the administration in stopping the inroads of the interior tribes; (v) if, inspite of the above measures, outrages were committed, armed forces to punish the offenders should be despatched without loss of time; and (vi) though the frontier officers should not attempt to bring the tribes under subjection, they should do all in their power to extend their influence over them and encourage them to trade with the plains, impressing upon them the strength of the government and the advantage of good behaviour and peaceful intercourse with the plains. All these depended upon the construction of a good system of roads to facilitate communication between the hills and the plains.[35]

The Government of India was generally in agreement with such a view. While approving the general lines of policy chalked out by the Government of Bengal, it emphasised the point that the object of the government should be not to extend the frontier but to consolidate the portion of the territory already under the possession of the government and to secure its good administration. It further pointed out that it must never be forgotton that while the Government of India acquiesced in the use of all such means of maintaining security on the border, these could be effective only if they were combined with the arrangements calculated at once to overawe and restrain the tribes from attacking the British subjects. "The better prepared we are in this respect, the further will our specific policy be moved from the chance of being misunderstood."[36]

But towards the close of the century, particularly, from the eighties, the need of a local officer functioning among the tribes was felt. The inadequacy of the native agency through which the Deputy Commissioners of Darrang and Lakhimpur conducted their relations with the hill tribes from a distance was realised. Sir Charles Elliot, the then Chief Commissioner of Assam, represented the need for the appointment of a separate officer at Sadiya to conduct the relations with hill tribes of the frontiers while reviewing the effects of the establishment of the Guards posts at Nizamghat on the Abor hills.[37] The issues raised by the proposal of the Chief Commissioner resulted in the appointment of an Assistant Political Officer at Sadiya in 1882.

This appointment, however, did not mean a departure from the traditional policy of the government. In fact, the Government of India under the British Crown did not pursue a policy essentially different from that of the East India Company. It tried to give a trial to the traditional policy by strengthening the administration and reorganising the border post forces as proposed by Col. Hopkinson.

Hopkinson's Proposal

As a matter of fact, Col. Henry Hopkinson, the then Commissioner of Assam, had written to the Government of Bengal in 1862 that "in restraining the savage tribes, which infest our frontier, reliance cannot be placed on one course of policy, but there must be a ready adaptation of expedients to suit evervarying circumstances: some times we must employ coercion pure and simple; sometime blockades; very often a judicious system of subsidising will keep the tribes quiet for a long while; but still the surest foundation on which to build our control over them will be their fear of us." "It is not coercion that has often failed us, but the failure to coerce."[38] "Gold has never yet prevailed in the long run, where there was not iron in reserve to support it," he observed elsewhere.[39]

Col. Hopkinson was the first British officer who had the farsight to see that by the annexation of Assam the British had accepted the obligation to undertake the administration of the tribes of the frontier and he criticised the government for creating a wall of separation between the hills and plains of the province. There would be no rest for the British, he held, in Assam till arrangements for administration of the hills were provided for.[40] In this, he had anticipated the recommdendations of Younghusband in his report submitted after the Tibetan expedition of 1904.[41] Col. Hopkinson wrote in his report to the Government of Bengal: "In taking possession of the country (Assam), we incurred a very distinct and positive obligation to administer it to the best of our ability, and at any expense to secure the most absolute protection to life and property by every means available to a civilised government; and it seems inconsistent with this view of our duty that we should have separated the people of the plains from the people of the hills and have made the former our subjects while we renounced the latter, and left them to prey upon those whom we had professed to take under our protection." "Shut out by us from all civilising or elevating influences but our own, we must be responsible for their condition; their murderous raids, their inhuman sacrifices, lie at our door, and we are as much answerable for their continuance in their present state as it used to be held that the States of North America were answerable for the continuance of slavery in the South."[42]

Col. Hopkinson recommended the construction of roads, which, he held, would "afford facilities for intercourse between the world external" and the world of the tribes. He urged the government to help and aid the missionaries in their work among the tribes.[43]

In reply, an Under Secretary to the Government of India wrote to Col. Hopkinson as follows: "I have seen the necessity of patience and forebearance, which I have studiously exercised towards them (hill tribes); these savages are utterly incapable of reasoning, and I fear they attribute our bearing towards them to timidity and either cannot, or will not understand our real motive." He went on to advice that "what is of utmost importance in dealing with the uncivilised tribes is patience. No one supposes that their civilisation is to be effected in a few years, and no one expects that in endeavouring to conciliate them, the government will not meet with occasional disappointment; but the policy is nonetheless on this account sound and intelligible."[44]

The recommendations of Col. Hopkinson for the reorganisation of the police forces of Assam and the withdrawal of the military and para-military forces from the borders was accepted by the government because it did not mean break with the past policy. He pointed out the inadequacies of the traditional arrangements for the defence of the frontiers of the regularly administered districts by employing the army in the Frontier Service. He observed that the actual frontier duty was performed by the Civil Police who pursued the marauding tribes even into the hills. "Our army administration, our military organisation, the quality of our troops, the conditions of their enlistment, their drill, their discipline, are all, I venture to think inappropriate to the exigencies of hill warfare on our Assam Frontier."[45] He recommended raising of a local force under the orders of the chief civil authority for the defence of the Assam frontier because the management of the frontier tribes was a responsibility of that authority.[46] This view seems to have been accepted by the Government of Bengal which requested the Supreme Government's saction of the proposal to raise a force like that of the Punjab.[47]

The Army did not share the view of Col. Hopkinson. Lt. Col. W. Agnew did not approve the idea of withdrawal of the troops and leave the defence of the province to the proposed Military Police.[48] But Col. Hopkinson held fast to his view. He pointed out that the tribal raids required prompt and quick action. But employment of the army required the sanction of the Government of India and orders through the army channel which meant delay and loss of time.[49] The Government of India was convinced of the necessity of the reorganisation as suggested by Col. Hopkinson. Accordingly, two battalions of Military Police were recruited; detachments of these were posted along the Inner Line and heavy concentrations were made at the district headquarters for march in emergency immediately.[50]

Direct Administration

Thus, so far the administration did not embark upon a new policy. The appointment of the Assistant Political Officer was required by the separation of Frontier Tracts from the regularly administered districts and notification of the Inner Line de-regulationised some parts of the province which now required an officer on the spot to administer those areas. Of course, he was appointed mainly to cultivate friendly relations with the tribal people and help the Deputy Commissioner in frontier politics. But his main duty was to manage the Frontier Tracts which were separated from the regularly administered districts for which purpose the Assam Frontier Tracts Regulation of 1880 had been passed. The reorganisation of the Police Forces or the creation of the Military Police was effected to activise the four planks of the frontier policy, namely, the system of payment of *posa*, the fairs or the safety-valve, the blockade, and the border posts to guard the inroads of the frontier tribes. The traditional policy initiated from the very beginning was given a chance to prove its efficacy.

The appointment of the Assistant Political Officer at Sadiya brought home the necessity of direct administration of the Frontier Tracts. So long the conduct of relations with the tribes was left with the Kotokis on whom the British officers put reliance and to whom they paid scanty attention. Now the British officer toured the tribal tracts and prepared reports which were read with care and attention and measures suggested by him were considered carefully. At the close of the century again the frontier policy was reopended for consideration by the Lt. Governor of Eastern bengal and Assam on the recommendations of Noel Williamson, the successor of F.J. Needham.[51]

Noel Williamson who joined as Assistant Political Officer at Sadiya in 1905 acted with indefatigable energy, courage, tact and enthusiasm in putting the frontier service on a new basis till his murder in the Abor hills in 1911. He carried on extensive tours, sometimes unaccompanied by the usual contingents of guards and pomp and splendour, and made good friends with the tribesmen. He had envisaged a course of gradual penetration of frontier hills which ultimately prevailed though the circumstances which burnt the pillars of the frontier policy were different. It was the flame of the fire of the breath of the Chinese Dragon which burnt the pillars of the frontier policy.

Like the realist Williamson the Lt. Governor of the new province of Eastern Bengal and Assam, Sir Lancelot Hare, was also a practical man. He lent his support for the Foward policy of his Assistant Political Officer in the Frontiers. In 1907, he wrote to the Government of India that the "policy of aloofness was foredoomed to failure", and advocated the adoption of the policy of direct and immediate administration of the British territories. Of course, he did not recommend the policy of advancing the administrative centres inside the hills as recommended by Williamson.[52] But the Government of India turned down his proposal in its entirely, and though they accepted the necessity of protecting the British territory, forbade expeditions to be sent beyond the Outer Line.

But the Chinese movement across the boundary (1908-11) became a matter of concern for the Government of Eastern Bengal and Assam. Reports of Chinese advance into the Aka hills, almost near the administrative boundary of the Assam district of Darrange, Adi hills and Mishmi hills forced the Government of India to propose to the Secretary of State for India to secure as soon as possible a sound strategic boundary between the two countries (India and Tibet) pending the question of demarcation till the explorations were over, as proposed by the Government of Eastern Bengal and Assam. The Government of Eastern Bengal and Assam, however, suggested the erection of a number of boundary pillars along the boundary between the two countries on the common trade routes following the traditional boundary of the two countries. The object of this measure was to be explained to the tribes.[53]

The proposal of the Local Government did not, however, suggest a third line beyond the so-called Outer Line; it meant the fixing up of the traditional boundary between India and Tibet, beyond the Outer Line, and not the shifting of the Outer Line from the foothills to the international boundary. In the second place, they proposed that in future the policy of the government should be one of loose political control, "having as its object the minimum of interference compatible with the necessity of protecting the tribesmen from unprovoked aggression, the responsibility of whose protection would have to be assumed by the government and at the same time preventing them from the violating either the administrative border or the Chinese territory". The tribes should be left to themselves as much as possible, but care should be taken to avoid any action or inaction as the case might be which might lead to inculcate in their mind any undue sense of independence as it had happened in the North-East Frontier. They suggested that before the finalisation of measures to be adopted with regard to them, it would be necessary to take effective steps to prevent the violation of the new external boundary as they had proposed.[54]

The Government of India accepted the recommendation but did not permit the extension of the administrative boundary beyond the existing line. They also sanctioned exploratory and survey expeditions to be sent to the Mishmi, Mishing and Nishi Hills. They addressed a despatch to the Secretary of State for India on the frontier issues recommending the lines of action proposed by the Government of Eastern Bengal and Assam, C.A. Bell and the General Staff of the Army. The Secretary of State, however, preferred not to push the posts within the tracts. The Government of India protested, for they contemplated to exercise loose political control over the tribes which could not be done from beyond the Inner Line boundary. The Secretary of State for India now concurred with the proposal and the hill tracts were subsequently divided into three sections as proposed in 1914.[55]

It is interesting to note that the Simla Conference, which the British Officers like Charles Bell and Henry McMahon utilised to finalise the Indo-Tibetan boundary, did not engage the attention of the Government of India insofar as they suggested creation of an administrative apparatus for the frontier region. In the Memorandum appended to the proceedings of the Simla Conference, Charles Bell had suggested the creation of new administration consisting of Bhutan, Sikkim, Tibet, Tawang and the North-Eastern Frontier Tracts. He held that though the frontier tribes were ethnologically different from the Tibetans, they had close relation with the Tibetans and it was imperative to pursue a common policy towards the frontiers. Besides one agency for the entire belt would result in economy and service in a large agency would be more popular than in smaller ones in different regions. He urged that in any case the frontier administration should be placed under the Foreign Department of the Government of India than under the Local

Administration of Assam and he recommended for the appointment of a separate discreet and tactful British Officer for Tawang.[56]

Sir Henry McMahon did not give much importance to what Charles Bell had suggested. He agreed that military aid should be given to the Tibetan authorities as Charles Bell had also suggested and recommended for the appointment of a separate British Officer for Tawang too. Next he thought of clearing the Chinese out of the Tibetan territories and set-up a strong British post at Gyantse.

But practically no arrangement was made for the proper and direct administration of the tribal tracts. The Government of India did not even forward the proceedings of the Simla Conference to the Local Administration and did not recommend any special measure for implementation of the recommendations of Henry McMahon or Charles Bell.[57] The Political Officers who continued to be under the Local Administration were instructed to exercise loose political control over the tribes. The wall of separation, the Inner Line, was also not removed. The Government of India was influenced by the "buffer" concept of Sir Henry mcMahon. They seem to have believed that it was not the boundary line which mattered in a tract like the North-Eastern Frontier; what was important was a "buffer" which meant a belt of neutral territory between the two countries. Moreover, Sir Henry McMahon had cautioned the Government of India not to offend the Tibetan vested interests in the tribal tracts south of the McMahon Line. McMahon's recommendation to send a British officer to proceed to the Tawang area and arrange for its administration, therefore, received no attention from the British Indian Government.[58]

Proposal for Simple Administration

Capt. Nevill who was in charge of the Balipara Frontier Tract, as the western section of the Frontier Tracts was known from 1919, paid a visit to Mompa territory and reported that in order to bring about a state of prosperity in this region and to promote the growth of trade it was necessary to establish some sort of simple administration within the Frontier Tracts by establishing outposts attached with dispensaries well connected by roads. Nevill tried to buttress his arguments to bring the hills under close control by evaluating the political developments in China and Tibet. He pointed out, "as soon as China settles down, this Tibetan frontier will become of great importance. China has still its eyes on Tibet and on Lhasa; the pro-Chinese party is growing in influence and should China gain control of Tibet, the Tawang country is particularly adapted for a secret and easy entrance into India. Russia is also trying to establish her influence in Tibet and, if successful, could safely and secretly send her emissaries into India by this route."[59] But then the Government of India dis not take interest in the affairs of the frontier tribes and they shelved the issue of frontier problem by sending a despatch to the Secretary of State.

After the First World War, a spirit of humanism spread far and wide in the world. People began to talk of human rights and protest against exploitation. The concept of 'Mandate' was developed for protecting the interest of the underdeveloped peoples under the supervision of the League of Nations. As a part of this worldwide change of outlook, the protection of tribal rights now caught the attention of the philanthropic people. In India, British administrators like J.P. Mill and J.H. Hutton who served in the hills in the north-east were struck by the exploitation of the simple tribal people by adventurers and businessmen which, if not actively patronised, was at least tolerated by the government. Essays appeared in journals to enlist popular support for stopping such practices towards the tribal people.[60] The government now adopted a more or less benevolent attitude towards the tribal people. But in an atmosphere of political tension between the rulers and the politically conscious sections of the Indian nation, the government solicitude for tribal welfare was utilised more for segregation of the tribal folk from the rest of the Indian community than for actual amelioration of their condition.

Isolating Tribal Areas from Regular Administration

The policy of segregation was given shape for the first time in the Reforms of 1919 although its beginnings may be traced in the late 19th century. It has already been observed that the Scheduled Districts Act was passed in 1874 to provide for the administration of the tribal areas in a rough and ready manner and the Inner Line Regulation of 1873 began to be applied to segregate tribal areas of the North-East Frontier from 1875 onwards. When Edwin Montagu, in concert with Lord Chelmsford, under the directions of the House of Commons, prepared their report on constitutional reforms in India, they recommended measures to be taken for reconstruction of the Indian Government, but the tribal issue was not given any new complexion. While recommending the increasing association of Indians in every branch of administration and "the gradual development of self-governing institutions with a view to progressive realisation of responsible government in India as an integral part of the British Empire", they did not deem it proper to either encourage the tribal people to participate in their own administration or to associate the Indian ministers and legislators with the administration of the tribal hills of the frontiers.[61]

The Mont-Ford scheme, which involved the division of functions of the Provincial Government between elected Indian Ministers and appointed Executive Councillors, proposed to keep the tribal areas separate from the regularly administered territory, on the ground that in those areas "there was no material on which to found political institutions."[62] It was held that the tracts mentioned in the schedules and appendices to the Scheduled Districts Act, 1874, with "certain exceptions and possibly certain additions, should be reserved for further consideration." But the "typically backward tracts (frontiers) should be excluded from the jurisdiction of the reformed provincial governments and administered by the head of the province."[63] In these areas, therefore, the old system was to continue, and the tribes were to be kept apart—ostensibly for their own welfare—from the people of the plains.

The reaction of the Government of India to the recommendations of the Joint Report was embodied in the Ninth Despatch on the Constitutional Reforms. The Government of India was anxious to limit exclusion as much as possible both in its local extent and in its degree. With this end in view, it estimated the degree of backwardness of each of the tracts and recommended varying degrees of exclusion to conform with such estimates. The recommendation that the backward tracts should be directly administered by the Governors was not finally carried out, except in the Shan States of Burma.[64] For Assam, the reserved half of the government was given full discretion to administer the tracts as per enactments under the Government of India Act, 1919.

The Government of India Act, 1915, as amended by the Government of India Act, 1919, which carried into effect the recommendations of the Mont-Ford Report provided, *inter alia*, that "the Governor-General in Council may declare any territory in British India to be a 'Backward Tract' and may, by notification, with such saction as aforesaid, direct that this Act shall apply to that territory subject to such exceptions and modifications as may be prescribed in the modifications."[65] When the Reforms were introduced in Assam in 1920, the frontiers affairs were placed under the reserved half of the government and the elected half of the government did not have any jurisdiction over them. This was a modified policy of segregation, for the reserved half of the government was not under the administrative or financial control of the Legislature.

Increasing British Influence

Meanwhile the government has pursued a policy of bringing

the frontier territory under its political influence. the tour reports of the Political Officers showed the popularity of the government in the tribal hills. A little good humour by the government officers endeared the government to the tribal folk. While the government officials in the plains dreaded the Indian Nationalists, they felt quite confortable in the tribal territory. Rather in Christian areas, like the Lushai hills and the Naga hills, they felt secure and firm. Step by step they developed the theory of exploitation of the tribal people by the Indians and they claimed to stand against such exploitation as friends of the tribal people.

By the time of the coming of the Statutory Commission, the officers serving in the frontiers and adjacent tribal hills, like the Lushai and Naga hills, had arrived at the conclusion that the British would withdraw some day from India and Burma, but if they could create a separate tribal belt along the North-East Frontiers they might continue to possess a foothold on Indian territory. The result of the policy of keeping the frontier tribes in isolation would be, they hoped, the perpetuation of the control in a part of this country. The conversion of the tribal people in the Lushai and Naga hills into Christianity had accustomed them to look upon the British as their co-religionists and upon the Indian people as heathens and exploiters. The Nagas put before the Simon Commission a demand to keep their areas excluded from the authority of the Indian Government, and anti-Congress ryots broke out in Shillong, the capital of Assam, which was located in the Khasi area.[66] In Burma, the British officers, by manipulating affairs in the Shan States and in the unadministered areas in the northern triangle of Burma on the Indian border, succeeded in developing in the local population a separatist outlook. The Burma Government wrote, "These.... areas are all unfit to participate in a constitution on representative lines suitable for Burma proper. Their peoples are educationally backward, and have evinced no desire to be linked with the Burmans, who in turn betray little interest in these hills tracts."[67] The calculating

British officers of the Assam Government now thought on the same lines and wanted to exclude the North-East Frontier hills from India.

Asked for opinions on the reforms and further changes in the mode of government, the officers of the frontiers as well as hills areas of Assam advocated exclusion of the hills tribes of the frontiers and the Hill Districts of Assam from the jurisdiction of the Indian ministers who, it was understood, would assume—on the abolition of the system of Dyarchy—control of entire provincial government. J.H. Hutton, Deputy Commissioner of Naga Hills District, wrote an exhaustive letter to the Government of Assam giving the history of the hill areas; basing his arguments on the social, economic, religious and cultural grounds of the region, he propagated the idea of a separate state for the hill tribes.[68] On the Burmese side, a similar proposal was made to unite the northern triangle of Burma and the Shan States with the hill areas on the north-eastern corner of India and create a separate state.[69] But the Government of Assam, as suggested by its Political Officers, urged retention of the frontier tracts under direct control and authority of the Governor-General in Council who would be responsible only to the British Parliament.

Development and Education of Tribals

In view of this trend of opinion in official circles the Simon Commission, which was appointed to report on further progress on constitutional reforms in India, did not find it possible to recommend the incorporation of the hill tracts of the North-East Frontier for administrative purposes in the province of Assam. It wrote that the "backward tracts of Assam are of great importance and extent, and nowhere in India is the contrast between the life and outlook of these wild hill-men and the totally distinct civilisation of the plains more manifest...." The report went on, "To the economic self-sufficiency of the indigenous hill races—the Nagas, Kukis,

Mishmis, and the rest the tea-planters and the immigrant Bengali alike—constitute a real damger."[70] The Commission recommended that the British Parliament should avow its special obligation for the tribal folk, educate them to stand on their own feet, give them protection against exploitation, and prevent their raids on the plains. The hills were, or course, not to be branded as backward tracts but termed as 'excluded areas'. For the administration of the tribal areas, excluded from the regularly administered districts of the province, the Governor-General in Council should use the agency of the Governor.[71]

The Commission expected that for developing the tribal areas and for educating the tribal people, huge money would be required. The money would not be forthcoming from the revenue of a poor State like Assam. Further the Commission apprehended that the representatives of the provincial legislature would not vote for the appropriation of money for development purposes in the hill tracts since that would not immediately benefit the constituencies of the members who would vote.[72] Perhaps the Commission applied a British analogy to an Indian perspective; in any case it overlooked the fact that the Federal Government could provide the money for development purposes and yet put the charge of the tribal affairs under the Provincial Government. The Government of Assam, controlled by the elected representatives, who came from the vicinity of the tribal tracts and who understood the tribal problems and possibilities much better, could undertake the development work more meaningfully and satisfactorily. In the prevailing atmosphere of distrust and political animosity, the British statesmen and administrators alike wanted to sympathise with the tribal folk and alienate them from the Indian people though the tribal people were a part and parcel of the myriad Indian population.

But inspite of the recommendations of the Simon Commission, the British Prime Minister disavowed any intention of the British Parliament to control any territory of British India; the hopes of the British officers in the tribal areas were thus dashed to the ground.[73] The Government of India now asked for reconsideration of the issues of Frontier administration by the Government of Assam since the previous scheme of retention of tribal territory under the British Parliament could not be worked upon after declaration of the British Prime Minister.[74] The Government of Assam, nevertheless, propsed the perpetuation of the separation of the tribal tracts of the frontiers from the regularly administered areas in the province of Assam. It wrote, "Its (tribal tracts) progressive absorption into the province of Assam in the past was forced upon the government by the unavoidable necessity of securing from the marauding and revengeful raids of its denizens, the safety of the plain districts for which the government had made itself responsible...what was needed for the future is a policy of development and unification on lines suited to the genius of the hill people, an object in itself of formidable magnitude."[75]

The formulation of such a policy could no longer be divorced from political factors. The Government of Assam pointed out that there had already developed in the hills an anti-Indian feeling, probably due to a fear of economic exploitation. It was even apprehensive that a change in policy with regard to the frontiers might provoke rebellion. Therefore, it recommended that in developing a scheme of administration for the hill tribes "the essence of the system in the administration of the definitely excluded areas would the personal rule of the Governor exercised through selected officers."[76] In couse of time, it suggested, an indigenous staff of officers of all ranks might be provided for the Hill Districts and frontiers.

The Government of India Act, 1935, which was passed after taking into consideration the Simon Commission's recommendations as well as the points of view of the provincial governments concerned with tribal areas, provided in sections 91 and 92 that His Majesty by an order in Council might declare some territory in India as "Excluded Area" or "Partially Excluded Area" and empower the Governor of a province to administer that area under the authority of the Governor-General. The Governor was given discretion to extend Acts or parts thereof passed by any provincial legislature or the federal legislature to the excluded areas which otherwise would not apply there. Moreover, the Governor was given the power to prepare and approve drafts of Regulations for the peace and good government of the excluded areas with the previous sanction of the Governor-General in Ccuncil.[77]

Gaining Influence in Tibet

Now the problem of the delineation of the Frontier Tracts cropped up when the question of notification of the boundary of the excluded areas and the definition of the Indo-Burmese boundary came up before the King in Council. In the meantime, an English botanist W.F. Kingdon-Ward, who toured the Dafla Hill areas, was arrested by the Tibetan authorities for crossing the Indian boundary. The British Government secured his release and said Kingdon-Ward, in an article, posed once again the problem of the McMahon Line.[78] The Government of India, which had almost forgotten the issue of McMahon Line and had not even informed the Local Government of Assam about the delineation of the boundary at the Simla Conference, was not at a loss. It was now found that the Russians had once again began—in view of the increasing Russo-Mongolian collaboration and the conclusion of the Russo-Mongolian Protocol of Mutual Assistance (1936) it now became imperative to pursue the Indo-Tibetan boundary as agreed to in 1914 in the Simla Conference—to gain influence in Tibet. As early as 1927, a Russo-Mongolian delegation visited Lhasa and another Military Officer remained in Lhasa in 1928.[79]

In view of these, the Governor of Assam Sir Robert Reid proposed that a tactful and discreet officer with knowledge of frontier diplomacy should be posted, at least for the summer months, at Tawang with instructions: (i) to collect a light tax, leaving to the people management of their own affairs, (ii) to offer an assurance to owners of private estates that their proprietory rights would be respected; and (iii) to give an under taking to the Tawang monastery that the Tibetan Government would be consulted whenever a new Head Lama was appointed.[80]

Capt. Lightfoot, who held the post of Political Officer in Balipara Frontier Tract, was authorised to lead an expedition to Tawang in 1938 and on his return he submitted a report which contained almost the same recommendations as were proposed by Capt. Nevill 24 years before, Capt. Lightfoot proposed that the Tibetan Government should be asked to withdraw their officials and assistants from south of the Mcmahon Line which would terminate automatically the exactions and forced labour and at the same time establish British title over the area. He advised to make the Tawang Monastery a purely Mompa affair in default of which the Tibetan intrigues would continue and also to abolish the system of payment in kind which entailed forced labour. He suggested to abolish the monopoly in salt and rice enjoyed by Tibetan officials. Further, he recommended establishment of a control area at Tawang and Dirangzong where Political Agents ought to be appointed who would manage tribal affairs through the Panchayats consisting of the representatives of the village headmen and monastic council and imposition of a house tax of Rs. 5 per annum in assertion of the British jurisdiction over the tribes of the area. The duty of the Agent would be to collect the house tax and hear appeals from the Panchayats. The Senior Agents were to visit the areas of the Junior Agents and reports were to visit the areas of the Junior Agents and reports were to be sent to the Political Officer whose subordinates the Agents would be. The Political Officer might hear appeals from the Political Agents.[81]

The acting Governor of Assam, Hogg, forwarded the recommendations of Capt. Lightfoot and observed that the existing situation in Tawang area was intolerable and should be terminated as early as possible. He also advocated the creation of control area within the Mompa hills under Political Agents as recommended by the Political officer and imposition of a house tax of Rs. 5 in substitution of the existing tax in kind. He recommended the proposal to reconstitute the Tawang Monastery excluding the Tibetan officials and abolition of salt and rice monopoly at Dirangzong. Further, he requested the Government of India to approve an expedition to Tawang even if the measures proposed were not approved for implementation.[82]

But the world was heading towards the Second Great War. Sir Henry Tuynam, acting Governor of Assam, in a letter to the Governor-General emphasised the risk of antagonising Tibet-China and financial involvement for the measure. The Government of India decided to implement the policy as proposed after one year and the proposed tour was not authorised since that might result in permanent occupation of the Mompa Tracts and, thus, entail an obligation to provide for its administration. When the World War broke out and the British were involved in it as a belligerent, they began to muster all their resources to win the war in Europe and for a time the affairs in the North-East Frontier were subordinated to war considerations. A Conference of Political Officers held in 1940 at Shillong decided not to pursue the occupation of Tawang area and offend the Tibetan sentiment over the issue.[83]

If the Government of India's attitude towards the Western Hills of the North-East Frontier was a little hesitating and procrastinating, its support for implementing the new policy in the Abor and Mishmi hills was not lacking. The British Government tried to build up a chain of outposts along the border of Abor and Mishmi hills and a number of control areas to exercise British jurisdiction.[84] Trading posts which benefited the people at large and reconciled them to the new government were opened in the interior as brigade tracks were constructed to connect the border from within the country. The Governor's proposal to extend control area as proposed by the Political Officer of Abor hills was approved by the Government of India in 1914, with the proviso that no extra cost should be incurred as it was then engaged in the Great War. The proposal of the Local Government to resist the Tibetan tax collectors from within the McMahon Line, of course, did not get approval of the Indian Government as it still followed the policy of good humouring China.[85]

The veil of the Frontier drama, however, was again lifted when the Japanese overran the whole of South-East Asia, and entered into India through Manipur and Nagaland in 1943. The rapid advance of the Japanese through the tribal territories surprised the british authorities and the difficulty of military movement through these hills made them aware of the backwardness of the region. Increasing Chinese activity in Tibet once again made the government uneasy over the situation in Tawang and as suggested by Chief of Staff Sir Reid, Governor of Assam recommended the occupation of Tawang to forestall Chinese advance in the region. J.P. Mill went up the hills and opened an advanced post in Dirang Dzong area.[86] The development of the area was undertaken immediately and to help and advise the Governor of Assam for development of the tribal region an advisor of the rank of Secretary to the Government was placed at his disposal, but the gradual recession of the Japanese invasion again removed priority on tribal development.

Preserving Influence Pockets before Departure

Meanwhile, when talks of transferring power to the Indians began, British politicians, scholars and administrators began to moot projects which would enable the British Crown to maintain a foothold in a part of the Indian territory in the name of protecting the tribal people and strengthening the defence of India. The union of the North-East Frontier, together with the Naga, Lushai and North Cachar Hills of India, with the northern triangle and Shan States of Burma seemed to them to provide a strategic platform wherefrom watch could be kept over Communist China, Burma, India and East Pakistan (now Bangladesh). Reginald Coupland, who had accompanied Sir Stafford Cripps, while delivering a talk at Oxford in 1945, developed on the British obligation to the tribal people of India as also of the British obligation for the defence of India.[87] The learned professor was still troubled by the thought of the white-man's burden in the East. He suggested the creation of a Crown Colony in the North-East of India. Including the Shan State and the northern triangle of Burma. He further advocated the encouragement of the Christian missions to undertake humanitarian and welfare measures in the area. In India and Burma, people scented a design by the British to keep under their domination portions of Indian and Burmese territory to serve as bases of British imperialism.[88] All suspicions, however, were laid at rest when the Labour Government that came to power in Britain after the World War, left the entire territory of India to the independent Indian Government on whom then developed the great task of harmonising tribal needs and aspirations with the larger interests and security of the country.

Conclusion

Thus reviewing the British policy in the North-East Frontier Agency Area, it can be concluded that, to begin with, the British policy was to wait and watch the existing conditions and then gradually they began to enter into a system of engagement with the hill tribes of the region. The engagements provided them an opportunity to sense the reaction of the cross-country Powers on British relations with the tribes and at the same time provided a basis of intercourse with the tribes. It may be mentioned in this context that the Mughals from whom the British gradually assumed sovereignty of India had similarly dealt with the indigenous potentates of India.[89] The petty chiefs of Hindustan were gradually brought under the complete control of the Mughal Emperors when the former began to assume obligations to the latter. The British Government in Assam introduced Mouzardi system for the collection of revenue in the Brahmaputra valley and thus created a class of people who were regarded by the local people as their representatives but were bound to the Government by the factor of their position.[90] In the frontier hills, they similarly entered into engagements with the different tribes and thus brought them under some obligations and later on, as and when necessary, the British imposed their control over them.

Again, a dividing line in British policy may be found in the year 1910. Till that year the British policy in relation to the North-East Frontier was to keep the frontier tribes in good humour by providing them some "blackmail" on condition of their good behaviour. They were hedged in by promulgating the Inner Line which was guarded by Frontier posts. But to provide for the economic requirements of the tribes, 'fairs' were held along their foothills. In case of any tribal raid on the plains villages on this side of the Inner Line, punitive expeditions were sent to chastise the attacking tribe. No interference was made in the purely tribal affairs. No agency operated for administration within the hills. But from 1910 this policy was substituted by the policy of direct control of the tribes from within the hills and the Indo-Tibetan border, which had remained undefined, was settled. The control of the Government was pushed to the border which was, of course, a strategic line drawn following the natural line of the Himalayas.

If the policy with regard to the tribal people in the North-East was that of non-interference in tribal affairs and non-exercise of jurisdiction, either political or administrative, beyond the Outer Line before 1914, after that year political jurisdiction was extended up to the international border which was now known and consequently, British jurisdiction now ran up to a definite area. Political and administrative agencies which did not operate before beyond the Outer Line, were now functioning beyond that line. Communication within the hills were neglected till now, but henceforth they began to be opened up and developed and this facilitated defence requirements but benefited the people of the region. Medical establishments with police posts were established in some places which won over the hearts of the people by their services. While the police succeeded in stopping Tibetan exploitation and inter-tribal blood feuds, the medicalmen became friends of the people by attending on the sufferers. The government, which disregarded the tribal rights and privileges, now posed as friends to protect the tribals from external aggression and internal enemies and diseases.

Major Sitaram Johri has rightly observed, "During and before the 19th century, the United States and of the United Kingdom's policy towards the aborigines of North America and Australia was to disregard their rights."[91] Pages of history are full of accounts of exploitation by the European colonists in United States of the Red Indians who were even hunted down and dispersed from the lands as the Frontiers men advanced towards the Pacific. The instances of British exploitation of tribal rights in India, particularly in Assam, are abundant. In fact, such things did not prick the conscience of the adventurers who ventured out of their home for riches. The commercial attitude, a legacy of the East India Company, was handed down to the British merchants in India whose interest the Supreme and Provincial Governments were bound to protect, even after the transfer of India to the Crown. No wonder, the appeal of T.M. Lewin in 1869, "let us not govern these hills for ourselves, but administer the country for the well-being and happiness of the people dwelling there", fell on deaf ears.[92]

REFERENCES

1. A. Mackenzie, *Memorandum*, p. 71.
2. *Ibid.*, p. 114.
3. Foreign Political Proceedings (India), 12 September 1838.
4. Bengal Papers in Assam State Archives, 1873-77, F. 22.
5. Judicial Proceedings (Bengal), June 1865, No. 71.

6. *Ibid.*
7. Mackenzie, *History*, p. 5.
8. Judicial Proceedings (Bengal), June 1865, No. 73.
9. *Ibid.*
10. L. Devi, *op. cit.*, p. 179.
11. S.K. Bhuyan, *Anglo-Assamese Relations*, p. 33.
12. *Ibid.*, pp. 91-95.
13. *Ibid.*, p. 96.
14. *Ibid.*, pp. 101-02.
15. Elwin, *The Art*, p. 16.
16. Foreign Political Proceedings (Assam), March 1885, No. 34.
17. Lakhimpur Deputy Commissioner's Collection, No. xii, F. 59, 1904-08.
18. G.C. Barua, *Ahom Buranji*, p. 61.
19. Foreign Political Proceedings (India), June 1866, Nos. 37-39.
20. Lakhimpur Deputy Commissioner's Collection, No. xiv, F. 36, 1910-12.
21. Report on the trade between Assam and the adjoining Foreign Countries, 1890.
22. Revenue Proceedings (Bengal), No. 5 of 11, August 1834.
23. Political Proceedings (Bengal), May 1864.
24. Report on the trade between Asam and the adjoining Foreign Countries, 1890.
25. *Ibid.*
26. S.K. Bhuyan, (ed.), *An Account of Assam*, p. 28.
27. Pemberton, (Capt.) R.B., *Report on the Eastern Frontier of British India*, p. 84.
28. H.F. Sinman, *A Monograph on Cotton.*
29. W.A.M. Duncan, *A Monograph on Dying.*
30. E.T. Dalton, *op. cit.*, p. 7.
31. Lakhimpur Deputy Commissioner's Collection, No. xii, F. 2, 1904-08.
32. Political Proceedings (Bengal), May 1864, 'B' Nos. 24-26.
33. Lakhimpur Deputy Commissioner's Collection, No. xii, F. 7, 1886.
34. Judicial Political Proceedings (Bengal), January 1870, No. 80.
35. *Ibid.*
36. Foreign Political Proceedings (India), June 1865, No. 82.
37. Lakhimpur Deputy Commissioner's Collection, No. xii, F. 59, 1904-08.
38. Political Proceedings (Bengal), June 1866, Nos. 37-39.
39. Foreign Political Proceedings (India), 1865, Nos. 80-82.
40. Political Proceedings (Bengal), June 1866, Nos. 37-39.
41. F. Younghusband, *India and Tibet*, p. 428.
42. Political Proceedings (Bengal), June 1866, Nos. 37-39.
43. *Ibid.*
44. *Ibid.*

45. *Ibid.*
46. *Ibid.*
47. *Ibid.*
48. Judicial Proceedings (Bengal), May 1870, No. 202.
49. Political Proceedings (Bengal), June 1866, Nos. 37-39.
50. L.W. Shakespeare, *op. cit.*, p. 8.
51. Lakhimpur Deputy Commissioner's Collection, No. xii, F. 6, 1904-08.
52. *Ibid.*, F. 59.
53. *Ibid.*, No. 204.
54. *Ibid.*
55. *Ibid.*
56. Foreign Political (Secret) Proceedings (India), May 1915, Nos. 36-50.
57. P. Mehra, *The McMahon Line and After*, p. 425.
58. Proceedings of the Governor's Secretariat, December 1937, Nos. 1-19.
59. Annual Administration Report, Western Section, North-East Frontier, 1927-28.
60. *Journal of Royal Asiatic Society of Bengal*, vol. lxix, p. LIII: Census Report of India, 1931, p. IV.
61. Report on Indian Constitutional Reforms, 1918, p. 1.
62. *Ibid.*, p. 129.
63. *Ibid.*
64. Report of the Indian Statutory Commission, vol. I, p. 159.
65. D. Basu, *Constitutional Documents*, vol. I, p. 91.
66. *Tribal Awakening*, p. 101.
67. Report of the Indian Statutory Commission, vol. II, p. 82.
68. Report on Constitutional Reforms, 1930, vol. XIV, pp. 111-17.
69. D. Woodman, *The Making of Burma*, p. 520.
70. Report of the Indian Statutory Commission, vol. I, pp. 75-76.
71. *Ibid.*, vol. II, pp. 109-10.
72. *Ibid.*
73. Political Proceedings (Assam), September 1931, Nos. 130-34.
74. *Ibid.*
75. *Ibid.*
76. *Ibid.*
77. D. Basu, *op. cit.*, p. 93.
78. P. Mehra, *op. cit.*, p. 420.
79. *Ibid*, p. 423.
80. Proceedings of the Government Secretariat, June 1940, Nos. 535-636.
81. *Ibid.*
82. *Ibid.*
83. K. Gupta, *The Hidden History of the Sino-Indian Frontier*, p. 86.
84. Political Proceedings (Assam), December, 1914, Nos. 19-54.

85. R. Reid, *op. cit.*, p. 264.
86. K. Gupta, *op. cit.*, p. 90.
87. R. Coupland, *The Future of India: Report on the Constitutional Problems in India*, pp. 164-65.
88. *Ibid.*
89. W.H. Moreland, "*The Revenue System of the Mughal Empire*," *The Cambridge, History of India*, p. 455.
90. M. Bora, *Assam in 1857*, p. 46.
91. S. Johri, *op. cit.*, p. 62.
92. V. Elwin, *North-East Frontier*, p. xix.

6

CONSTITUTIONAL AND ADMINISTRATIVE GROWTH OF ARUNACHAL PRADESH

Independent India inherited a precarious legacy in the North-East Frontier. The tribes had lived, as we have seen, a 'life unaffected by the current of history' and had developed an isolationist psychology and attitude.[1] No regular attempt had been made to raise them in the scale of civilisation or to provide any system of direct administration, though the Frontier Tracts were divided into three charges in 1914; and in 1919 the names of the Eastern and Western Sections of the Frontier Tracts were changed into Sadiya Frontier Tract and Balipara Frontier Tract, respectively. Roads, postal communication, schools, hospitals etc. did not exist. Practically the tribes were living in a paradise of their own almost ignorant of the outside world.

The course of the Second World War did not affect in any way the tribes of the North-East Frontier, though a road was constructed to connect through the present Tirap District, across the Pathkye range and Upper Burma to connect Nationalist China.[2] But the Japanese invasion of India through the Naga Hills, adjacent to the Tirap and Tuengsang districts, had a dangerous sequel. For the First time the British felt the necessity of developing the tribal territories in the North-East Frontier and it was at that time that an Adviser was placed under the Governor of Assam in

1943 to aid and advise on the development of the tribal territories.[3] Further by a Regulation Eastern tracts of the Sadiya Frontier Tract was separated and a new independent charge of Tirap Frontier Tract was created with Margherita as its headquarters; and in 1946 Balipara Frontier Tract was subdivided into two units named, Sela Sub-Agency and Subansiri Area.[4] Otherwise the North-East Frontier territories remained quite unaffected by the Great War.

The crude agency created by the British to administer the tribal territories began to develop after independence. At the time of independence there were altogether three Political Officers for the Frontier territories and a few substaff to cater to the needs of their offices.[5] Immediately after the independence the administration of the Frontier Tracts was placed at the disposal of the Government of Assam by Indian Independence Act, 1947, and in 1948 Sadiya Frontier Tract was bifurcated into two charges of Abor Hills and Mishmi Hills.[6]

The Constituent Assembly of India viewed the problem of Tribal development carefully and appointed a Committee to investigate and report for a rational administration of the tribals of Assam.[7] The Committee headed by late Gopinath Bordoloi toured the tribal areas of Assam but could not proceed to the Frontier Tracts for lack of communication. Yet after a thorough probe and understanding of the problems they recommended a system of administration in which the tribal people were to be given to administer their tribal issues applying their tribal custcms and conventions, leaving the overall planning and development and administration to the Government of Assam.[8] The Committee did not recommend immediate application of the same system for the North-East Frontier tribes but they envisaged gradual extension of the same system in the Frontier Tracts. These recommendations took the shape of Sixth Schedule (Part B) of the Indian Constitution.[9] The Constitution placed the administration of the tribal tracts of the Frontier under the Governor of Assam acting as an Agent of the President of India not the

Government of Assam, as under the British.[10] The idea was to pace up the development of the Frontier Tracts which they thought would be best done by the Union Government with its plentiful funds, than the meager resources of the Assam Government.

The administration of the Frontier as an integrated agency was created under the Governor of Assam who was assisted by an Adviser of the rank of a Senior Secretary to the Government, technically under the Ministry of External Affairs.[11] The headquarter of the Administration remained in Shillong, the capital of Assam at that time. The Chief Minister of Assam had nothing to do with the administration of the Frontier; but as an architect of the Sixth Schedule with his varied experience and influence, he played a very prominent role in the shaping of the administration of the North-East Frontier.[12] Sir Akbar Hydery, the Governor, and Sri Gopinath Bordoloi, the Chief Minister of Assam, together dreamt ultimate integration of the Hills and Plains of Assam in a single Government, as did the immediate past English Governor Sir Robert Reid who had carried deep research on the issue.[13] On the recommendation of the Chief Minister Gopinath Bordoloi, Sir Akbar Hydery, the Governor, began to replace the European Officers from the Frontier by placing the best Assamese or Indian Officers in the Frontier Administration with a view to create a good impression upon the tribal people of the Indian Officers.[14] Fortunately, the first batch of Political Officers were remarkable people and were welcomed by the tribal people cordially. Sri Gopinath Bordoloi succeeded in 1951 in transfering and integrating more developed areas of the Frontier Tracts to Assam as he had dreamt while recommending the Sixth Schedule.[15]

Independent India thus took some time to realise the magnitude of the Tribal problem and yet took time to plan a course of action for the development of the tribal areas. As the Chinese invasion of Tibet in 1910 had forced the British Government of India to consider the problem of defence of the North-East Frontier and bring the Frontier Tracts under the direct and immediate administration of the Government delimiting the territorial boundary of the British Empire in the North-East the Chinese occupation of Tibet in 1950 again made the Indian Government conscious of the problems of the Frontiers.[16] Meanwhile the problem of communication of the Frontier territories was highlightened by the earthquack of 1950.[17] New Delhi now evinced an interest in the Frontier which so long had been left to the care of the Governor of Assam under the nominal control of the Ministry of External Affairs.

The Constitution had of course, directed the Government to take up the cause of the tribal development. Formula evolved in the Constitution was to deal with the tribal problem scientifically and provide for smooth integration of this vast body of population within the fold of the Indian society.[18] Article 339 enjoined the President of India to appoint and from time to time Commission to review the development of the tribal people. With a view to draw up a clear and scientific programme of development, the Government of India convened a Seminar of the Ministers and experts in the field of tribal affairs of the different States of Indian Union in 1952.[19] Sociologists, anthropologists, tribal leaders and administrators assembled in New Delhi in the Central Hall of the Parliament to chalk out a programme of tribal development.[20]

The Conference held between 7th and 9th of June 1952, discussed mainly three problems, viz. Education, tribal economy and grant-in-aid for the tribal development.[21] The then President of India Dr. Rajendra Prasad, Prime Minister Sri Nehru and Home Minister Dr. Katju agreed with the Scholars of the Conference that the development of the tribes should be so planned as to raise them without destroying their culture and basing their development programme on the basis of their past heritage.[22] Prime Minister Nehru later wrote in his foreword to V. Elwin's *Philosophy for NEFA* "I had a feeling that we should help them to grow in their own way".[23] They recommended that "the tribe will be served best if they were helped to retain their culture and at the same time helped to assimilate the better elements of the culture of the surrounding population". Prime Minister Nehru had suggested at the Seminar that the approach to the tribal problem should be one of learning from them and having learnt to try to help and cooperate.[24] He also pointed out that he neither wanted to keep the tribes as specimens for anthropological study nor would he suggest forcible assimilation in the name of development. What he suggested was to provide a sort of protection to the tribes so that they could develop of their own on the foundation of their past heritage.[25]

The scheme adopted by the Seminar was given an idiological framework in the book *A Philosophy for NEFA*. As enunciated by V. Elwin in his five principles of tribal development, it held: (i) People should develop along the lines of own genius and government should avoid imposing anything on them. (ii) Tribal rights in land and forest should be respected. (iii) Government should try to train and build up a team of their own people to do the work of administration and development. Some technical personnel from outside will be doubt be needed, especially at the beginning. But attempt should be made to avoid introducing too many outsiders into tribal territory. (iv) Nor should there any attempt to over administer these areas or overwhelm them with a multiplicity of schemes; rather development should be through, not in suppression of, their own social and cultural institutions. (v) Govern-ment should measure the results of the progress not by statistic or the amount of money spent but by the quality of human character that is evolved.[26]

Elwin's view as expressed in *A Philosophy for NEFA* is, of course, based on the assumption that the British Government inclined, on the whole to leave the tribes to themselves; the tribesmen on the other hand should not be ashamed of his own culture and religion and thus feel an inferiority complex which is a political as well as social danger. Yet isolation was neither possible nor desirable. He too agreed to the principle-let the tribes grow in their own way on their own heritage, according to their own genius and tradition.[27]

But, New Delhi had remained practically unconcerned and took little interest in the affairs of the Frontier and the administration of the Frontier was left to the Governor of Assam and his Adviser as before. Fortunately both the new Governor Sri Jairamdas Daulatram and the Adviser Nari Rustomji were very sympathetic to the tribal people and discharged undifatigable energy and tact and understanding of the problems in dealing with the tribal affairs.[28] Jairamdas expressed his ideas of tribal development in the followings words "Each section of our large population contributes to the making of the nation in same manner as each flower helps to make a garden. Every flower has the right to grow according to its own laws of growth; has the right to enrich and develop its own colour and form and to spread its own fragrance to make up the cumulative beauty and splendour of the garden. I would not like to change my roses into lilies nor my lilies into roses. Nor do I want to sacrifice my lovely orchids and rhododendroms of the hills".[29] Jairamdas had determination and staying power and it was mainly due to his inexhaustible initiative and drive that the new policy of development and integration of the Frontiers was so speedily and effectively put in motion. He meticulously devoured the tour diaries of the officers in the frontier and to encourage them put his remarks by the side of their reports.[30]

During Jairamdas Daulatram's time a systematic plan for the administration was laid down. The blue-print for future Government was prepared and working of the plan was put in motion. Major achievements of Jairamdas Daulatram were the standardisation of the terminology of the administrative units and shifting of the headquarters of the administration of these units within the Tracts themselves at vantage positions.[31] Hitherto the administrative units were known as tracts Districts, Areas and Sub-Agency; these were by

Regulation of 1954 termed Divisions and named after the principal rivers of these divisions.[32] Thus instead of Balipara Frontier Tract we had Kameng Frontier Division, for Abor Hills District Siang Frontier Division, for the Mishmi Hills Lohit Division, for Sela Sub-Agency Subansiri Frontier Division, and for the Naga Tribal Areas Tuensang Frontier Division. Tuengsang Frontier Division was subsequently transferred to Naga Hills Administration as the people were more akin to the Nagas Nagaland and the Triap Frontier Tract became Tirap Frontier Division. The headquarters of these Divisions were transferred from foothills to centrally located places within the hills of the Division.[33] Thus the headquarters of Kameng Division was now located at Bomdila, Subansiri Division at Ziro, Siang Division at Along, Lohit Division at Tozu and the Tirap Division at Khelee from which it was later named to Khonsa. Tuensang was separated from NEFA in 1957. Frontier Administration was given a new name as North East Frontier Agency or NEFA in short.[34]

The Divisions were further subdivided into Sub-Divisions.[35] Thus Kameng Division was divided into Tawang sub-division, Bomdila sub-division, Sopla sub-division and Chayangtajo sub-division; Subansiri Division was sub-divided into Kolariang Hapoli or Ziro sub-division, Sagaloo sub-division, Siang division was divided into ten sub-division, i.e., Taksing, Nacho, Dapo-Rijo, Neelhaka, Tuting, Along, Basar, Pasighat, Dosing and Maryang sub-division; Lohit Division was subdivided into five sub-division of Anini, Roing, Hayuliang, Namsai and Tezu sub-division; and finally Tirap Division was split-up into three sub-divisions of Khonsa, Naiusa and Changlang sub-divisions. These sub-divisions were further sub-divided into a number of Circles and Checkposts. Altogether there were five Divisions, 28 sub-divisions and 81 Circles or Checkposts.[36]

Each of the Frontier Division was placed under the charge of a political officer or Indian Frontier Administrative Service, Grade-I and important sub-divisions were placed as independent sub-division under charge of Additional Political Officers of the same cadre.[37] Initially Pasighat in Siang and Anini in Lohit were made independent sub-division and later Dapec-Rajo was also placed under Additional Political Officer as an independent sub-division. The sub-divisions were generally under the charge of Assistant Political Officers, Grade-II of Indian Frontier Administrative Service and the Circles and Checkposts Base-Superintendents.[38]

The enthusiasm and the services of Jairamdas Daulatram earned for him much esteem and love of the people he served and a place in the present Tirap District was named after him in recognition of his services.[39] Above Jairamdas Daulatram, the Joint Secretary of the Home Ministry of the Government of India Sri T.N. Kaul, who had done some research on tribal developments in Soviet Russia took initiative in organising a separate service to be recruited from the retiring defence service personnel for tribal administration as in the USSR especially in the frontier. In 1953 this services was created and to aid and advise the personnel of the administration Mr. Elwin who had earned fame as loader of the tribal people, was appointed.[41]

Elwin's view as expressed in *A Philosophy for NEFA* was based on the assumption that the British Government inclined, on the whole to leave the tribes men alone... "but detribalisation leads to make the tribesman ashamed of his own culture and religion as so creates that inferiority complex which is a political as well as social danger. Yet isolation was neither possible nor desirable. He too agreed to the principle—let the tribes grow in their own way on their own heritage, according to their own genius and tradition.

Nari Rustomji who had distinguished himself as the first Indian Advisor to the Governor of Assam for Frontier particularly in the relief works of 1950 transferred from that position was detained and requisitioned for training the personnel of the new administration.[40] The Governor's Frontier Administrative Staff was brought under a new setup to be called henceforth North-East Frontier Agency or NEFA in short as already noted.[41]

Till then no special service existed for the Frontier Administration. The Officers in the service on the Frontier were drawn from the existing All India Service cadres of Assam.[42] In few cases selected Extra Assistant Commissioners of Assam Civil Service were appointed as Political Officers or Assistant Political Officers in the Frontier Service.[43] Thus the cadres of administration fell under two heads: Frontier Civil Service consisting of posts of Base Superintendents, Assistant Political Officer and Indian Administrative Service personnel in the post like Political Officer. When the Indian Frontier Service was created in 1953 a new cadre of Frontier Administration emerged for the Frontiers.[44] But the expedient of providing a separate cadre for an extremely limited service proved in expedient as practically no avenues of proportion which is an inactive for work, existed in the new cadre. As a result the Indian Frontier Administrative Service had to be amalgamated with the Indian Administrative Service.[45] Thereafter again the Government of India created a separate service cadre for the Union Territories to provide personnel of the Frontier Service.[46]

But the tempo of development and administration of the Frontiers receded from limelight with the adjustment of Sino-Indian points of view with regard to Tibet and Nehru-Mao Treaty of 1954, commonly known as the *Pancha Sila.* As the United States threat on China from Taiwan and on India from Pakistan receded India and China drew closer and the border tribes of India no more drew that much of attention as they deserved.

With recesion of the tide of popular applause of Sino-Indian friendship and decline in the threat of Pakistani aggression on India with United States, support, India began to appreciate the political dangers on the North-East Frontier. And when the Chinese ruthlessly suppressed the Tibetan rebellion and the Dalai escaped from Lhasa to take refuse in India, Government of India began to take positive steps for defence and administration development of the Frontier territories.[47] Outposts for patrolling the borders on the MacMahon Line which had not been demarcated on the ground since 1914, opening of base of administration like Circles and Sub-division, clearing of tracts for communication and construction of air strips all were taken up in the right earnest. Even the terms of reference of the Dhebor Commission which was appointed by the President in 1960 to report on the 5th Schedule tribes were changed to accommodate enquiry into and report on the 6th Schedule Areas as well.[48]

After the Government of India had given Political asylum to the Dalai the Sino-Indian friendship took the turn of enimity and without declaration of war regular fighting broke out at the onset of 1962 winter. The Chinese with due preparation with massive manpower and supplies of sophisticated weapons swept away the Hindustani troops, mostly fighting with backdated 2nd World War-time weapons.[49] Moreover the Indian Army Command damped the morale of the army; the Chinese carried everything before them. But the Divine helped the Indian cause. Thanks God the Chinese at the hight of their success declared unilateral ceasefire on 22.11.62 and retreated from all most all the territories they had occupied of the North-East Frontier.[50]

The Government of India took no time to rectify the past mistakes and integrate the administrative structure of the NEFA administration with that of the State of Assam. All the territories south of the MacMahon Line apportioned into different administrative units and the officers employed in them were renamed following the administrative practice in Assam.[51] The five administrative Division were now termed Districts which had been split-up into Sub-divisions and the Sub-divisions split-up into Circles and Checkposts.[52]

The nomenclature of the officers were changed to assimilate them with the administrative officers of the Assam Government. The Political Officers and Base Superintendents were now known as Deputy Commissioners and Circles officers. Development Blocks, coterminous with the circles were created to encourage the tribal people in undertaking development promgramme under Government direction and guidance.[53] The guidance and control of NEFA was transferred from External Affairs Ministry to that of Home on August 1, 1965.[54]

The structure of the territorial administrative jurisdiction thus consisted of circles consisting of some 30 to 40 villages; Sub-division consisting of one or more circles and Districts consisting of several sub-divisions. Usually a circle is held by a circle officer who is also the Block Development officer of his circle; Extra Assistant Commissioners were placed in charge of sub-divisions; and Deputy Commissioners are posted at the headquarters of the Districts.[55] But in some independent sub-divisions Additional Deputy Commissioners held charge of the sub-division to expedite the tempo of development.[56]

Although the pattern of circles, sub-divisions and Districts followed what exists in other parts of India, the duties allotted to circle officers, Extra Assistant, Assistant and Deputy Commissioners very quite a lot and to cope with the local circumstances. They have been given full powers, to deal with local affairs, as laid down in the Assam Frontier (Administrative of Justice) Regulation of 1945. Besides, these officers have been given full powers to act as local heads for all subjects within their jurisdication development work, community development schemes, revenue works, socio-cuntural works, etc., and they exercise authority over the various installations and schemes of the various technical departments like schools and college, hospitals and despensaries, roads and buildings, agriculture and forests, and so on and so forth.[57] From the Administration point of view, the overall head provides a single authority to help resolve interdepartmental overlapping in the area and generally gives an integrated out look to each administrative unit within its territorial jurisdiction.[58] It also enables the unsophisticated tribal people to take their complaints and difficultires to the head of the administration for appraisal and solution.

The conception of Additional Deputy Commissioner's charge in independent sub-divisions in peculiar to NEFA—Immediately following the India-China War of 1962 and after it was felt necessary to develop some areas on the borders at fast rate and for the purpose six such charges were created.[59] There the Additional Deputy Commissioners were vested with the full powers of a Deputy Commissioner to render these effective in planning and sanctioning administrative business and three of these were placed directly under NEFA administration to enable them to make quick reference and get decision there on quickly.[60] The experiment proved successful in developing remoter places. Subsequently, however, the Districts sub-division were further sub-divided and converted into new Districts and Sub-division. In 1980 all district except Tirap was devided into two Districts, viz. Kameng into East Kameng and West Kameng; Subansiri into Lower and Upper Subansiri; Siang into East and West Siang District and Lohit District into Dibang Valley and Lohit Valley Districts.[61] Tirap became an independent District in 1980, 1984 again Tawang was separated from West Kameng and made a new District and Changlang sub-division gained the status of District separated from Tirap in 1987. On the eve of Election of 1990, there were 11 District, 28 Sub-divisions and 101 Circles in Arunachal Pradesh.[62]

Though North-East Frontier was an integral part of the territory of the Republic of India the people of the area hitherto did not enjoy the democratic rights and privileges of a citizen of the Indian Republic. The North-East Frontier people did not elect their representative in the Parliament, the representative from this area was nominated by the President of India.[63] There was almost in every locality or village a local headman either elected by the people themselves or hereditary who performed much useful work, but the people did not enjoy any right of participation in the working of this local self-Government of statutory provisions. Moreover, there was no liaision between the Administration and the people. To remove these Sangs Government of India set-up a committee for Administrative Reforms in NEFA under the Chairmanship of late Daing Fring, the nominated member of Parliament from NEFA.[64] The Committee recommended a three tier system of local self-Government. The Panchayat Raj Regulation of 1967 was drawn up accordingly and promulgated on 2nd October 1969.[65]

The Panchayat Raj Regulation of 1967 created statutory Local self-Government in all the districts of North-East Frontier.[66] First there is an Anchal Samity in every one of the 43 blocks which are coterminous with the community Development Blocks.[67] Next there are 5 Zilla Parishads in every one of the five districts;[68] and finally there was the Pradesh Council at the North-East Frontier Agency level.[69] The Agency council was named Pradesh Council of 30 members with a responsible cabinate after NEFA was constituted in to a Union Territories in 1972.[70]

An Anchal Samity consists of their representatives of the Gram Panchayats who elect four member each, (ii) representative of the cooperative societies within the jurisdiction of the Anchal Samity, and (iii) not more than five members nominated by the Deputy Commissioner of the District to represent the tribes.[71] The Sub-Divisional Officer in whose subdivision the Anchal Samity is situated is the ex-officio chairman of the Anchal Samity and the Deputy Commissioner has been given the power to nominate such other officers whom he deems necessary, for the smooth and effective functioning of the Samity.[72] The Vice-President of Anchal Samity is elected and in the absence of the S.D.C. who is ex-officio president looks after and conduct of business of the Samity.[73]

The idea behind the indirect election of the Anchal Samity and official direction of the affairs of the Samity is to train the tribal people gradually in running their own administration in broader perspective of regional planning and mutual understanding. The tribes till recently were living an exclusive life without much consideration of the need of the other tribes. So it is necessary to give them some sort of guidance in the initial stages to develop wider outlook. Moreover, the technicalities and formalities of modern administration requires some degree of sophistication which again is lacking among the simple tribesmen. Therefore, official tutelage in the initial stages have been taught essential.[74]

The powers and functions of the Anchal Samity are those which are necessary to promote health, safety, education, comfort, convenience or economic or social well-being of the residents of the area.[75] It has been given the control and management of roads, bridges, culverts and water courses; it may layout and make new roads and water courses and construct new bridges and culverts.[76] An Anchal Samity has been given to maintain hospitals, dispensaries and for the promotion of public health and prevention of epidemic it has been given wide powers to inocculate and disinfect residential houses, maintain proper drainage, to clear any land of thick vegetation, undergrowth and jungle, remove patients suffering from epidemic disease and close markets to prevent spread of disease.[77]

The Anchal Samities are implementing the works of the local bodies like the Gram Panchayats and such particular work to works assigned to a Gram Panchayat and pays money for their extension.[78] Thus to some extent an Anchal Samity co-ordinates and distributes the works of the Gram Panchayats within its jurisdiction.

The satisfactory functioning of an Anchal Samity requires some financial resources. But the resources in the initial stages would be meagre for it can have only little revenue from licences and taxes within its jurisdiction; vary little money may be raised from loans. Therefore, the resources were to be provided by the administration.[79] Coordinated planning and effective execution are essential for the success of the Panchayat Raj. The Act has provided for the purpose close cooperation of the officials of the

Government with the Samities.

Next, with a view to coordinate to district works the Anchal Samities of each district have been brought under another organisation viz. the Zilla Parishad. Every Zilla Parishad consists of the Vice-Presidents of the Anchal Samities of the district, ex-officio, one representative of every Anchal Samity in the District, to be elected by its members from amongst themselves, not more than six persons to be nominated by the Chief Commissioner from the tribes which have not secured presentation on the Zilla Parishad and the Deputy Commissioner of the District is the ex-officio president.[80] The elected members serve a term of three years which is again the term of office of the member of the Parishad.[81] It is the duty of the Zilla Parishad to advise the Chief Commissioner of the province on all matters concerning the activities of the Gram Panchayats and Anchal Samities situated within the District, particularly recommend the budget estimate of the Anchal Samities and coordinate the plan and works of the Gram Panchayats and Anchal Samities within the district.[82] The Zilla Parishad meet as frequently as necessary but not more than six months shall elapse between two meetings of a Zilla Parishad.[83] This has been done with a view to activise the Zilla Parishad in the matter of control and co-ordination of the works of the different Gram Panchayats and Anchal Samities of the District.

Finally the Act provided for an institution called Agency Council to coordinate the plan and works of the entire province under the guidence of the Chief Administrator of the Province.[84] The body consists of the Chief Commissioner of the province, the member of the parliament representing the Province, vice-presidents of all the Zilla Parishads of the province, and members elected from each Zilla Parishad and not more than three persons to be nominated by the Chief Commissioner from other tribes which had not been represented in the Council.[85] The Council advised the Chief Commissioner on matters of administration involving general questions of policy of the province, the Five Year Plan and

Annual Development Plans of the province, estimate budget expenditure, proposal for undertaking general legislation for the province on matters enumerated in the seventh schedule of the constitution of India and any other matter which the Chief Commissioner may refer to it.[86] The Council has been provided for as a sort of legislature for the province. The members of Council were accorded the right of asking questions on general policy in the Chief Commissioner was given the discretion to disallow any thing he thinks fit.[87] Moreover, the Chief Commissioner had the right to appoint not more than five Counsellors from amongst the members of the Pradesh Council for consultation on any matter relating to the administration of the province and given views on such issues.[88] The opinions of the Councillors are in no way was binding on the Chief Commissioner who might or might not accept them at his own discretion.[89]

Behind this structure of three tier system of government stood the NEFA Administration under the control of the President of India exercising powers through the Ministry of External Affairs and the Governor of Assam aided by an Advisor as already mentioned till 1965 when the control of the Agency Administration was transferred from the External Affairs Ministry to the Ministry of Home.[90] The Administration was conducted like a Union Territory as provided in paragraph 18 of the 6th Schedule of the Constitution of India. The Union Ministry delegated powers to the Governor and then to the Chief Commissioner from 1972 who delegated powers to the district and departmental heads as and when necessary. As usual the Local Administration had two wings:[91] First the complement of Secretaries, Judicial Officers and the Financial Adviser; secondly, there were the different Heads of the Administrative Departments. After that attainment of Status of Union Territory Arunachal Government by 1981 had as Chief of the State a Lt. Governor, one Chief Secretary, one Commissioner and a Development Commissioner besides a complement of thirteen Secretaries to the Government and

Twenty-eight Heads or Administrative Departments.[92] The fact that the business of the Local Administration was under the direction and control of the Governor of Assam who was more or less like a Chief Secretary to the Union Government in this regard.[93] The post of Adviser to the Governor ceased to exist when Chief Commissionership was constituted and the Chief Commissioner took charge of the Local Administration in the place of Governor of Assam.

A Parliamentary delegation headed by the Deputy Speaker of the Lok Sabha visited NEFA in May 22-29, 1966 and recommended the transfer of headquarters of Local Administration from Shillong to NEFA territory.[94] Accordingly steps were taken to shift the capital by stages to Itanagar situated centrally in Lower Subansiri district of Arunachal Pradesh from 1972 onwards. The transfer is now complete practically, only the Department of Statistics has remained in the Shillong Secretariat Building.[95]

Thus we see that NEFA strode towards democracy step by step and the tribes of NEFA developed wider outlook so as to think in terms of fellow tribes and the province of NEFA. The progress was found to be satisfactory and warranted a further step towards constitutional development. Therefore, by an amendment act of Parliament NEFA was constituted into a Union Territory under a Chief Commissioner and a Legislative Assembly of 30 members with a responsible cabinet and the name Arunachal Pradesh which was adopted as the name of the province by the Agency Council in it first meeting, became the name of the new Union territory which came into being on 20th January, 1972.[96] Initially, however, the Agency Council was converted into a Pradesh Council to serve as a Provisional Legislature and the five Councillors to the Chief Commissioner were designated as a provisional Council of Ministers on 1975.[97] The status of the Chief of the state was raised to that of Lt. Governor on August 15, 1975.[98] Adult franchise was introduced in Arunachal in 1972 and representation to the Union Parliament from Arunachal was increased to two members now to be elected under this franchise.[99] The first election to the Parliament and Arunachal Legislature took place in 1977.[100] In 1987 Arunachal gained statehood and the membership of the Legislative was increased to sixty by redistribution of seats.[101] The Chief of the State's status was elevated to the rank of Governor at same time.[102]

The North-East Frontier territories as a separate entity began to developed gradually since 1875-76 when the Inner Line Regulation of 1873 was drawn up. A state began to emerge gradually, perhaps imperceptibly, out of the then territories of the Assam Administration. The British did not bother much about the requirements of the tribes; they were only concerned with the safety of the Indian Empire and thus without burdening themselves with the administration of the territories which yeilded no revenue, remained content by enforcing "loose political control" over the tribes on the border of the Indian Empire. The Republic of India envisaged a planned development of the territories on the border and requirements on the border tribes warranted the creation of a separate province on the frontiers.

REFERENCES

1. V. Elwin, *A New Deal for Tribal India*, p. 17.
2. N. Rustomji, *Enchanted Frontiers*, p. 72.
3. *Ibid.*
4. The Evolution of the Administrative Jurisdictions of the North-East Frontier Agency 1914 onwards.
5. *Ibid.*
6. M.L. Bose, *Historical and Constitutional Documents*, p. 158.
7. *Ibid.*, p. 159.
8. *Ibid.*
9. *Ibid.*, p. 183.
10. *Ibid.*
11. P.N. Luthra, *Constitutional and Administrative Growth of NEFA*.
12. *Ibid.*
13. N. Rustomji, *The Enchanted Frontiers*, pp. 48-117.
14. *Ibid.*
15. *Ibid.*
16. *Ibid.*

17. *Ibid.*
18. Proceedings of the Conference for the Development of the Scheduled Caste and Schedule Tribes Areas, New Delhi, 1952.
19. *Ibid.*
20. *Ibid.*
21. *Ibid.*
22. *Ibid.*
23. V. Elwin, *A Philosophy for NEFA*, Preface.
24. Proceedings of the Seminar.
25. *Ibid.*
26. V. Elwin, *A New Deal for Tribal India*, p. 17.
27. *Ibid.*
28. N. Rustomji, *A Philosophy for NEFA*, p. 11.
29. V. Elwin, *A Philosophy for NEFA*, p. 11.
30. N. Rustomji, *op. cit.*, p. 131.
31. *Ibid.*
32. M.L. Bose, *Historical and Constitutional Documents*, pp. 185-90.
33. *Ibid.*
34. *Ibid.*
35. The Evolution of the Administrative Jurisdiction.
36. *Ibid.*
37. *Ibid.*
38. *Ibid.*
39. N. Rustomji, *op. cit.*, pp. 114-37.
40. *Ibid.*
41. *Ibid.*
42. *Ibid.*
43. *Ibid.*
44. *Ibid.*
45. *Ibid.*
46. *Ibid.*
47. Report of the Administrative Reforms Commission, New Delhi, 1969.
48. V. Elwin, *A New Deal for Tribal India*, p. 1.
49. N. Maxwell, *Indo-China War 1970*; J.P. Dalvi, *The Himalayan Blunder*, 1969.
50. *Ibid.*
51. M.L. Bose, *Historical and Constitutional Documents*, pp. 188-90, also letter of Advisor to the Governor of Assam letter No. PLB. 262/63 dated 24.12.69.
52. *Ibid.*
53. *Ibid.*
54. *Ibid.*
55. P.N. Luthra, *op. cit.*
56. *Ibid.*
57. *Ibid.*

58. *Ibid.*
59. *Ibid.*
60. *Ibid.*
61. *Ibid.*
62. *Ibid.*
63. *Ibid.*
64. Report of the Administrative Reforms Commisison, 1969.
65. P. Dutta, *Arunachal Pradesh—An Overview*, p. 16.
66. M.L. Bose, *Historical and Constitutional Documents*, pp. 190-227.
67. *Ibid.*
68. *Ibid.*
69. *Ibid.*
70. *Ibid.*
71. *Ibid.*
72. *Ibid.*
73. *Ibid.*
74. *Ibid.*
75. *Ibid.*
76. *Ibid.*
77. *Ibid.*
78. *Ibid.*
79. *Ibid.*
80. *Ibid.*
81. *Ibid.*
82. *Ibid.*
83. *Ibid.*
84. *Ibid.*
85. *Ibid.*
86. *Ibid.*
87. *Ibid.*
88. *Ibid.*
89. *Ibid.*
90. *Ibid.*, p. 188.
91. *Ibid.*
92. *Infra.*
93. *Infra.*
94. Ram Rahul, *The Himalayan Borderland*, New Delhi.
95. Statistical Hand Book, 1880-81.
96. M.L. Bose, *Historical and Constitutional Documents*, p. 262.
97. *Ibid.*
98. P. Dutta, *op. cit.*, p. 16.
99. Statistical Hand Book 1980-81, pp. 179-82.
100. *Ibid.*
101. The Telegraph, March 8, 1990.
102. P. Dutta, *op. cit.*, p. 16.

7

NEW PROFILE OF ARUNACHAL

Laying between latitude 26°28'N and 29°30'N and longitude 91°30'E and 97°30'E on the extreme North-East Arunachal Pradesh covers an area of 83,743 sq. km with a population of 631,839 souls of which 69.82 per cent are tribals of Indo-Mangolian origin spread over 6 townships and 325 villages as per 1981 census.[1]

The well known term NEFA, short form of North-East Frontier Agency of 1954, yeilded to Arunachal Pradesh in 1972 when it was renamed by its own people.[2] It became a Union Territory in 1972[3] and in 1987 it gained the Status of full-fleged State of the Union of Indian States.[4] Indian Constitution had defined the territories of Arunachal in Part B of the Sixth Schedule as: (1) North-East Frontier Tract, Tirap Frontier Tract, Abor Hills District and Mishmi Hills District; and (2) Naga Tribe Area. These were brought under an Administrative Agency called NEFA in 1954.[5]

In the British period it was a closed land and in a sease it continues to be so as travel across the Inner Line of Arunachal Pradesh in not allowed even now; a person has to obtain a pass to cross the Line from a competent authority. Arunachal had remained virtually a hidden land in the colonial period and all sorts of mysterious and absurd stries were associated with the life and culture of the people living there. From nineteenth century onwards Indian nationalist movement and social and cultural reforms revived and rejuvenated the people of India and fostered unity and national consciousness among the Indians. But Frontier remained unaffected as political parties were not allowed to carry on their activities in the region.[6] Consequently the struggle for freedom from the foreign-rule did not create. In the Frontiers any change in the out-look and North-East Frontier remained out of the stream of Indian national development.[7]

The general policy of the British Government was to maintain status quo in the frontier and as such they did not allow the life of the people in the frontier to be disturbed by any new idea or development. The proselytising activities of the Christian Missionaries so fruitful and vigorous among the tribes of the hills of the south bank of the Brahmaputra did not affect the tribes on the hills of the north bank of the river.[8] Their initial interest in the Dibang and Lohit valley and belated interest in the Siand valley did not leave behind any considerable impression except in the Siang valley where few people still follow the religion of Chirst.[9]

Government of free India attempted a uphil task of planned and systematic opening up of Arunachal inspite of the inaccessible difficult terrain and age-old tradition of its people[10] i.e., modernisation and yet keep a continuity of its traditions the genius of its people who had not been accustomed to any change at all. Yet regular administration started penetration deeper and deeper into the hills and brought entire territory under administration. A number of Government Agencies and socio-cultural organisations started acculturation process to bring in a synthesis of culture of the frontier people. Changes have began in political, economic, social and cultural life of the people. The static period of aloofness and isolation has yeilded to a modern period of dynamism which is "shaking off the dust and rust of ages" for a brighter future of the people of this kaleidoscopic land.

In the initial stage the task before the government was to penetrate deep into the area by setting up of administrative centres within the hills of the Frontiers. In 1965 the entire territory was divided into five districts, 26 Sub-divisions and 82 Circles;[12] in 1980 again the larger districts were divided into two each and in 1984 Tawang subdivision of West Kameng and Changlang Subdivision of Tirap district were made in 1987 districts.[13] Meanwhile some more subdivisions were created out of larger sub-divisions and a few more Circles came into existence. Now there are some 11 Districts 28 Sub-divisions and 101 Circles in the State of Arunachal Pradesh.[14] The Administration and territory were separated from Assam to give a distinct identity of its own. Government and administration has now reached every nook and corner of the State where there were no administrative agency practically within Arunachal territory before Independence. Now there were some 16,912 persons serving the Arunachal Government in 1981 with a team of 4542 tribal people.[15]

Independent India to speed up development on a systematic way adopted development planning to speed-up development; Five years planning was extended to Arunachal as well. For the development of communications, agriculture, cottage industry, health, education and community development the plan allocation were as follows:[16]

Ist 5 Year Plan	Rs.	20.1	millions
2nd 5 Year Plan	Rs.	35.6	"
3rd 5 Year Plan	Rs.	92.0	"
4th 5 Year Plan	Rs.	215.7	"
5th 5 Year Plan	Rs.	630.0	"
6th 5 Year Plan	Rs.	2058.50	"
7th 5 Year Plan	Rs.	4000.00	"

To bring in close cooperation between the Government and people Panchayat Raj was introduced in 1969.[17] Elections under Adult franchise were held for three tier system of Local Government in 1972[18] and this resulted in the creation of 704 Gram Panchayats, 54 Anchal Samities, 11 Zilla Parishads with 48 Community Development Blocks.

Agency Council of NEFA was substituted by the

Pradesh Council and in 1975 the latter became a Provisional Legislature;[19] nominated members to the Union Parliament were replaced by duly elected members in 1977 when elections were held for the State Legislature.[20] The Councillors to the Chief Commissioners were turned into Council of Ministers and a fully responsible Cabinet assumed office in 1977.[21] Again General Elections were held in 1987 and 1990.[22] The status of Chief of the State under went changed from Chief Commissionership to Lt. Governor and Governorship to recognise the new political personality of the State.

That politicisation is complete in Arunachal is evident from the fact that where the tribes were living in perpetual enimity and warfare and did not know anything about democracy and parliamentary elections have become conscious of their political rights and voted responsible in the elections for three-tier system of Local Government and a elections of the State Assemblies and Union Parliament held in 1977, 1980, 1987 and in 1990 with due election propaganda and campaigns of the All India Political Parties.[23] In the first Parliamentary Election Sri P.K. Thungon, Congress (I) candidate was elected uncontested in the West Constituency and in the East Constituency Sri Sobeng Tayeng also Congress (I) candidate faced a triangular contest and was elected by a slender majority receiving 34,864 votes from an electorate of 1,14,616 of which 78,311 votes were cast.[24] In the general election of 1980 for the West Constituency there was a five cornered fight and number of the electorate was 1,51,450, 1,04,598 voters cast their votes of which 98,260 were found valid Sri P.K. Thungon (Congress-I) candidate was elected receiving 41,736 votes defeating his nearest rival Sri Kuru Hassang (UPP) who polled 37,381 votes.[25] For the East constituency there was a triangular contest among an electorate of 1,14,616. Sri Sobang Tayang (Cong-I) was elected by a slender majority receiving 34,864 votes defeating his nearest rival Sri Bakin Pastin (UPP) who received 32,429 votes of out of a total of

78,311 votes polled.[26] Five Political Parties contested the election besides the independents in the Parliamentary and Assembly elections of 1980.[27]

In the General Election of 1978 for the State Assembly and mid-term poll of 1980 for thirty seats an electroate of 239,945 and 266,726 went to polls respectively and of these in 1978 itself 158,988 votes were found valid and in 1980, 170,816.[28] In the State Election of 1987, Assembly polls of 1990 same 167 candidates belonging to different Congress Parties, Janata Dal Janata Party and Independents went to poll on 5th March 1990 for sixty seats.[29] Congress (I) candidates bagged 37 seats, Janata Dall 11 and Janata Party one while the Independents got eleven seats (Eco of Arunachal, March 6, 1990).[30]

The impact of the establishment of Administrative posts within the Inner Line covering the entire territory and transfer of headquarters of Government in Itanagar and Naharlagun were momentus on the life of the people of Arunachal Pradesh. The administrative posts and capital offices in Naharlagun and Itanagar had potentials of urbanisation and synthesis of culture. Administrative headquarters—buildings are houses of bricks and morters and corrugated iron-roofs or concrete roofs built keeping the local styles in view for accommodation of offices and officers. The people in these places required necessaries of life and office equipments. These led to setting up of shops and markets where tribal goods and modern manufactures are available. People around now moved towards these posts and began to live a life in new houses in the style of the office holders. The result was growth of towns and different mode of living adjusting to new environment by a new society with a radically different society and yet keeping a link with the past heritage. It may be mentioned that Arunachal Pradesh has now five townships above five thousand population and one Bomdila below five thousand.[31] But all administrative headquarters have potentials of further urban growth.

Tribal economy of Arunachal was consumption oriented

and barter was the mode of exchange in general. People around the administrative posts now are growing crops and vegetables not only for their consumption but for sale to the office holders as well. Economy has been thus mentioned. In fact Administration brought in far-reaching agricultural reforms in Arunachal. It did not forbid jhuming but encouraged improved methods within the traditional framework[32], e.g. increasing cycle of rotation of jhuming sites and plantation of seedlings, instead of broadcasting in the dearings better-seeds and use of labour savings implements teracing and watering by irrigation, encouraging production of vegetable and fruit gardens. As per 1981 census 1,336 hectares of land were brought under permanent cultivation; there were same 1,254 horticultural gardens owned by the people; 6,191 hectares of land were brought under high-yeilding variety of seeds and 1,309 hectares of land utilised chemical fertilisers green manuring in 1695 hectares and pesticides were used in 9,123 hectares of land; 6,283 hectares of land utilised minor-irrigation facilities provided by 142 minor-irrigation projects of the State.[33]

Allied with agricultural development in the department Animal husbandry and veterinary and fisheries departments. There are some 67 veterinary dispensaries, 76 veterinary aid centres and 9 cattle breading farms with 6 mobile dispensaries who are trying to improve the live-stock poultry of the people.[34] Besides there are some 33 fish-ponds which produce 410 tonnes of fish annually. Cumulative effect of these agricultural and allied departments is the self-sufficiency of Arunachal in food and it contributes even a quantity of its surplus to Government storage. Through its arable land is only 4 per cent of which 70 per cent are under Jhuming.[35]

Forest is the greatest gift nature has endowed on Arunachal. It is the highest revenue yeilding source of Arunachal Government. Total area under forest is 51,549 Sq. kms of which 11,934.75 are Reserved forest.[36] Many forest based industries have developed in the State and cash crops like tea, coffee, cardamom etc. are being produced.[37] An amount of four crores of rupees are earned as revenue of the forest in Arunachal. In view of its importance Forest Corporation has been set up to improve and cordinate forest development activities.[38]

Survey of Natural resources of Arunachal is not yet complete but it can be assumed that it has tremendous potential for industrial growth. Industrialisation is slow because of lack of infra-structural facilities besides capital and entrepreneurship.[39] Inspite of that some medium and small-scale industries like saw and veneer mills, plywood factories and mini-cement factories have come-up. Altogether there are 13 medium size industries, 1426 small scale industries, 32 crafts Centres, 30 weaving centres and 25 sericulture centres.[40] The first industrial Estate of the State has started in Itanagar, the capital town of the state. A total of 41401 non-agricultural and industrial population is supported by those industries and business enterprieses.[41]

Industry and commerce in Arunachal are ran, by and large, by Arunachal people themselves through cooperative societies. They have a tradition of self-reliance and cooperation. There are, of course, licensees who run retail shops and stores all over but the principle and practice of the Government is to provide facilities to people to create a class of entrepreneurs of the people of Arunachal itself. With that end in view cooperative movement was launched in 1957.[42] These societies run factories, distribute essential commodities to retailers, purchase the bulk of surplus produce of the people, ply transport buses and even through these other commodities are brought to Arunachal from other states of country for sale in the state. Its achievements can be guessed from the fact that some 161 such cooperatives are functioning with a membership of 32000 persons; their business capital is 1568 lakhs of rupees.[43]

Administration in Arunachal Pradesh has created a cultural ferment and an atmosphere of change. The greatest gift that the Administration has brought however, is the gift of peace.[44] For centuries the people here had been living in constant state of inter-tribal and inter-village war; they have had a long history of crisis and anxiety. Women and children could not go abroad without an escort and the mist of fear hung heavily above the workers in the fields. Government has brought to an end head-hunting and kidnapping of children as slaves, smuggling of opium, putting an end to cruel punishment, and human sacrifice.[45] Women and children go freely and happily about the country side, former enemies feast together in amity and inter-village and inter-tribal cooperation is a common thing in social life of Arunachal to-day. Slavery has been abolished from Arunachal only after independence though the British Government as a party to the International slavery convention of 1962 tried to apply its clause to Frontier in 1938 unsuccessfully.[46] Many of the former slaves to-day have a social positions and distinction as leaders in Arunachal society.

A new class-alignment is emerging and traditional class-hierarchy has yeilded to new social order. In pre-independence period practically there was no caste or class distinction in Arunachal society. Of course the tribal priests or monks among the Buddhists and the Gams or village headmen could emerge from any family and they could claim no hereditary caste or class-privilege except certain privileges of office conferred on them by the people for service to them. In the new environment created by the Administration after independence new class alignment in the offing; the ministers and legislators, officers and employees in the Government service, the newly educated people in society have began to live a different and distinctive life of their own forming a class of elites of society. Their mode of living in newly built houses in separate blocks, made of bricks and morthers, corrugated iron-roofs or R.C.C. buildings, furnished with upto date furniture and with door and window curtains, gadgets like T.V. sets and V.C.R., radiograms and tape-recorders, electric and gas hotplates, room-heaters and aircoolers or airconditioners, their dress and dietary are all new and separate from the rank and file who are still living age-old life in the changing environment; their wives and children go about the market places or bazars in uptodate model cars and play new games and enjoy new paste-times. A promise of total change is there in the air in society.

In the old days people were little clothing usually little above the west. Now many go clothed as if they are Europeans dressing for chilly spring. Dress is something much more than a mere protection of the body against the weather. In fact three points are marked in dresses: hierarchy, utility and attractiveness. Educated moderns in Arunachal prefer European dressing. Tribal dress varies greatly from place to place and yet dress-fashions depend on the principle of utility. But Arunachal dress has charm, variety and colour.[47] The effect of alien dress has not created a sense of shame and embrassment to the people of Arunachal and they have not thrown off their tribal dress. Tribal weaving and fashions have been improved by research. European and tribal have been synthetised—European trousers and shirts beautified by tribal jackets and shawls.[48] For example, for Pasighat High School an excellent blazer has been designed. It is based on Adi coat, handwoven on Adi loom but is better fashioned, the sleeves being longer, it has a coller, buttons and two pockets.[49] Similar coats, based on local designs are being made for other schools of Arunachal Pradesh.

Educational objectives in Arunachal were two-fold[50]: First to discover and develop promising boys and girls to train them up to the highest standard possible, to make them future leaders and administrator of their own people; second a simple and basic sort of education for the masses suitably adjusted to the local conditions and need. Therefore, while establishing modern schools and colleges as in other parts of the country Arunachal Administration tried to make use of the existing institutions like the Buddhist gompas and Bapuchangs and the morangs and dormitories.[51] Attempts were made to adjust education to tribal life as a whole so that children do not learn to despite their own religion and culture, forget their traditions, dances and songs and art, for it would be barbarous to twist a child's nature and kill his joy in preparing him for future which may not be his.[52] Attempts have been made to create a literature for its people based on their own dialect, with local stories and pictures and traditions.[53]

That considerable progress has been achieved is evident from both the quality of the present day leaders and administrators of the state as well as educational statistics. Beginning from primary schools there are different grades of schools and colleges and for highest education a University has been functioning now. There are one university, four degree colleges, 23 Higher Secondary schools, 41 Secondary schools, 151 Middle schools, 998 Primary schools, 249 Pre-primary schools and 29 others educational institutions were 4097 teachers, 67 college teachers imparting education to 120600 students.[54] Besides many students of Arunachal are studying medical, engineering, journalism and law in others states outside. The growth in education and literacy has resulted in the development of journalism and press and popularity of libraries in the State. Arunachal publishes two English dailies from its capital 'Arunachal Eco' and the 'Arunachal Times' besides a host of other periodicals and vernacular news papers.[55]

The major difficulty the medical and health service people faced was that the people of Arunachal had a system of diagnosis and treatment of their own and they believed that disease was caused by hostile spirits, the ghosts of the dead or the breach of some taboo. Therefore, they preferred to go to their own priests for cure than to the medical staff of the Government.[56] But the medical staff by tactfull attitude to tribal customs and local physicians have succeeded in changing the attitude of the people, they feel that the hospitals and dispensaries are their own.[57]

The beginning of the health services was difficult for

lack of communication facilities and trained personnel who refused to serve in the interriors. These have been overcome as was the indifference of the people to medical treatment. Arunachal to-day enjoys one of the highest ratios of doctors and in-door beds per thousand of population. From one hospital to few dispensaries in 1947, Arunachal has now 10 hospitals, 65 dispensaries, 53 health centres, 17 medical teams, one H.O. Sanatorium, 3 T.B. hospitals and one Ayurvedic dispensary with 356 Doctors, 154 pharmacists, 36 Staff nurses, 148 Auxiliary Nurses for its 2185 authorised beds.[58]

Starting with curative services, Health Department now has become an integrated service of curative, preventive and health promotional service and through net work of hospitals dispensaries, Health Centres and mobile units mortality rate has been reduced, Malaria eradicated completely, goitre and eye diseases reduced and people in every part of the State is provided with specialist services.[59]

After independence there has been an astonishing renaissance of the traditional art throughout India. Lovely textiles from Rajasthan, Uttar Pradesh, Maharashtra, Orissa and Bengal have earned renown throughout the World. In North Eastern India, particularly in Assam efforts are there to revive traditional patterns of weaving and designs of ornamentation.[60] The art of wood-carving has come again into its own and many beautiful musks, toys and other objects together with terrocotta stone being made throughout India.[61] People every-where are turning towards simple but attractive products of craftsman who is thus being encouraged to increase and improve his handicrafts. Arunachal Government through its Research Department and Museum has been endeavouring to revive and improve art, music, dance, songs and manifold enjoyments of life.[62]

To the people Arunachal art and recreation are not luxuries, rather these are duty. Rightly guided and inspired weaving, wood-carving, busketry and host of others artistic pursuits have become mainspring of a joy and happy life.[63]

"Dance, Music and songs have been systematically encouraged and developed to gain celebriety and popularity in all parts of the country" for "A nation needs joy as much as food and knowledge".[64]

The advance of administration has thus created an atmosphere of change and cultural ferment. A new world of ideas, a new freedom from fear, new foods grown, new sensations to enjoy, new ways to live more healthily but without destroying the culture and art of the people and their own ideas and customs and breeding any sense of inferiority-complex have made life opulent and rich. People educated in modern educational institutions have adopted western dress, acquired a taste for modern luxuries; holders high posts in administration or political status find life in an interior village intolerable but the seldom they despite their tribal heritage and ancestry. The breaking of tribal loyalty has led to bewilderment, disillusion followed by social degeneration and crime; education for the mass acted like a corrosive in the community, undermining the solidarity of the tribal peoples in Mexico, United States, Africa and South Asian countries.[65] But in India the objective that "the tribes should develop their own culture and made their contribution to the cultural richness of the country" with a feeling that they have perfect freedom to live their own lives and to develop according to their wishes and genius and realise that they are part of India and have equality with other people of India, has come true.

REFERENCES

1. N. Shanker, "A Profile of Arunachal Pradesh", *Resarun*, Vol. XIV, Nos. 1 & 2, 1988.
2. *Ibid.*
3. *Ibid.*
4. *Ibid.*
5. M.L. Bose, *Historical and Constitutional Documents*.
6. V. Elwin, *New Deal for Tribal India*, p. 9.
7. *Ibid.*
8. V. Elwin, *A Philosophy for NEFA*, p. 1.

9. *Ibid.*
10. P. Dutta, *Arunachal Pradesh, Itanagar*, 1988, p. 50.
11. *Ibid.*
12. The Evolution of the Administration Jurisdictions of the North-East Frontier Agency, 1914 onwards.
13. *Ibid.*
14. *Ibid.*
15. Statistical Hand Book of Arunachal Pradesh, 1980-81, p. 182.
16. P. Dutta, *op. cit.*, p. 51.
17. M.L. Bose, *Historical and Constitutional Documents*, p. 190.
18. P. Dutta, *op. cit.*, p. 16.
19. *Ibid.*
20. *Ibid.*
21. *Ibid.*
22. *Ibid.*
23. Statistical Hand Book of Arunachal Pradesh, pp. 179-82.
24. *Ibid.*
25. *Ibid.*
26. *Ibid.*
27. *Ibid.*
28. *Ibid.*
29. *Ibid.*
30. *Ibid.*
31. Statistical Hand Book , 1980-81, p. 29.
32. V. Elwin, *A Philosophy for NEFA*, pp. 22-23.
33. Statistical Hand Book , 1980-81, pp. 107-33.
34. *Ibid.*
35. P. Dutta, *op. cit.*, p. 52.
36. *Ibid.*, p. 55.
37. *Ibid.*
38. *Ibid.*
39. *Ibid.*, p. 53.
40. Statistical Hand Book, 1980-81, p. 183.
41. *Ibid.*
42. P. Dutta, *op. cit.*, p. 56.
43. *Ibid.*
44. V. Elwin, *op. cit.*, pp. 90-99.
45. *Ibid.*
46. *Ibid.*
47. *Ibid.*, pp. 59-62.
48. *Ibid.*
49. *Ibid.*
50. *Ibid.*
51. *Ibid.*
52. *Ibid.*
53. *Ibid.*

54. Statistical Hand Book, 1980-81, pp. 84-94.
55. *Ibid.*
56. *Ibid.*
57. *Ibid.*
58. Statistical Hand Book, 1980-81, p. 76.
59. P. Dutta, *op. cit.*, pp. 53-54.
60. V. Elwin, *op. cit.*, pp. 32-50.
61. *Ibid.*
62. *Ibid.*, pp. 22-35.
63. *Ibid.*
64. *Ibid.*
65. *Ibid.*, p. 4.

APPENDICES

APPENDIX-A

THE INNER LINE REGULATION, 1873[1]

Regulation under Act XXXIII Vic, Chap. 3, Sec. I.

A Regulation for the Peace and Government of certain districts on the Eastern Frontier of Bengal.

Whereas the Secretary of State for India in Council as by resolution in Council declared the provisions of the Q Vict. Act XXXIII, Chap. 3, Section 1, to be applicable to the districts of Kamrup, Darrang, Nowgong, Sibsagar, Lakhimpur, Garo hills, Khasi and Jaintia hills, Naga hills, Cachar and Chittagong hills;

And whereas the Lieutenant Governor of Bengal has proposed to Governor-General in Council a draft of the following Regulation, together with the reasons for proposing the same, for the peace and good government of the said districts;

And whereas the Governor-General in Council has taken such draft and reasons into consideration and has approved of such draft and the same has received the Governor-General's assent:

The following Regulation is now published in *Gazette of India* and will be published in the Calcutta Gazette, and thereupon will have the force of law under thirty-third of Victoria, Chapter III;

1. Bengal Papers in Assam Archives, F. No. 521 of 1873.

1. This Regulation shall extend to the districts named in the preamble, and shall come into force on the Ist of November 1873.
2. It shall be lawful for the Local Government of Bengal, with the previous sanction of the Governor-General in Council, from time to time alter by notification in the *Calcutta Gazette*, a line to be called "The Inner Line" in each or any of the above named districts. The Local Government may, by notification in the *Calcutta Gazette*, prohibit all British subjects, or any class of British subjects, or any persons residing in, or passing through such districts, from going beyond such line without a pass under the hand and seal of the executive officer as be may authorised to grant such pass; and the Local Government may from time to time cancel or vary such prohibit.
3. Any British subject or other person to prohibit who goes beyond the 'Inner Line' fixed in accordance with Section 2 of the Regulation, after its notification, in the *Calcutta Gazette*, without a pass, shall be liable on conviction before a Magistrate to a fine not exceeding Rs. 100 for the first offence and to a fine of not exceeding Rs. 500 or to simple or rigorous imprisonment for a term not exceeding three months, or to both for each subsequent offence.
4. The Local Government may, from time to time prescribe, by notification in the *Calcutta Gazette*, a form of pass for each district and may in such form of pass fix such restrictions or conditions the Local Government may deem fit and may require the payment of such dues and fees for such passes as the Local Government may deem proper. Any holder of such pass shall on breach of any such restriction or conditions be liable on conviction to a fine not exceeding Rs. 100 for a first offence and to a fine not

exceeding Rs. 500 or to simple or rigorous imprisonment which may extend to three months or to both for each subsequent offence.

5. Any rubber, wax, ivory or other jungle product found in possession of any person convicted of an offence under this Regulation may be confiscated to the Government by an order to be passed at the time of conviction by the Magistrate.
6. The Chief Executive Officer of any district comprised in any notification as aforesaid may, subject to the approval of the Local Government, authorise, by a written instrument under his hand, any public servant to arrest and bring before him with the least practicable delay:

   Firstly—Any person prohibited from crossing the Inner Line prescribed for such district if such person shall be found beyond the line and when asked to produce his pass shall refuse or be unable to do.
   Secondly—Any person to whom a pass may have been granted, and who has committed any infraction of its conditions.

7. It shall not be lawful for any British subject, or other persons not being a native of the district comprised in the preamble of this Regulation to acquire any interest in the land or the product of land beyond the said Inner Line without the sanction of the Local Government officer as the Local Government shall appoint in this behalf. Any interest so acquired may be dealt with as the Local Government or its said officer shall direct. The Local Government may also by notification in the Local Gazette extend the prohibition contained in this section to any class of persons natives of the said districts and may from time to time in like manner cancel or vary such extension.

8. Wherever, without the written permission of the officers authorised by the Local Government to grant such permission kills or captures or attempts to kill or capture, or abets the killing or capturing of a wild elephant in any of the districts to which this Regulation extends, shall be liable to a fine not exceeding Rs. 200 for each elephant so killed or captured and any elephant so killed or captured shall be confiscated to Government provided that no person who kills or abets the killing of an elephant in protection of himself, his house or his crops, shall be liable to punishment; and provided also that every person who in the like case captures, or abets the capture of an elephant shall not be liable to fine, but shall be bound to surrender such captured elephant to the government or to pay such royalty thereon as the Local Government may from time to time direct.
9. It shall be competent for the Local Government to make rules for the issue of licence to kill or capture elephant and for all purposes connected with the capture of elephant.
10. The prosecution for every offence punishable under section 8 of the Regulation shall be commenced within 6 months after the offence is committed.
11. Offences against this Regulation may be tried by Magistrate of the first or second class and shall be bailable.

APPENDIX-B

INDIA-TIBET FRONTIER, 1914; EXCHANGE OF NOTES BETWEEN THE BRITISH AND TIBETAN PLENIPOTENTIARIES[1]

To
Lonchen Shatra, Tibetan Plenipotentiary,

In February last, you accepted the India-Tibet frontier from the Isu Razi Pass to the Bhutan frontier, as given in the map (two sheets), of which two copies are herewith attached, subject to the confirmation of your Government and the following conditions:

(a) The Tibetan ownership in private estates on the British side of the frontier will not be disturbed.

(b) If the sacred places of Tso Karpo and Tsari Sarpa fall within a day's march of the British side of the frontier, they will be included in Tibetan territory and the frontier modified accordingly.

I understand that your Government have now agreed to this frontier subject to the above two conditions. I shall be glad to learn definitely from you that this is the case.

You wished to know whether certain dues now collected by the Tibetan Government at Tsona Jong and in Kongbu and Kham from the Mompas and Lopas for articles sold may still be collected. Mr. Bell has informed you that such details will be settled in a friendly spirit, when you have furnished him the further information which you promised.

---

1. Foreign Political (Secret) Proceedings (India), October 1914, Nos. 136-396.

The final settlement of this India-Tibet frontier will help to prevent causes of future dispute and thus cannot fail to be of great advantage to both Governments.

A.H. McMahon

Delhi 24th March, 1914 British Plenipotentiary

(Translation)

To

Sir Henry MacMahon,

British Plenipotentiary to the China-Tibet Conference.

As it was feared that there might be friction in future unless the boundary between India and Tibet is clearly defined, I submitted the map, which you sent to me in February last, to the Tibetan Government at Lhasa for orders. I have now received orders from Lhasa, and accordingly agree to the boundary as marked in red in the two copies of the maps signed by you subject to the condition mentioned in your letter, dated 24th March, sent to me through Mr. Bell. I have signed and sealed the two copies of the maps. I have kept one copy here and returned herewith the other.

Sent on the 29th day of the Ist month of the Wood-Tiger year (25th March 1914) by Lonchen Shatra, the Tibetan Plenipotentiary.

Seal of Lonchen Shatra

APPENDIX-C

SCHEDULED DISTRICTS ACT, 1874[1]

An Act to ascertain the enactments in force in various parts of British India, and for other purposes.

Whereas various parts of British India have never been brought within, or have from time to time been removed from, the operation of the general Acts and Regulations and the jurisdiction of the ordinary Courts of Judicature;

And whereas doubts have arisen in some cases as to which Acts or Regulations are in force in such parts and in other cases as to what are the boundaries of such parts;

And whereas among such parts are the territories specified in the first schedule hereto annexed, and it is expedient to provide readier means than now exist for ascertaining the enactments in force in such territories and the boundaries thereof, and for administering the law therein;

And whereas it is expedient to declare that certain Acts are in force in a tract of land lying between the Railway Station at Satna and the eastern boundary of the Jabalpur Division;

(It is hereby enacted as follows:)

1. This Act may be called the Scheduled District Act, 1874.

   This Act extends in the first instance to the whole of British India other than the territories mentioned in the first schedule hereto annexed, and it shall come into force in each of the Scheduled Districts on the

---

1. Luthra (Col.) P.N., *Constitutional and Administrative Growth of NEFA*, (Shillong, 1972).

issue of a notification under section 3 relating to such district.

In this Act the term "Scheduled Districts" means the territories mentioned in the first schedule hereto annexed; and from the date fixed in the resolution next hereinafter mentioned, it shall also include any other territory to which the Secretary of State for India, by resolution in Council may declare the provisions of the 33rd of Victoria, chapter 3, section 1, to be applicable.

2. The enactments mentioned in the second schedule hereto annexed shall be repealed.

3. The Local Government**** may from time to time, by notification** in the local Gazette**:

   (a) declare what enactments are actually in force in any of the Scheduled Districts, or in any part of the any such district,
   (b) declare of any enactment that it is not actually in force in any of the districts or in any part of any such district,
   (c) correct any mistake of fact in any notification issued under this section:

   Provided that a declaration once made under clause (a) or clause (b) of this section shall not be altered by any subsequent declaration other than a declaration under clause (c) of this section.

4. On the issue, under section 3, of the notification declaring what enactments are in force, or not in force in any Scheduled District, the enactments so notified shall be deemed to be in force or not in force, according to the tenor of the notification, in such district, and every such notification shall be binding on all courts of law.

5. The Local Government*** may, from time to time, by notification*** in the local Gazette*** extend to any

of the Scheduled Districts or to any part of any such district, any enactment which is in force in any part of British India at the date of such extension.

5A. In declaring an enactment in force in a Scheduled District or part thereof under section 3 of this Act, or in extending an enactment to a Scheduled District or part thereof under Section 5 of this Act, the Local Government**** may declare the operation of the enactment to be subject to such restrictions and modifications as that Government thinks fit.

6. The Local Government may from time to time:

(a) appoint officers to administer civil and criminal justice and to superintend the settlement and collection of the public revenue, and all matters relating to rent and otherwise to conduct the administration, within the Scheduled District,

(b) regulate the procedure of the officers so appointed; but not so as to restrict the operation of any enactment for the time being in force in any of the said districts,

(c) direct by what authority any jurisdiction, powers or duties incident to the operation of any enactment for the time being in force in such district shall be exercised or performed.

7. All rules heretofore prescribed by the Governor-General in Council or the Local Government for the guidance of officers appointed within any of the Scheduled Districts for all or any of the purposes mentioned in section 6, and in force at the time of the passing of this Act, shall continue to be in force unless and until the Governor-General in Council or the Local Government, as the case may be, otherwise directs.

All existing officers so appointed previous to the date on which this Act comes into force in such districts shall be deemed to have been appointed hereunder.

8. Whenever any question arises as to the line of boundary between any of the Scheduled Districts and other territory, such officer as the Local Government or (where the said district and the other territory are not subject to the same Local Government) as the Governor-General in Council from time to time appoints, may consider and determine such line of boundary; and the order made thereon by such officer, if confirmed by the Government which appointed him, shall be conclusive in all Courts of Justice.

9. Any person liable to be imprisoned or to be transported beyond sea under any order or sentence passed by any officer appointed under section 6 may (subject to such rules as the Local Government may from time to time prescribe in this behalf) be imprisoned in such jail or transported to such place as the Local Government directs.

10. Acts No. III of 1867, *** and No. XXV of 1869 are hereby declared to be in force in the tract of land ceded to the British Government in the year 1863 and lying between the Railway Station at Satna and the eastern boundary of the Jabalpur District.

11. Nothing contained in this Act or in any notification issued under the power hereby conferred shall be deemed:

    (a) to affect the criminal jurisdiction of any Court over European British subjects, or
    (b) to effect any law other than laws contained in Acts or Regulations or in Rules made in exercise of powers conferred by such Acts or Regulations.

THE FIRST SCHEDULE

See Section I

Part I

Scheduled Districts, 5 Madras
1—In Ganjam

Part X

The Chief Commissionership of Assam

APPENDIX-D

ASSAM FRONTIER TRACT REGULATION, 1880[1]

Whereas it is expedient to provide for the removal of certain frontier tracts in Assam inhabited or frequented by barbarous or semicivilized tribes from the operation of enactments in force therein; It is hereby enacted as follows:

1. This regulation may be called the Assam Frontier Tracts Regulation, 1880.

It extends to such frontier tracts within the territories (for time being) administered by the Chief Commissioner of Assam (as he) may, by notification in the (local Gazette) from time to time direct;

and it shall come into force in each of such tracts on such day as (he) in like manners directs in this behalf.

2. When the Regulation has been extended in manner hereinbefore prescribed to any tract, the Chief Commissioner may from time to time**** by notification in the local Gazette, direct that any enactment in force in such tract shall cease to be in force therein, but not so as to affect the criminal jurisdiction of any Court over European British subjects.

3. Whenever any question arises as to the line of boundary between any tract to which the provisions of this Regulation have been extended as aforesaid and the adjoining territory in British India, such officer as the Chief Commissioner of Assam from time to time appoints may consider and determine such line of boundary; and the order made thereon by such officer, if confirmed by the said Chief Commissioner, shall be conclusive.

---

1. Foreign Proceedings (Assam), April 1884, No. 1.

APPENDIX-E

RULES FOR THE ADMINISTRATION OF JUSTICE IN THE DIBRUGARH FRONTIER TRACT[1]

Administration of the Dibrugarh Frontier Tract

No. 7751P—In exercise of the powers conferred upon him by section 6 of Act XIV of 1874 (the Scheduled Districts Act), the Chief Commissioner is pleased to prescribe the following rules for the administration of justice in the Dibrugarh Frontier Tract. This concels all previous orders on the subject, but does not affect the rules published with Notification No. 142J, dated the 23rd December 1888:

I. GENERAL

1. The administration of the Dibrugarh Frontier Tract is vested in the Chief Commissioner of Assam, the Political Officer, Central and Eastern Sections, North-East Frontier, his Assistants, and the native village authorities, or such other officer or officers as the Chief Commissioner may see fit from time to time to appoint in that behalf, subject to the restrictions and rules hereinafter recorded.

2. The Political Officer shall nominate and appoint the village authorities, if any, subject to the confirmation of the Chief Commissioner and shall assign to them their respective functions under these rules, and define, so far as may be necessary, the local limits within which such duties shall be exercised by each, respectively, and may cancel or modify any such order. When no village authorities have been so

---

1. Foreign Proceedings (Assam), April 1884, Nos. 1-38.

nominated and appointed, the powers and duties assigned to them by these rules shall be exercised and performed by the Political Officer or by such other officers as he may depute for this purpose.

II. POLICE

3. The ordinary duties of policy in respect of crime will be discharged by the village authorities. They shall arrest all criminals and maintain peace and order within their respective local limits.

4. It shall be the duty of the village authorities to report to the Political Officer or such other officer as may be authorised by him in that behalf, at the earliest practical moment, all crimes, violent deaths, and serious accidents occurring within their respective local limits, and all occurrences, whether within or beyond such limits, which may come to their knowledge and which are likely to affect the public peace; and to deliver up offenders as soon as may be to the officer authorised to try them.

5. The village authorities shall watch and report, or apprehend and deliver up, all vagrants or bad and suspicious characters found within their respective local limites.

Administration of the Dibrugarh Frontier Tract

6. On the occurrence of any heinous crime* or of offences under the Arms Act or Excise Act within their local limits, the inhabitants of the village shall at once, if possible, apprehend the offender, and in any case shall at once inform the chief village authority, who, if the offender has not been apprehended, shall proceed without delay to the place where the crime occurred, and enquire into the matter. He shall further, as soon as possible, report any such offence to the

* Heinous crimes are—

Arson, Cattle Stealing, Counterfeiting coin or passing it, Dacoity, Wounding to the danger of life or limb, House breaking, Murder, Rape, Rebellion, Robbery, and Riot.

Political Officer or such other officer as may be duly authorised by him in that behalf, whether the offender has been apprehended or not.

7. The village authorities may pursue an offender fleeing beyond their jurisdiction and arrest him, but shall not ordinarily attempt to arrest an offender beyond their own jurisdiction without the cognisance and co-operation of the village authorities within whose limits the offender has fled. When an offender is traced from one jurisdiction to another, it will be sufficient to point him out to the village authorities within whose limits he may be found, aiding them, if required, to effect his capture.

8. When the village authorities are unable to arrest an offender, they shall apply to the Political Officer or such other officer as may be duly authorised by him in this behalf for the aid of the regular police.

9. All inhabitants of the tract are bound to aid the village authorities when required to do so for the maintenance of order or apprehending offenders, and are liable to fine for failing to give such assistance; the fine to be adjudged by chief village authority to the extent of his powers in criminal cases, or by the Political Officer or his Assistants. And if it appears that the community is to blame, and that particular offenders cannot be discovered a fine may be imposed upon the community, but by the Political Officer only.

10. Misconduct on the part of the village authorities in police matters shall be punishable by the fine which may extend to Rs. 500, or by simple imprisonment to the extent which would be awardable under the Penal Code or other law for a like offence, or by both. Imprisonment may be awarded in lieu of fine in accordance with the provisions of the Penal Code or any other law in force.

11. An appeal shall lie from all orders of the chief village authority in police matters to an Assistant Political Officer authorised by the Political Officer in that behalf, and from him to the Political Officer, whose orders are final; but

the Chief Commissioner may at any time call for the proceedings, and modify or reverse any order of the Political Officer.

III. CRIMINAL PROCEDURE

12. Criminal justice shall be ordinarily administered by the Political Officer and his Assistants and by the chief village authority duly authorised in this behalf.

13. The Political Officer shall be competent to pass sentence of death, transportation, or imprisonment up to the maximum amount provided for the offence, of whipping, and of fine up to any amount: Provided that all sentences of death or transportation or imprisonment for a term of seven years and upwards shall be subject to the confirmation of the Chief Commissioner.

Administration of the Dibrugarh Frontier Tract

The Chief Commissioner or Political officer may call for the proceedings of any officer subordinate to him and reduce, enhance or cancel any sentence passed or remand the case for retrial; but no offence shall be punished by a sentence exceeding that awardable under the Indian Penal Code. The Assistant Political Officers shall exercise such powers not exceeding these of a Magistrate of the first class as defined in the Criminal Procedure Code, as they may be invested with by the Chief Commissioner.

14. The chief village authorities may themselves dispose of the cases of persons residing within their jurisdiction charged with the following offences:

Theft.
Injury to property of whatever kind.
Injury to person not endangering life or limb.
House-trespass.
Affronts of whatever kind.

15. The chief village authorities may impose a fine for any offence which they are competent to try up to a limit of Rs. 50 and may award restitution or compensation to the extent of the injury sustained. Fines may be enforced by distraint of the property of the offender.

16. The chief village authorities may not decide in cases:

(a) where their father, mother, son, daughter, their wife, or the children, husbands, or wives of any of these are concerned; or
(b) where the defendant does not reside within their jurisdiction;
(c) where the offence is one against the State or of causing death or danger to life or limb, or of robbery of any sort with violence or of arson or of making or passing counterfeit coins or of making fraudulent documents, or offences under the Arms Act or Excise Act, and generally any offences of a heinous nature.

17. The chief village authorities shall decide all cases in open Darbar in the presence of at least three witnesses and of the complainant and accused whose attendance they are empowered to compel.

18. The chief village authority may carry out his decision as soon as pronounced, unless the accused person appeals. If the sentence is fine, and the accused person does not pay, he shall be sent to the Political Officer or any Assistant authorised by him in that behalf to be dealt with while the fine is being realised.

19. Either party may appeal from the decision of the chief village authority at the time the decision is pronounced. The case shall then be tried de novo.

20. An appeal shall lie from the decision of an Assistant Political Officer to the Political Officer if preferred within thirty days.

21. No appeal shall lie as a matter of right from any sentence passed by the Political Officer involving less than

three years' imprisonment. An appeal shall lie to the Chief Commissioner against sentences of three years' imprisonment and upwards, and from all sentences of death or transportation. Appeals must be presented within thirty days of the date of the order appealed against excluding the time required for procuring copy of the order; Provided that an appeal from a sentence of death shall be preferred within seven days from the data of the sentence.

Administration of the Dibrugarh Frontier Tract

22. The Political Officer and the Assistant Political Officers shall be guided in regard to procedure by the principles of the Code of Criminal Procedure so far as they are applicable to the circumstances of the district and consistent with these rules. The chief exception are:

(a) Verbal orders or notice only shall be requisite in any case except when the regular police are employed, or when the person concerned is not a resident of or in the tract at the time; but orders or summonses shall in every case be for a fixed day, and the order shall be made known to the person concerned or to some adult member of his family, and failing this shall be openly proclaimed at the place where he is, or was last known to be, in sufficient time to allow him, if he sees fit, to appear.

(b) The proceedings of the chief village authorities need not be recorded in writing, nor shall it be necessary that examinations before the Political Officer and the Assistant Political Officers be signed by the parties examined; but the Political Officer may require the chief village authorities to report their proceedings in any way which appears to him suitable.

(c) There shall be no preliminary enquiries by regular or village police unless the Political Officer or Assistant Political Officer see fit to directions.

(d) Recognisance to appear shall not be taken unless it appears necessary to the Political Officer or Assistant Political Officer.

(e) Examinations and proceedings generally shall be recorded in English only.

(f) Oaths shall be administered to parties and witnesses in cases where the accused is charged with murder, but not in other cases unless the Court or either party so require. It is, however, at all times optional with the Court to put witnesses on oath; but witnesses, whether on oath or not, shall be punishable for giving false evidence. In all cases where oaths are administered, all persons shall be sworn in the mode most binding on their conscience.

IV. CIVIL PROCEDURE

23. The administration of civil justice in the Dibrugarh Frontier Tract shall be conducted by the Political Officer, the Assistant Political Officers and the chief village authorities.

24. The chief village authorities may try cases in which plaintiff and defendant are living in their jurisdiction without limit as to amout, but with the following reservations.

25. The chief village authorities may not try suits in which their fathers, mothers, sons or daughters, uncles or aunts, sisters or brothers, the children of any of the foregoing, their wives, or persons in the above relationship to a wife, or any near relative, are concerned.

26. All suits shall be decided in open Darbar in the presence of the parties, and at least three respectable witnesses.

27. The chief village authorities shall have power to compel attendance of parties to any suit and witnesses, and to fine up to a limit of Rs. 50 to persons failing to attend when ordered to do so. They have power to award all costs, also compensation to defendants for unfounded or vexatious suits brought against them.

Administration of the Dibrugarh Frontier Tract

28. All proceedings shall be viva voce, but the Political Officer may require the chief village authorities to report their proceedings in any way which appears to him suitable. After hearing both parties and their witnesses, if any, they shall, with or without the opinion of assessors, as they may see fit, forthwith pronounce a decision.

29. The chief village authorities may carry out their decisins at once, if necessary, by destraint of any property belonging to the person found liable, to pay (unless appeal is made, or security given to the chief village authorities' satisfaction); but if an appeal is made at the time of decision, the chief village authority shall send up the parties and their witnesses to the Political Officer or any other officer authorised by him in that behalf forthwith, as soon as may be. He shall either accompany them himself or send at least one respectable person who has been present at the trial with them.

30. The political Officer and the Assistant Political officers shall not ordinarily hear any suits triable by the chief village authorities; but suits which under these rules the chief village authority cannot try shall be tried by the Political Officer or an Assistant Political Officer.

31. The Political Officer and the Assistant Political Officers shall in all cases coming before them, in which the parties are indigenous inhabitants of the frontier tract, endeavour to induce them to submit their case to a Panchayat. In that event, each party shall name an equal number of arbitrators, and the Court shall either choose, or leave the arbitrators to choose an umpire. The name and residence of the arbitrators and umpire and the matter in dispute shall be recorded before their proceedings commence, and the Court shall direct the chief village authority, or some other person, to assemble the Panchayat and witnesses within such reasonable period as the Court may fix. When the case has been decided, the umpire shall appear with the parties

before the Court, which shall proceed to record the decision and enforce it as its own. From such decision there shall be no appeal.

32. On appeals to the Political Officer from a decision of the chief village authority, a record shall be made of the matter in dispute, and of the decision of the chief village authority; if necessary, the Court shall examine the parties, and, if the decision appears to be just, it shall be affirmed and enforced by the Court as its own. If, on the other hand, the Court sees grounds to doubt the justice of the decision, it shall try the case *de novo*, or refer it to a Panchayat, as provided above.

33. Decrees against persons resident beyond the jurisdiction of the Court in the Dibrugarh Frontier Tract, if satisfaction cannot be obtained within the Dibrugarh Frontier Tract, shall be tranferred for execution to the Court having jurisdiction.

34. Houses, needful clothing, or cooking utensils, or implements whereby the owner or his family subsists, shall not be attached, soil, or tranferred in execution of a decree, unless the house or other thing above exempted is the actual subject-matter of the suit. Land may be sold or temporarily transferred where custom admits of individual right in it being recognised.

35. There shall be no imprisonment for debt, excepting when the Political Officer is satisfied that fraudulent disposition or concealment of property has taken place. In such case the debtor may be detained for a period not exceeding six months.

Administration of the Dibrugarh Frontier Tract

36. The Chief Commissioner or a Political Officer may, on application or otherwise, call for the Proceedings of any case decided by any officer subordinate to him and pass such orders as he may deem fit.

37. An appeal shall lie to the Political Officer against

any decision of an Assistant Political Officer, and to the Chief Commissioner against an original decision of the Political Officer, if the value of the suit be rupees five hundred or over, or if the suit involve a question of tribal rights or customs, or of right to, or possession of, immoveable property: Provided that the petiton of appeal accompanied by a copy of the order appealed against and by a clear statement of the grounds of appeal be filed within thirty days from the date of decision, excluding the time required for obtaining a copy of the decision. An appeal which lies to the Chief Commissioner may be presented to the Political Officer, who shall, if it be in order and presented in due time, endorse upon it the date of receipt and transmit it with the records of the case to the Chief Commissioner.

The decree of the Appellate Court shall be transferred to the Court passing the original order for execution as a decree of its own.

37. The Courts of the Chief Commissioner, Political Officer and Assistant Political Officers, shall be guided by the spirit, but not be bound by the letters of the Code of Civil Procedure.

38. No professional pleader or mukhtar shall be allowed to appear in any case except with the sanction of the Court. Near relatives may appear for persons incapacitated by age, sex, or sickness.

39. Oaths shall not be administered to parties or witnesses in suits unless the Court or either party to a suit so require. In all cases where oaths are administered, all persons shall be sworn in the manner most binding on their conscience. It is at all times optional with the Court to put witnesses on oath; but witnesses whether on oath or not, shall be punishable for giving false evidence.

40. The Political Officer is empowered to try suits up to any amount. The Assistant Political Officers shall hear and decide original civil suits up to a value of Rs. 1,000 and shall hear and decide appeals from the decision of the chief village authorities up to a value of Rs. 300.

BIBLIOGRAPHY

PRIMARY SOURCES

1. UNPUBLISHED RECORDS

(i) *Proceedings of the Government of Bengal:*

(a) Political Department, 1824-1873;
(b) Judicial Department, 1824-1873;
(c) Police Department, 1824-1873.

(ii) *Proceedings of the Government of Eastern Bengal and Assam, Political Department, 1905-12.*

(iii) *Proceedings of the Government of Assam:*

(a) Foreign Proceedings of the Chief Commissioner of Assam, 1874-1905.
(b) Political Proceedings of the Chief Commissioner of Assam, 1912-20.
(c) Political Proceedings of the Government of Assam, 1921-37.
(d) Proceedings of the Tribal Affairs Department, Governor's Secretariat, 1937-47.

(iv) *Foreign Political Proceedings of the Government of India, 1824-1915.*

(v) *Lakhimpur Deputy Commissioner's Collection, 1874-1947.*

2. PUBLISHED RECORDS, REPORTS AND GAZETTEERS

(i) Aitchison, C.U., *A Collection of Treaties,*

Engagements and Sanads Relating to India and Neighbouring Countries, (Calcutta 1862).

(ii) *Survey of India Records, 1874-75.*

(iii) *Selection from the Records of the Bengal Government, XXIII, 1855.*

(iv) *White Papers of the Government of India (On India-China Border Issues), vols. I-XIV.*

(v) A.J.M. Mills' *Report on Assam, 1854.*

(vi) *Census of India Reports, 1881-1941.*

(vii) *Annual Political Reports on the Frontier Tracts, 1874-1945.*

(viii) *Assam Administration Reports, 1874-1946.*

(ix) *Report on Indian Constitutional Reforms, 1918.*

(x) *Report of the Indian Statutory Commission, Vol. I&II, 1930.*

(xi) *Report of the Officials of the Government of India and the People's Republic of China on the Boundary Question.*

(xii) *Assam Government Hand Book, (Shillong, 1938).*

(xiii) *Assam District Gazetteers, (Shillong, 1906).*

(xiv) *Imperial Gazetteer, vol. IV, 1905.*

(xv) *Statistical Hand Book of Arunachal Pradesh, 1980-81.*

3. MAPS

(i) *Atlas of the Northern Frontier of India, Ministry of External Affairs, New Delhi, 1960.*

(ii) *Augusto Gansser's Geology of the Himalayas Maps.*

(iii) *Evolution of the Administrative Jurisdictions of the North-East Frontier Agency, Shillong, 1965.*

4. NEWS PAPER—ARUNACHAL ECHO, 1990

SECONDARY WORKS

Aidye, (General) Sir J., *Indian Frontier Policy* (London, 1897).

Amanatulla (Khan Choudhury), Ahmed, *A History of Cooch Behar*, (Cooch Behar, 1936).

Bailey, F.M., No Passport to Tibet, (London, 1957).

—, China, *Tibet and Assam* (London, 1945).

Banerjee, A.C., *Eastern Frontier of British India*, (Calcutta, 1943, 3rd edition 1954).

—, Annexation of Burma (Calcutta, 1944).

Barooah, N., David Scott in North-East India 1802-31, *A Study in British Paternalism* (New Delhi, 1970).

Baruah, G., *Ahom Buranji* (Gauhati, 1930).

Barua, H., *Asom Buranji* (Gauhati, 1930).

Baruah, T., *The Idu Mishmis*, (Shillong, 1961).

Basu, D., *Constitutional Documents*, vol. I, (Calcutta, 1969).

Baveja, J.D., *Across the Golden Heights of Assam and NEFA*.

Bell, C., *Tibet—Past and Present* (London, 1924-48).

Beresford, G.W., *Notes on the North-East Frontier of Assam*, (Shillong, 1881), reprinted 1906).

Bhuyan, S.K., *Anglo-Assamese Relations, 1771-1826* (Gauhati, 1947).

Buckland, C.E., *Dictionary of Indian Biography*, (London, 1906).

Butler, John, *Travels and Adventures in the Province of Assam*, (London, 1855).

Chakravarti, P.C., *Evolution of India's Northern Borders* (New Delhi, 1971).

Chakravorty, B.C., *British Relations with the Hill Tribes of Assam since 1858* (Calcutta, 1964).

—, *India-China Relations*, (Calcutta, 1965).

Chakravorty, L.N., *Glimpses of the History of Arunachal Pradesh*, (Shillong, 1973).

Chowdhury, J.N., *A Comparative Study of the Adi Religion* (1971).

—, *The Hills Miris* (Shillong, 1970).

—, *Arunachal Panorama* (Shillong, 1973).

Dalton, E.T., *Descriptive Ethnology of Bengal*, (Calcutta, 1872, 1960).

Dalvi, (Brigadier) J.P., *The Himalayan Blunder*, (Bombay, 1969).

Devi, L., *Ahom-Tribal Relations*, (Gauhati, 1968).

Duff-Sutherland-Dunbar, G., *Abors and Galongs (Memoirs of Asiatic Society of Bengal*, vol. V, 1913-17).

Dun, G.W., *Preliminary Notes on Daphlas* (Simla, 1896).

—, *Preliminary Notes on Miris* (Simla, 1896).

Dutta, P., *The Tangsas of the Namchik and Tirap Valley*, (Shillong, 1959).

—, *Arunachal Pradesh—An Overview* (Itanagar, 1989).

Elwin, V., *A Philosophy for NEFA* (Shillong, 1957, 1959).

—, *Democracy in NEFA* (Shillong, 1965).

—, *India's North-East Frontier in the Nineteenth Century* (Oxford, 1959, 1962).

—, *Myths of the North-East Frontier of India* (Shillong, 1958).

—, *The Art of the North-East Frontier of India* (Shillong, 1959).

—, 'The North-East Frontier Agency of India', (*Geographical Magazine*, vol. XXIX, 1956, pp. 405-16).

—, *The Tribal World of Verrier Elwin* (Oxford, 1964).

Furer-Haimendorf, C. Von., 'Agriculture and Land Tenure among the Apa Tanis' (*Man in India*, vol. XXVI, 1946, pp. 20-49).

—, *Ethnographic Notes on the Tribes of the Subansiri Region* (Shillong, 1947).

Gait, E., *A History of Assam*, (Calcutta, 1926).

Gansser, A., *Geology of the Himalayas*, (New York, 1964).

Gogoi, L., *The Tai Khamtis*, (Namsoon, NEFA, 1971).

Grierson, G., *Linguistic Survey of India*, vols. I-IV (Calcutta, 1905).

Gupta, K., *The Hidden History of the Sino-Indian Frontier*, (Calcutta, 1974).

Hamilton, F., *An Account of Assam*, compiled between 1907-14; edited by S.K. Bhuyan (Gauhati, 1940).

Hannay, S.F., Sketch of the Singphos, or the Kakhyens of Burma; the Position of the Tribes as regards Bauno and the Inland Trade of the Irrawaddy with Yunan, followed by an Account of the Shans (Calcutta, 1847).

Hesselmeyer, C.H., 'The Hill Tribes of the Northern Frontier of Assam' (*J.A.S.B.*, vol. XXXVII, 1968, pp. 192-208.

Hunter, W.W., *A Statistical Account of Assam* (London, 1879).

Hutton, J.H., *A Primitive Philosophy of Life* (Oxford, 1938).

—, 'Head Hunters of the North-East Frontiers' (*Journal of Royal Society of Arts*, vol. LXXXII, 1936, pp. 134-44).

Ilbert, (Sir) Courtenay, *The Government of India* (London, 1915).

James, O.E., *The Beginning of Religion* (New York), 1958).

Johri, (Major) S., *Where India, China and Burma Meet*, (Calcutta, 1962).

Kennedy, R.S., *Ethnological Report on the Akas, Khoas, and Mijis and the Membas of Tawang* (Shillong, 1914).

Lahiri, R.N., *Annexation of Assam* (Calcutta, 1954).

Lamb, Alastair, *India-China Border: The Origins of the Disputed Boundaries* (London, 1964).

—, *The MacMahon Line: A Study of Relations between India, China and Tibet 1904-14*, (London, 1966).

Luthra (Col.) P.N., Constitutional and Administrative Growth of NEFA, Shillong, 1969.

Mackenzie, A., *Memorandum on the North-East Frontier of Bengal*, (Calcutta, 1869).

Mackenzie, A., *History of the Relations of the Government with the Hill Tribes of the North-East Frontier of Bengal* (Calcutta, 1884).

Maxwell, N., *India's China War*, (Bombay, 1970).

Mehra, P., *The Younghusband Expedition*, (Bombay, 1968).

—, *The MacMahon Line and After*, (Madras, 1974).

Mehta, K.L., 'The North-East Frontier Agency Today' (*March of India*, vol. VIII, 1956, pp. 8-12).

Mills, J.P., *The Mishmi Hills of the Lohit Valley* (Reprint, Shillong, 1962).

Mishra, S.D., *Rivers of India*, NBT, (New Delhi, 1970).

Pemberton, R.B., Report on the Eastern Frontier of British India, (Calcutta, 1835).

Rahul, Ram, *The Himalaya Borderland*, (Delhi, 1970).

Rao, K. Krishna, *The Sino-Indian Boundary Question and International Law* (New Delhi, 1963).

Reid, R., *History of the Frontier Areas bordering on Assam from 1883-1941*, (Shillong, 1942).

Reid, R., *Years of Change in Bengal and Assam*, (London, 1966).

Richardson, H.E., *Tibet and Its History*, (Oxford, 1962).

Robinson, W., *A Descriptive Account of Assam* (London, 1841).

Rustomji, N., *Tribal Administration in the North-East Frontier Agency*, (Delhi, 1955).

Rose, L.E., and Fisher, M.W., *North-East Frontier Agency of India*, (California, 1967).

Shakespeare, L.W., *History of the Assam Rifles*, (London, 1929).

Sharma, S.P., *The India-China Border Dispute: An Indian Perspective*, (New Delhi, 1967).

Sing, (Buragohain) P., *Asom Buranji, Transcript No.* 109 (Director of Historical & Antiquarian Studies, Gauhati).

Sing, R.L., (ed.), *India—A Regional Geography*, (Varanasi, 1971).

Thomas, M.M. and Taylor, R.W., (ed.), *Tribal Awakening: A Group Study*, (Bangalore, 1965).

Younghusband, F., *India and Tibet*, (London, 1910, Reprinted, 1971).

INDEX

Abors, 13, 17, 148
expedition, 59
Acharya Permanand, 83
Adis, 73-74, 112, 126, 158, 162
Hills, 10-12
Administration, 59
experiments in, 182-84
Africa, 261
Agreement, 2, 61, 78, 112, 118, 156
Agriculture, 29-30
Agricultural,
ceremonies, 38
demonstration, 183-84
economy, 33
Ahom authorities, 55
Ahom Buranji, 85
Ahom Rajas, 57
system, 154
Aitchinson, 54, 140, 147
Akas (tribes), 7, 57, 60, 63, 72, 112, 148, 201
Akasi Ganga, 41
Anchal Samity, 242, 243, 244, 252, 254
Anglo-Burmese War (1824-26), 60, 88, 135
Anglo-Chinese Adhesion agreement, 131
Anglo-Chinese convention, 133, 145
Anglo-Russion convention (1907), 132
Anglo-Tibetan Boundary agreement, 144
Anglo-Tibetan negotiations, 143
Annual pensions, 62
Anti-congress ryots, 216
Apa-Tanis, 8, 19, 65
Arunachal Pradesh,
Administration, 256
Communication facilities, 15-16
Constitutional and administrative growth, 230-35
economy, 29-30
educational objectives, 258-59
festivals, 25-26
industry and commerce, 256-57
intelligence service, 155-56
languages, 21-24
natural resources, 256
new profile of, 250-60
religious philosophy, 39
tribal society, 21-24
Assam, 157, 172
rule in, 157-58
Assam Frontier Police Regulation, 165
Assam Frontier Tract Regulation (1880), 59, 101, 172, 174, 179, 180, 208, 275
Assam Land and Revenue Regulation, 173
Assam Light Infantry, 162
Autonomy, 133

Backward Tract, 215
Balipara Frontier Tract, 212, 221, 230
Ballantine, W.T.H., 180
Bangladesh, 224
Bangni, 67
Banges, 9, 28
Banskota Daflas, 158
Barpani, 10
Beeha settlement, 76
Bell, C.A., 125, 126, 135, 136, 211, 268
Bengal Presidency, separation of, 166-68
Bengal Regulation, 160
Bhairou Kund, 40, 92
Bhutan, 1, 4, 10, 71, 113, 119, 126, 127, 132
Bhutias (tribes), 7, 33, 55, 57, 58, 74, 158, 162, 198
Bhuyans (tribes), 42
Blackmail, 67, 68, 97, 195
Bomdila, 5, 8, 236, 254
Border tribes, 127
Boundary agreement, 142, 143
Brahamputra valley, 8, 11, 16, 19, 20, 21, 34, 42, 47, 74, 91, 118, 119, 162, 225
Brahmanism, 36
Bride-price, 23
British administration, 70
    crown, 149
    government, 54, 55, 56, 57, 60, 116
    influence, 215-16
    museum, 87
    negotiation, 133
    Parliament, 218-19
Buddhism, 26, 35
Buranjis, 96
Burma, 1, 14, 45, 112, 127, 216

Cachar Levy, 162
Calcutta Gazettee, 265
Callaghan, T.P.M.O., 180
Cambodiya, 45
Chakmas (tribes), 14
Chakravarty, L.N., 41
Changland, 14
Changnoi Nagas, 98
Charduar, 56, 57, 58, 60
Chatterjee, S.K., 43
China, 18, 34, 46, 122, 127, 157, 213, 230
China-Tibet Conference, 269
Chinese,
    aggression, 132
    allegations, 144
    dragon, 209
    invation, 232
    revolution (1911), 131
    troops, 127
Christian Mission, 224
Chulikata Mishmis, 13, 84
Chutias (tribes), 40, 42, 45
Civil procedure, 282
Clarke, W.S., 116
Coal mines, 100
Cottage industry, 32
Communication facilities, 260
Consolidation, 203-04
Court Fees Act, 172
Crimes, 156-57
Criminal Procedure, 270-80
    refugees, 78
Cross-country trade, 33

Daflas (tribes), 29, 66, 72, 113, 148
Dalai Lama, 5, 122, 131, 132, 133, 136
Dalton, E.T., 202
Daphalas (tribes), 9
Darjeeling, 126
Darrang district, 7, 59, 113, 153
David Scott, 60, 67, 74, 154

Defence, 161
army, 162-63
military police, 163-66
Defence of Plains, 161-62
Devi, L., 57
Dibang Valley, 13
Dibrugarh, 8, 15, 70, 75, 100, 150, 163
Dibrugarh Frontier Tract, 172, 175, 178, 276, 279
administration, 276-77, 281-82, 283-84
Dikrang, 10
Direct administration, 208
Direct collection, 155
Diphuk Pass, 137
Disputes, 70, 87, 92, 89
Drawing of Boundary, 111-14
Dundas, W.C.M., 82, 130, 138, 179
Dwaraka, 40

East India Company, 2, 34, 148
Economy, 29-32
Edgor, J.W., 203
Elapion mishmi, 82
Elections, 252, 253
Elephant Preservation Acts, 174
Elphinstone, Mountstuart, 168
Elliot, Charles, 79, 164, 175, 205
Elwin, V., 35, 233, 234, 237
Employment, 100, 160
Enactments, 173-75
Excavations, 40, 41
Excluded areas, 185, 219
Expedition, 64, 72, 80, 86, 128, 155
Exploitation, 213, 218
Extra-Bhutan Bhutias, 54-55, 197
Fairs, 32-33, 200
First Anglo-Burmese war (1824-26), 2, 96, 193
First World War, 164, 213
Forze, T.Z., 180

Gallong, 9, 55, 56
Garo (tribes), 169
Gauhati, 98
Jail, 61
General election, 253, 254
Ghasi Merees, 158
Ghasi Mishings, 80
Goods exchange, 202-03
Gopinath Bordoloi, 231, 232
Gordon, J.T., 58
Gorkha Regiment, 165
Graham, A.M., 66
Gram Panchayat, 242, 243, 252
Grierson, George A., 18
Gumming, R.C.R., 20
Gurkha Rifles, 65

Harkaras, 156, 181
Hat (weekly market), 69
Hazarikhowas, 60
Herrelmayer, C.H., 18
Hill tribes problems, 114
Hopkinson, Henry, 163, 199
proposal, 205-06
Hos (tribes), 170
Hukanjiri tea garden, 98
Hutton, J.H., 213, 217

Independent tribes, 139
Indian Arms Act (1879), 173
Indian Stamp Act (1899), 172
India-China war (1962), 241
Indo-China Border controversy, 142-45
India-Tibet Frontier, 268
Indo-Tibetan border, 124, 128, 135, 137
Indo-Tibetan Agreement, 137
Inner line, 33, 114-15
regulation, 59, 115-16, 122, 170, 179, 214, 247, 264

Inter-tribal disputes, 70

Jaintia, 44, 69
rebellions, 166
Jairamdas Daulatram, 235, 237
James, E.O., 36
Jamadar, 156
Janata Dal, 154
Janata Party, 254
Jhum cultivation, 138
John Lawrence, 168
Joypore, 93, 98

Kacharis, 14, 44
Kalingpong, 4, 124
Kalikapurana, 41
Kalitas, 42
Kameng Valley, 5, 6, 17
Kamrup, 59
Kashmir, 11, 145
Capt. Kennedy, 19, 45
Khamptis, 13, 24, 46, 87-90, 156, 198
Khasis (tribes), 18, 169
Khawa Gohain, 89
Khonds, 170
Kingdom-ward, W.F., 220
Kotokis, 155, 157, 158, 181
Kuber, 44
Kukis, 217

Ladakh, 34
Lakhimpur, 9, 67, 71, 97, 98, 117, 156
Lakhimpur Armed Police Battalions, 164
Lakhimpur Frontier Tract, 100, 101, 172, 178, 186
Lakhimpur Inner Line, 119
Lakhimpur Military Police, 80
Languages, 161
Lasbax, Emile, 37
Lohit district, 13, 17, 46, 124
Loose Political control, 87, 247
Lord Chelmsford, 214
Lord Curzon's letter, 144
Lord Hardings, 121
Lord Minto, 128
Lord Siva, 40
Luthra, P.N., 270

McMahon line, 7, 12, 19, 82, 133-34, 186, 220
MacCabe, R.B., 65
Mackenzie, Alexanders, 33, 57, 193, 203
Mahabharata, 44
Mahalders, 71
Maharashtra, 260
Malayan Archipelago, 45
Management, 28
Maxwell, P., 64
Maxwell, R.M., 80, 158
Mexico, 261
Miaos, 14
Migration, 16
Militus, P.G., 159
Mills, J.P., 20, 186, 213
Mishings, 72-75, 126, 211
Miris, 148
Mission, 71, 128
Mishmis, 5, 12, 13, 17, 82-84, 126, 148, 162, 211, 218
clans, 24-25
mission, 128
Modernisation, 251
Mopas (tribes), 7, 28, 148, 198
Mongolia, 124, 134
Monogamy, 23
Mont-Ford Reforms, 185
schemes, 214
Montagu, Edwin, 214
Morangs, 24
Mutiny, 3

Nagas, 18, 96, 169, 217

affairs, 100
Naga Hills Military Police, 80
Nagaland, 1, 14, 236
Namche Barwa, 11
Namasangias, 14
Nari Rustomji, 235, 237
Needham, Jack Frances, 79, 85, 86, 176, 209
Negotiations, 55, 57, 62, 68, 70, 77, 151
Nehru, J.L., 142, 233
Nehru-Mao treaty, 238
Nepal, 127, 132
Nepalees coolies, 63
Nevill, G.A., 66, 71, 129, 140
Nishis (tribes), 8, 57, 63, 66, 112, 126, 199, 200
clans, 19
Nishis Bhutias khels, 68
Nizamghat, 79, 114, 175, 205
Noctes, 24
North-East Frontier Agency (NEFA), 1, 40, 140, 236, 245, 246, 250
administration, 239
intelligent, 159-60

O'callaghan, 87
Occupation, 24, 127, 222
Obligation, 31, 75, 125, 222
Orang, 158
Orissa, 260
Ornamentation, 260
Outerline, 120-24
Ownership of land, 31

Paiks, 53, 67
Pakistan, 238
Pancha Sila, 238
Panchayats, 221
Panchayati Raj, 252
regulation, 242
Parasuram Kund, 12, 13, 42, 116
Paterson, A.H., 163
Patkai, 20, 96-100
ranges, 14-16
Peking, 128
Political Agent, 156
duties, 156
Political Jamadar, 181
Political organisation, 28-29
Poll-Tax, 95, 101, 181
Posa, payment, 195-96
Pratap Singha, 53, 60, 73
Protection, 206
Punjab, 208
Purander Singh, 154, 193
Pughe, J.R., 164

Rajasthan, 260
Rajendra Prasad, 233
Rajgurh Ali, 118, 119
Rangpangs Nagas, 101
Regulation province, 157
Regular administration, 214-15
Reid, Robert, 232
Religion and culture, 35-39
Reserved Forest, 255
Reservations, 282
Restriction, 199, 265
Revolutions, 17
Robinson, 9, 16, 17
Robbery, 70
Rungpore Light Infantry, 162
Russia, 213
Russo-Chinese agreement, 131
Russo-Mongolion collaboration, 220

Sacrifices, 37
Sadiya Agency, 154, 156
fairs, 85
Sadiya Frontier Tract, 186, 230
Salt manufacture, 201
Santhals, 170
Sarkari Nagas, 14, 100

Sat Raja, 28, 29, 54, 56, 57
Sati, W., 131
Scheduled District Act (1874), 174, 270
  declaration of, 169-70
Second Anglo-Burmese war (1852), 2, 75, 95, 112, 157
Second World War, 60, 186, 230, 239
Sherdukpen, 7, 19, 28, 57, 198
Shillong, 216
Shifting cultivation, 39
Siang, 11, 12
Sikkim, 4, 132
Sikkim-Tibet frontier, 135
Simla agreement, 147-48
Simla conference, 133, 135, 136, 142, 143, 145, 149, 184, 211, 220
  convention, 145, 147
Simon Commission, 185
Simple administration, 212
Singphos, 12, 20, 24, 46, 90-93
Siwalik sediments, 5
Slavery, 26-28, 71, 257
Smuggling, 257
Sepoy mutiny, 160
Srimad Bhagavata, 40
Subansiri, 9, 36
Subsidies, 78
Surma valley, 162, 164
Switzerland, 16
Sylhot Light Infantry, 162

Tagin Daflas, 9
Tamreswari temple, 40
Tangsas, 24
Tawang, 7, 60
  monestry, 221
  tract, 129
Taxation, 181
Tea garden, 117, 118
Terrace cultivation, 30
Tezpur, 19
Thailand, 18
Third Anglo-Burmese War, 112
Tibet, 10, 122, 157
  gaining influence in, 220-21
Tibet and China, revolution, 149
Tibet National Assembly, 131
Tibet Trade regulation, 145
Tibetan plenipotentiaries, 268
Tippum Raja, 93, 94
Tirap, 14
Tirap Frontier Tract, 231
Trade, 31-32
  agreement, 135
Transfer of Property Act, 172
Tribes,
  customs of, 26
  immigration of, 18-19
  migration, 16-18
  occupation, 54, 127, 222
Tribal,
  affairs, 125
  administration, 170
  craft, 201
  development and education, 217, 19
  economy, 31-32
  houses, 26-27
  languages, 21-22, 161
  religious practices of, 35
  society, 23-25
Tributaries, 10, 47

Udalgiri, 33, 54
Union Parliament, 253
United States, 261
Urga Convention, 132
Uttar Pradesh, 260

Vaishnavism, 36
Capt. Vetch, 55

Victoria, 271
Vidarbha, 40
Village community, 24
Village council, 28, 29, 31, 60
Violation, 56, 196
Vishnu Purana, 41

Wade, J.P., 44
Wanchos, 20, 24
Waste Land Grant Rules, 121
Weekly Bazars, 32
Wet Rice cultivation, 30, 184
Whipping Act, 174
Capt. White, 57, 68
Williamson, Noel, 34, 81, 87, 95, 101, 124, 128, 177, 178, 209, 210
Woodthrope, R.G., 78

Yaksas, 41
Yandabu treaty, 111
Yobins, 14
Younghusband, 124, 206
  mission, 131, 132
Yunan, 34

Zayul Chu Valley, 128
Zilla Parishad, 242, 244, 245, 252
Zoji La, 11
Zyul-chu, 127